Bible Stories
for
All Ages

with activities for the very young

Year A

Collected from over 10 years of the
phenomenal Christian education curriculum
and worship resources *The Whole People
of God*, and *Seasons of the Spirit*, these
volumes offer tried and true material in easy-
to-use format. These are proven resources
with a theology and approach that thousands
have come to trust.

Other books in the series:
Bible Stories with Songs and Fingerplays
52 Crafts for the Christian Year
Live the Story: Short Simple Plays for Churches
Youth Spirit: Program Ideas for Youth Groups
Youth Spirit 2: Program Ideas for Youth Groups
Worship for All Ages: Services for Special Sundays

Bible Stories for All Ages

WITH ACTIVITIES FOR THE VERY YOUNG

Compiled by Margaret Kyle

WoodLake

Editor: Cathie Talbot
Cover and interior design: Margaret Kyle
Cover art: www.photos.com, adapted by Lois Huey-Heck
Proofreader: Merlin Beltain

WoodLake is an imprint of Wood Lake Publishing, Inc. Wood Lake Publishing acknowledges the financial support of the Government of Canada, through the Book Publishing Industry Development Program (BPIDP) for its publishing activities. Wood Lake Publishing also acknowledges the financial support of the Province of British Columbia through the Book Publishing Tax Credit.

At Wood Lake Publishing, we practise what we publish, being guided by a concern for fairness, justice, and equal opportunity in all of our relationships with employees and customers. Wood Lake Publishing is an employee-owned company, committed to caring for the environment and all creation. Wood Lake Publishing recycles, reuses, and encourages readers to do the same. Resources are printed on 100% post-consumer recycled paper and more environmentally friendly groundwood papers (newsprint), whenever possible. A percentage of all profit is donated to charitable organizations.

Library and Archives Canada Cataloguing in Publication
Bible stories for all ages: with activities for the very
young: lectionary year A/compiled by Margaret Kyle.
Includes index.
ISBN 978-1-55145-546-4
1. Bible stories, English. 2. Christian education – Activity programs.
I. Kyle, Margaret
BS550.3.B52 2007   220.9'505   C2007-901820-3

Published by WoodLake
An imprint of Wood Lake Publishing Inc.
9590 Jim Bailey Road, Kelowna, BC, Canada, V4V 1R2
www.woodlakebooks.com
250.766.2778

Printing 10 9 8 7 6 5 4 3 2 1

Printed in Canada by
Houghton Boston, Saskatchewan

Table of Contents

Acknowledgements

The stories and resources in this book are compiled from the rich archives of *The Whole People of God* and *Seasons of the Spirit* curriculum and worship resources, published by Wood Lake Publishing, that have been written, edited, and prepared over the years by an international team of writers, editors, artists, and graphic designers.

Thanks must go to the writing and editing teams of both these curriculum resources who worked to discuss, explore, and imagine the lectionary readings into life. They spent a week together three times a year away from their homes and families to do this. Often the pace was gruelling in order to cover all the readings in the allotted time. But it was also an enriching experience shared between people of diverse denominations, countries, and backgrounds. After the group consultation time, writers would return to their homes to write the material and send it to the editorial team and illustrator.

A special thanks must go to all of the writers of the Nursery and Beginner materials for *The Whole People of God* and the *Ages 3-5* materials for *Seasons of the Spirit,* and to Donna Scorer, who has been the editor for both of these curriculum resources.

Thanks also to illustrators Barbara Forbes, Barbara Houston, Tina Prichard, and Katherine Carlisle.

Introduction

This book is organized to follow the weekly *Revised Common Lectionary* readings for Year A, beginning with Advent and ending with the Season after Pentecost. The complete three-year cycle of the lectionary provides a framework to explore the major themes of the Bible, the life of Jesus, and the birth of the church.

The church year cycle of Advent, Christmas, Epiphany, the Season after the Epiphany, Lent, Easter, Pentecost, and the Season after Pentecost, follows the flow of Jesus' life, death, resurrection, and the birth of the church. The church year cycle also follows the ebb and flow of preparation, celebration, growth, and inward and outward transformation into action and service.

This book contains one and sometimes more than one story for each Sunday of the year. Sometimes there is more than one version of the same story, to offer choices in various situations and in storytelling methods. This book also contains photocopiable activities for young children, to help them experience and remember the story. Sometimes the props used by the storyteller can be duplicated for the children so they can then tell the story themselves.

The stories in this book are taken from the best of the Nursery and Ages 3–5 session material from *The Whole People of God* and *Seasons of the Spirit* curricula and worship resources. Though written for small children, they can be easily and imaginatively adapted to any age level or group and are especially helpful in small congregations with a small number of children. This resource can be used in a home setting as a means of sharing faith stories in an interactive and memorable way.

This book is meant to be a storytelling tool and a spark for the imagination. Read the stories and become familiar with them before telling them in an intergenerational setting or with a group of young children. Experiential learning expert Tim Scorer has found that these stories, though written for young children, also interest and ignite the imagination of adults when shared in an engaging way.

Here is what Tim says about using these stories in an intergenerational worship setting:

> What I have discovered is that there is as much payoff for the adults in the [young children's] storytelling approach as there is for children and youth. The feedback from the adults has been staggering. They talk about hearing familiar passages "for the first time;" about being captivated by the power of the insight at the heart of a semi-familiar story; and about feeling that the stimulation of their imaginations and creativity has brought an aliveness to their participation in worship that has long been absent.
>
> Speaking of imagination and creativity, you might still need to exercise these yourself as you decide how to adapt this storytelling material to your own worship situation. For instance, one method I used was to create a story frame for a certain period of time that was held together by a visiting "God-Talker." Each week, God-Talker would visit and tell the story as presented in the storytelling materials.

The stories often use storytelling techniques and resources that are made for a small group activity, not a large sanctuary. So in the adaptation from small group to sanctuary a stick puppet might become a large piece of fabric. To make this work, you might have to discover and nurture the storyteller in you or in someone else from the congregation. Do it! This material holds such promise for you as storyteller that it would be a shame not to make the most of it.

A couple of final pointers. It's fine to invite children to come to the front of the sanctuary to be able to participate better in the congregational story time, but extend the invitation to people of all ages, never to the children alone. Over just a few weeks you will be able to transform "children's time" into "congregational story time." And finally, if teachers have a concern about children hearing the story in worship as well as in the church school, remind them that children love the repetition of story and learn it at a much deeper level the second time around. In fact, they acquire confidence having heard the story once in one version, and then in another version in a different setting.

Somewhere in you, there may be a biblical gremlin ringing alarm bells about the congregation receiving scripture in storytelling form, rather than word-for-word from the text. Send that gremlin packing and welcome in a Spirit of storytelling that can transform how people in your faith community hear scripture, both individually and collectively. [1]

Many of the stories in this book use actions, sounds, or storytelling props to help the listener become engaged with the story. This method of storytelling has proven to be more memorable and fun. Using all the senses and involving the body in movement and sound sparks the imagination and helps to integrate the story's message into everyday experience.

Telling, rather than reading, stories to children can be both fun and enjoyable if you keep in mind a few simple techniques. Importantly, make the story your own. Read it carefully, noting the flow of the story. Jot down key words. This will help you remember. Then, knowing the story well, you will be able to tell it in your own words. It is important to tell the story as you feel it. If you enjoy it, others will too. Expect interruptions, and hope for lively participation and free self-expression. Children love being invited to join in the story; if they can move, see things develop, are able to shout, laugh, sing, and talk, they begin to feel they are part of the story. And remember that story times do not always go well. Be patient. Children absorb far more than may be apparent.

All the activities in this book can be photocopied. This will give an opportunity for congregations with no Sunday school to offer activities to children during the worship service, which will help them further experience the story at their own level.

[1] Adapted from *New Ways to Tell the Story: Using Ages 3–5 Story in Worship*, by Tim Scorer, in *Congregational Life* Lent – Easter 2006. Copyright © *Seasons of the Spirit*, Wood Lake Publishing, Inc., Kelowna, BC, www.woodlakebooks.com. Used by permission.

Advent/Christmas/Epiphany

The "Christmas cycle" begins with the four weeks of Advent, moves through the seasons of Christmas and Epiphany, and culminates immediately before the start of Lent in the Sunday called Transfiguration. The Christmas cycle is the cycle of spiritual affirmation. It is the part of the church year which lends itself to growing into the fullness of selfhood, to become the special gift God intends.

ADVENT The four-week period leading to Christmas is called the season of "Advent." During Advent we wait for holiness to come as a baby, the child who comes to be known as Jesus Christ. What a marvellous time of year, and what a challenge! In this age of neon Santas and so many "me first" wish books, how can we find a quiet centre of expectancy and await with hope the gift of Jesus Christ? How can we still our busy hearts to welcome Christ into our lives?

The key to Advent is to heighten the sense of expectancy while avoiding commercial fuss and hype. Amidst the gathering frenzy of the commercial Christmas season, we seek an Advent time of intimacy, tenderness, and simplicity. Visual symbols might include, an advent wreath, the angel's trumpet, the root or tree of Jesse, and the plea: "Maranatha: Come, Jesus, come." Figures from the journey to Bethlehem can also make their appearance. If you can, save some Christmas carols for the season of Christmas. Lovely Advent carols are available to us now. We can add them to our repertoire and enjoy them.

CHRISTMAS At the end of Advent, the visual environment changes dramatically for Christmas Eve. Now, textures, garments and banners are fine and elegant, shimmering with white and gold brilliance. Symbols can include the manger, angels and shepherds, the star of peace, and images from Christmas carols. If decoration has been ongoing through the season of Advent, Christmas Eve is the time to turn on shining lights and light all the candles in the room. Refresh the Advent wreath, and lay the infant Christ in the manger. In the warmth and the wonder of exchanging gifts at Christmas, we celebrate the light that is born in human hearts through receiving and sharing the gifts of God. "Light" and "gift" are central symbols of the Christmas cycle.

Christmas is the season to give thanks for the presence of holiness in the material world. Now is the time to give thanks for Christ among us. All is one. Thanks be to God!

EPIPHANY The season of Epiphany is a time of dazzling light and revelation. Imagine a crowd in the darkness of night, waiting for a fireworks display. When the starbursts begin, there's a collective "Ooh-Aah!" That's Epiphany!

The word "epiphany" comes from a Greek term meaning "manifestation" or "showing forth." God's love is shown in Jesus, and the people watch and see – "Ooh-Aah!" In the season of Epiphany we read stories of the mission and the ministry of Jesus, which show us the radiant light of God. Like the people of Israel, we too watch and see – "Ooh-Aah!"

The weeks between the feast of Epiphany and Lent are sometimes called Epiphany Season, or in some churches, just "ordinary time." There can be as few as four weeks or as many as nine, depending on the dates of Lent and Easter. In these weeks, the ordinary is transfigured by wonder through stories of the ministry of Jesus. We learn how to watch for God, as we see Christ at work in the world.

During the weeks between Epiphany and Lent, we move with Christ's followers from our Christmas spirituality, where holy love is born in us, to an Epiphany spirituality of discipleship. The word "disciple" actually means "learner." So we too engage our own learning. These weeks are "working time" in the Christmas cycle of spiritual affirmation, a time to grow into the fullness of personal selfhood so we can pour ourselves out.

On the Sunday immediately before the start of Lent, the revelation of Christ as holy light for the world finds its zenith in the story of Jesus' shining "transfiguration" on a mountain.

– excerpted from *Living the Christ Life: Rediscovering the Seasons of the Christian Year*, by Louise Mangan, Nancy Wise, and Lori Farr. Copyright © 2001 Wood Lake Publishing Inc., www.woodlakebooks.com. Used by permission.

Ideas and Routines Suggested
for Advent, Christmas, Epiphany

1. The Jesse Tree

History of the Jesse tree

The origins of the Jesse tree can be found in Isaiah 11:1. There, Isaiah prophesied that a shoot would spring from the stump of Jesse. Jesse was the father of King David, an early ancestor of Jesus. The Jesse tree is similar to a family tree with Jesus as the new shoot. The symbols that are put on the tree represent biblical events leading up to the birth of Christ and may include symbols of Jesus' life. A description of each symbol is found on page 13.

Ideas and routine for using a Jesse tree

The Jesse tree can be used each week during Advent/Christmas/Epiphany. During the four weeks of Advent, Jesse tree symbols may be placed on the tree. Nativity and magi pictures (from greeting cards) may be added between Christmas and Epiphany.

Branch with foliage
in can

Preparing a Jesse tree

There are a number of ways to make a Jesse tree. One can be drawn on a large piece of poster board or cut out of construction paper or cloth and attached to a wall or bulletin board. The tree can be made with foliage or with bare branches. An alternative is to use a real tree branch which can be anchored in wet sand (or plaster of Paris) inside a plant pot or large coffee can.

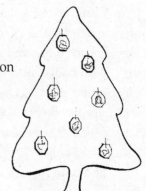

Cut from felt or
material

Symbols: cut out the symbols on pages 11 and 12. These can be used as is or you may wish to mount them on paper circles or leaf-shaped cutouts. If you will be hanging your symbols, punch a hole in each one and tie on a loop of yarn.

Routine: each week place the required dated symbols in a basket. Share with the children the name of the biblical character of each symbol. Hang the symbols on the tree together. You may want to end with the singing of "O Jesse Tree." On December 30 and January 6, the symbols with nativity scenes and magi pictures (from greeting cards) can be added.

Bare branch in can

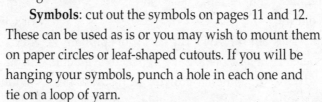

O Jesse Tree
(tune: "O, Christmas Tree")
O, Jesse tree, O Jesse tree
Your branches tell of God's dear son
O Jesse tree, O, Jesse tree
God's love and peace for everyone

Jesse Tree Symbols #1

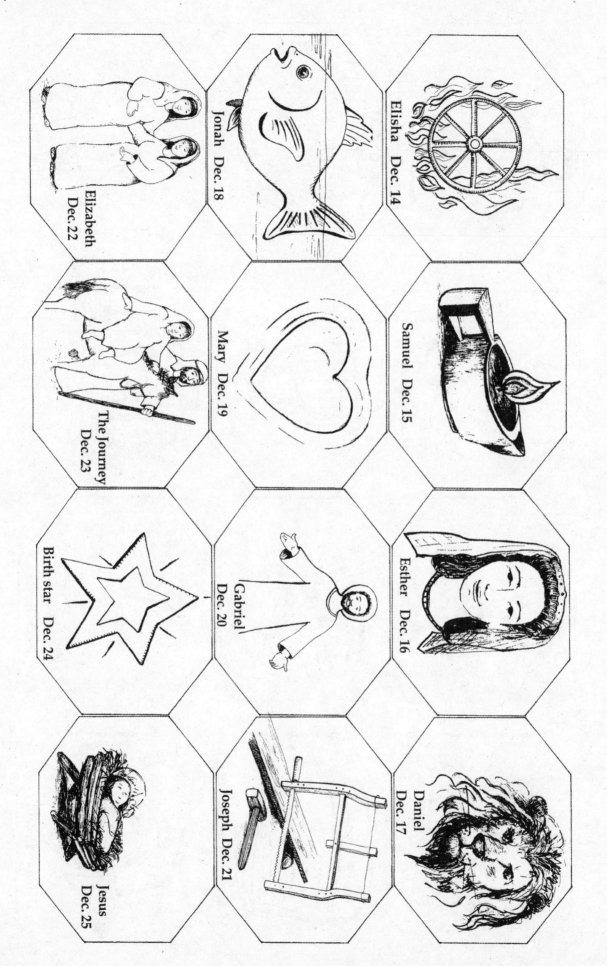

Jesse Tree Symbols #2

Elizabeth Dec. 22

Jonah Dec. 18

Elisha Dec. 14

The Journey Dec. 23

Mary Dec. 19

Samuel Dec. 15

Birth star Dec. 24

Gabriel Dec. 20

Esther Dec. 16

Jesus Dec. 25

Joseph Dec. 21

Daniel Dec. 17

Description of Jesse Tree Symbols

December 2 – Noah: builds the ark, saves animals and birds, God's promise in a rainbow

December 3 – Abraham and Sarah: built an altar, mother and father of a nation

December 4 – Jacob: cheated his brother, ran away, had a dream of a ladder up to heaven

December 5 – Joseph: given a fancy coat, sold by his brothers, becomes Pharaoh's chief assistant

December 6 – Moses and Miriam: led the Hebrew people out of Egypt and out of slavery

December 7 – Ruth: faithfully cares for Naomi by gathering grain; great grandmother to King David

December 8 – David: fights Goliath with a sling and smooth stones, composes psalms, becomes king

December 9 – Isaiah: called people to walk in God's light; prophesied about the coming of "Emmanuel"

December 10 – Deborah: prophet, wise judge, and leader of the Hebrew people

December 11 – Jesse: father of King David, stump from which the new branch would spring

December 12 – Solomon: wise king, builder of a magnificent temple

December 13 – Elijah: prophet who showed the power of God in sun, rain, and drought

December 14 – Elisha: prophet who faced an army with visions of fiery horses and chariots from God

December 15 – Samuel: prophet who was a child when God called him

December 16 – Esther: queen who risked her life to save her people

December 17 – Daniel: angered the king by praying to God; was thrown to the lions but kept safe

December 18 – Jonah: prophet, didn't do what God asked; swallowed by a great fish; did God's work

December 19 – Mary: young girl with a pure heart, faithful to God, Jesus' mother

December 20 – Angel Gabriel: sent by God to tell Mary she would have a baby

December 21 – Joseph: carpenter, Mary's husband, protected and cared for Mary and Jesus

December 22 – Elizabeth: Mary's cousin, mother of John the Baptizer

December 23 – The journey: Mary and Joseph travel to Bethlehem; must sign up to be taxed by Rome

December 24 – The star: shone above the place where Jesus was born; later the Magi followed it

December 25 – Jesus: Emmanuel, God with us, the Messiah, born for all

2. Using the Storytelling Figures in This Book
There are several ways you can use the story figures to help you tell a story.

Flannelgraph Glue pieces of felt to the back of each figure. As you tell the story, place each figure on a flannel-covered board.

Magnetic board Attach a small piece of peel-and-stick magnetic tape to the back of each figure. As you tell the story, place each figure on a metal storyboard, a metal tray, or even a baking sheet.

Puppets Attach each figure to a cardboard tube, craft stick, or small box. As you tell the story, hold the puppets or stand them on a flat surface.

Storyboard Make a storyboard from heavy paper folded in half or thirds so it will stand by itself. If you wish, use paint or markers to colour background scenery such as sky or desert. As you tell the story, use a small piece of tape to attach the figures to the board.

Storytelling box Cut out the figures. To reinforce them, you may want to glue each figure to heavy paper and cut it out again. Decorate a small box and place the story figures in the box. Remove the figures as you tell the story.

3. Isaiah Stories

For the first three weeks of the Advent season the stories centre around the prophet Isaiah and the promises and messages he brought from God. Each week you may invite the children to join you in Isaiah's place to hear a story about Isaiah's messages to the people. There are several figures on page 15 to use with the stories.

Isaiah's place can be created in a number of ways. Spread a blanket on the floor or mark a boundary with rope, yarn, or tape to help set apart the space as somewhere special. Create a sign that says "Isaiah's Place," or "Welcome to Isaiah's Place."

Isaiah

Isaiah's walking stick (used as storytelling prop for story on page 20)

Materials: large dowel or handle removed from a broom or mop, ribbons, feathers, glitter, stickers
Use the materials to decorate the dowel or handle.

Jesus

Andrew

Simon

John

another disciple

Dove

Storytelling Figures

4. Wood Block Nativity Set

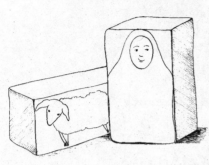

Your church may decide to create these figures as an activity during advent. The blocks may be kept at church in an individual box for each child. The set may be used by children to re-enact the story on Christmas Eve, and then be taken home. Magi figures can be made on the first week in January and sent home.

Materials: wooden blocks ranging in size from 10–15 cm(4–6 in.) x 7 cm (3 in.), felt or other heavy fabric pieces in various colours, assorted buttons or beads, glitter, permanent markers, yarn, a small box for each child.

Preparation: Sand the wooden blocks well to eliminate slivers. Round and smooth the corners. Use the patterns or draw your own to create figures. The basic body shape for most characters is the same. Faces are a simple oval. Scraps of felt can be used to create props such as magi crowns, shepherds' staffs, etc. Decorate with glitter or beads. Make facial features with permanent markers.

People face

Animal face

Manger

Animal Body
(cut from fake
fur or fuzzy
fleece fabric)

Basic Body Shape

Cut here for smaller people

5. Family Advent Wreath

Instructions
- colour and cut out wreath
- tape or glue it to the top of an inverted paper plate.

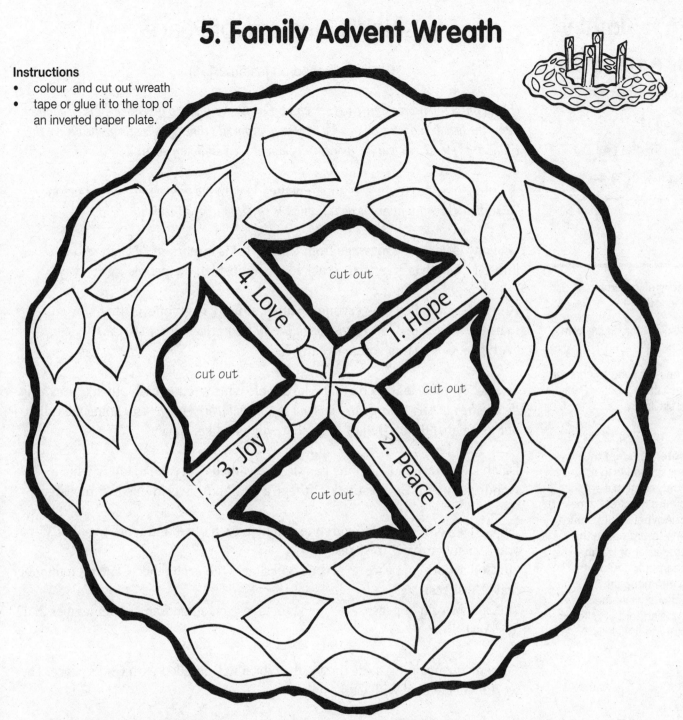

4. Love

1. Hope

cut out

cut out

cut out

3. Joy

2. Peace

cut out

cut out

The following letter can be sent home with children, if you are using this activity.

Dear families,

Today your child will bring home an Advent wreath that you will be able to use together for the remaining three weeks of Advent. Talk a little about waiting. Your child will have heard that we use Advent wreaths to remind us that we are waiting to celebrate Jesus' birth. Each Sunday bend up one candle. You may also want to read a portion of the nativity story found in Luke's gospel or sing a familiar Advent song as these candles are "lit."

Making a wreath part of your Advent celebration will help children understand that Advent is a time of waiting and getting ready. Sometimes this can get lost in the bustle of Christmas celebrations – a few moments of quiet time together as a family may help to focus on the amazing gift of Jesus. The candles represent Hope, Peace, Joy, and Love.

First Sunday of Advent

Isaiah 2:1-5

Psalm 122

Romans 13:11-14

Matthew 24:36-44

Storytelling props needed:

• Isaiah story figure from page 14

• one toy people figure for each child (Fischer Price™ or similar)

Note: To adapt the Isaiah stories in a congregational setting during the first 3 weeks of Advent, invite someone to dramatize the character of Isaiah – the character could either pantomime the actions while the story is being told or tell the story themselves.

Isaiah's Message of Peace

(based on Isaiah 2:1–5)

(Hand out a toy people figure to each child. Encourage them to give their figures names. Have the Isaiah story figure nearby. At the appropriate times in the story, encourage the children to stand and say the words in bold and then sit down again.)

Long, long ago there was a man named Isaiah. He was a very wise person. *(Show the story figure Isaiah. Invite the children to greet Isaiah.)*

One day Isaiah got a message from God. "This is important," Isaiah said to himself. "God has given a message to me. I must tell the people right away."

And so Isaiah called to everyone, "Gather around, everyone. Gather around to hear God's message." *(Children gather all their people close to Isaiah.)* "Listen, everyone. God wants you to live in peace."

The people looked at each other. The people whispered to each other. *(Encourage the children to have their figures pretend to talk and whisper together.)* Someone called out to Isaiah, "Peace? Tell us what that will look like, Isaiah."

Isaiah looked around at all the people. He wanted everyone to know what a wonderful world God wanted for them, a wonderful world filled with peace.

"In God's world of peace, everyone will help each other and work together. Can you remember that?" **Yes! Yes!**
"In God's world of peace, everyone will share with each other. Can you remember that?" **Yes! Yes!**
"In God's world of peace, everyone will love each other. Can you remember that?" **Yes! Yes!**

"When you are doing these things, the world will be filled with God's peace. The world will be filled with God's light."

The people looked at each other again. Then the people cheered! **Hurray! Hurray!**
They wanted to live in a world of peace. **Hurray! Hurray!**
They wanted to love and care for each other. **Hurray! Hurray!**

"Let's tell all our friends," they said. "Let's tell everyone about God's world of peace. Thank you for telling us God's message, Isaiah. Thank you for teaching us about peace." *(Encourage the children to place their figures close together on a table or the Communion table.)*

Isaiah felt happy. He had delivered God's message to the people.

Other ideas for exploring the lectionary readings (Advent 1)

1. The considerate thief (Matthew 24:36-44)

In today's gospel reading Jesus uses the image of a burglary to remind his disciples to be on their guard, always ready for his return. The idea that a thief would let the owner of the house know when he is coming is an absurd one and certainly catches our attention!

Talk about having visitors. What sort of things do we do to get ready? What is it like when people drop by unexpectedly? You might share an amusing or uncomfortable experience you have had with unexpected guests. It helps to be prepared, doesn't it?

Holding your Bible in your hand briefly talk about the gospel reading. Explain that Jesus promised that one day he would return, but no one knows when that will be. *(Note: Help people understand that Jesus' return is something to look forward to, not something to be scared of.)* Jesus told a silly story about how the owner of a house needs to be ready all the time, in case a thief decides to call. This was Jesus' way of telling his disciples they should always be ready for his return.

2. Changing swords into plowshares (Isaiah 2:1-5)

In advance: locate a picture of the "Swords into Plowshares" sculpture located on the grounds of the UN headquarters in New York. You can download one from www.un.org/Pubs/CyberSchoolBus/ untour/subswo.htm.

Hold a Bible on your lap open to Isaiah 2. Have a conversation about the sculpture. What is the man doing? Talk about swords and ploughs – what are they used for? What would it mean if you were changing your sword into a plough? Where did the artist get the idea for the sculpture? Read Isaiah 2:4b. Talk about Isaiah and his vision of a world filled with God's peace. Wonder together about what it would be like to live in a world where there is no war. You may want to finish by having a short discussion about the ways in which we can help to bring God's peace.

3. Get ready (Introduction to the Season of Advent)

Materials: Mary and Joseph figures and an empty stable (see page 16 or 31 or bring figures from a nativity set)

Have a brief conversation about Advent. Show the pieces from the crèche scene and explain that we get ready to celebrate the birth of Jesus. Invite children to choose a place to set up the stable and the manger. Start Mary and Joseph on their long journey to the stable by placing them some distance from the stable. Explain that every Sunday in Advent Mary and Joseph will move closer to the stable, until they arrive on Christmas Eve. *(Each week move Mary and Joseph closer to the stable, and encourage the children to find the two travellers.)*

Prayer

Dear God,
as we get ready to celebrate Jesus' birth,
we are very excited.
Help us as we get ready to welcome you. Amen.

Second Sunday of Advent

Isaiah 11:1-10

Psalm 72:1-7, 18-19

Romans 15:4-13

Matthew 3:1-12

Storytelling props needed:

• walking stick as on page 14

• Isaiah figure from page 14 and animal figures from page 21

Isaiah Shares Good News

(based on Isaiah 11:1–10)

(Have Isaiah and animal figures nearby. As you tell the story use Isaiah's walking stick.)

Isaiah hurried down the road towards the gathering place. *(Show Isaiah.)* He carried his walking stick and swung it as he walked. He knew the people would be in the gathering place. He had another message from God to share with all the people. Isaiah hoped the children would be there. This time he had a special message just for them!

There they were! The people were waiting for him. Isaiah raised his walking stick over his head and waved it at the people. "Greetings, dear friends!" Isaiah called out.

"I'm glad you are here together. Listen to this wonderful message I have for you." The people made a special place for Isaiah to sit. "Gather the children close," said Isaiah. "And," Isaiah smiled at all the people, "gather the animals close too."

The people looked at each other. The children? The animals? But the people knew Isaiah brought special messages from God. They did what Isaiah asked and made spaces for the children and animals right in front of Isaiah. They put the cats over here. They put the dogs over there. They put the goats standing on one side. They put the cows standing on the other side. *(Invite the children to place all the animal figures around your space.)* At last they were ready to hear the message.

Isaiah spoke to the people, "God wants such a wonderful world for us. God is sending someone to teach us all about this wonderful world. This person will teach us how to love and live together in peace. In the kind of world God wants, everyone will care for each other. Even the animals will love each other. *(As each pair of animals is named, invite the children to place them side by side.)* The wolves and lambs will live together. The cows and the bears will share their food. The leopards and goats will lie down together. The lion will eat straw just like the ox. All the animals will live in peace together. We will live in peace together." Isaiah smiled a great big smile. "Here's the best part!" he said. Isaiah laid his walking stick down in front of the children. He gently touched the heads of two children. "A little child will lead them," said Isaiah. "A little child will show the way to love and peace."

The people were amazed. What a message from God! Peace for everyone! "Let's celebrate!" they said. So Isaiah invited a child to hold his walking stick. "Lead us in a parade," Isaiah said to them. "Lead us in love and peace. Bring the animals, everyone. Let's go!"

So the children led everyone in a parade. They sang about God's love and peace. Everyone felt so happy as they celebrated. *(Encourage the children to hold the animal figures and join in a parade around the room. Invite the children to take turns leading the parade with Isaiah's walking stick.)*

A Peaceful World

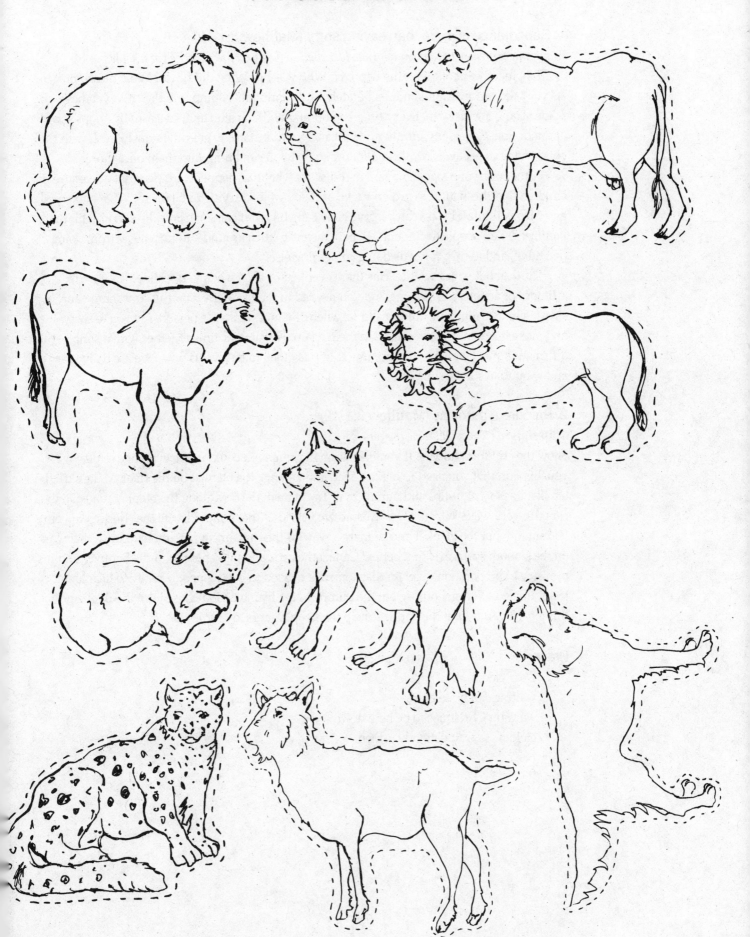

Other ideas for exploring the lectionary readings (Advent 2)

1. Repentance is more than saying sorry (Matthew 3:1-12)

In advance: prepare this option with an older child so they won't be surprised at what happens.

Talk together about John the Baptizer. Who was he? What did he do? What did he preach? As you talk, move around and deliberately, and continually, bump into the child you have made arrangements with. Every time you bump into them stop and say casually, "oops sorry" and move on. Consider hamming this up a bit, until it starts to get ridiculous! Finish with the child trying to get away, while you follow so that you can bump into them once more!

Gather everyone together again and discuss what had happened. If necessary, reassure the children that this had been pre-arranged and you weren't trying to be mean! What happened here? Do you think I was really sorry? How can you tell if someone is really sorry? John the Baptizer called people to "repent." Repent means to turn around – to turn away from doing one thing, and to turn towards doing something else.

Think about your own life. Has there ever been a time when you realized your own attitudes or actions were wrong and you needed to repent? Reflect on this and share your story. Re-enact your skit; only this time, when you bump into the person, say you're sorry and make it a point not to bump into them again. Finish your time together with a simple affirmation that God loves us very much, and is quick to forgive us when we are truly sorry and want to live in God's way.

2. Prepare a pathway (Matthew 3:1-12)

Materials: a blanket and some toy cars

Show the children the cars. If you have a small group you could invite everyone to play with you. Explain that you need to make a road and arrange the blanket on the floor. Make sure the blanket has lots of lumps and bumps in it. Try to push the cars along the blanket road. Do the cars run very well? Why not? How could we get rid of the bumps? Invite the children to help you smooth out the blanket and prepare a way for the cars. Encourage them to push their cars on the smooth surface. Is that better? Collect the cars, and talk about John the Baptizer and his ministry of preparation. Explain that someone needed to get the people ready to hear about Jesus, this was like smoothing out the bumps in the blanket. God chose John the Baptizer for this job. How did John the Baptizer help the people get ready for Jesus?

Prayer

Dear God,
waiting can be so hard –
we want Christmas to be here now!
Help us to wait patiently. Amen.

Celebrating with Isaiah

(based on Isaiah 35:1–10)

Third Sunday of Advent

Isaiah 35:1-10

Psalm 146:5-10

  or Luke 1:47-55

James 5:7-10

Matthew 11:2-11

(Have a container of sand, some flowers and greenery, and the storytelling figure of Isaiah nearby. At the appropriate times in the story, encourage the children to stand, shout "Rejoice," excitedly wiggle their bodies, and then sit down.)

Isaiah lived long ago. The sun was usually shining where Isaiah lived. Isaiah could look around in the sun and see sand everywhere. *(Place the container of sand in the circle. As you tell the story slowly lift handfuls of sand and let it run through your fingers.)* He could see sand and more sand. There were no streams or rivers. There were no lakes. Just lots and lots of sand. This was a desert. *(Invite the children to feel the sand, letting it run through their fingers.)*

One day Isaiah hurried through the desert to join the people. *(Invite a child to place the figure of Isaiah in the sand.)* "Come quickly, everyone! Come and listen!"

The people were glad to hear Isaiah calling them. God's people were having a hard time. They were not getting along with the people who lived in the country next to theirs. They knew God wanted to help them. They stopped what they were doing and hurried to Isaiah. *(Invite the children to wave and call out greetings to Isaiah.)* Isaiah had a big smile on his face. He looked so excited.

The people stood all around Isaiah. "Why are you so excited, Isaiah?" they asked. "Do you have another message for us?"

"Oh, dear friends," said Isaiah. "I do have a message for you. I want you to rejoice with me! Listen, everyone, to this promise from God."

"Flowers will grow in the desert. Rejoice at this good news!" **Rejoice!** *(Hand out the flowers and greenery.)*

"It will be like the desert singing and shouting for joy." **Rejoice!**

"The mountains will be so beautiful." **Rejoice!**

"Everyone will see how wonderful God is, they will see how powerful God is!" **Rejoice!**

"It will be a safe place where all people will come together in God's love." **Rejoice!**

(Invite the children to place the flowers in and around the container of sand.) **Rejoice!**

"This sounds wonderful!" the people shouted. "This is good news! Let's celebrate! Isaiah, how can we rejoice with you?"

"Sing! Dance!" said Isaiah. "Join hands and say thank you to God for this wonderful promise."

So the people joined hands. They said thank you to God. They sang. They danced. They rejoiced with Isaiah.

Storytelling props needed:

• container of sand, flowers, and greenery

• storytelling figure of Isaiah from page 14

REJOICE!

Materials
- unsharpened pencils or lengths of dowelling
- tape

Instructions
- Decorate the circles.
- Place one of the circles face-down.
- Tape an unsharpened pencil or a piece of dowelling to the middle of the face-down picture.
- Place the other circle face-up over the pencil. Tape or glue the edges of the circles together enclosing the pencil or dowelling inside.
- Hold the pencil or dowelling between your palms and roll it back and forth very quickly.

The desert is blooming!

Other ideas for exploring the lectionary readings (Advent 3)

1. A world transformed (Isaiah 35:1–10)

Materials: a picture of a desert wilderness and another picture of a lush green fertile land. You may also wish to bring in two potted plants, one that is well watered and one that has been allowed to dry out.

Show the pictures and/or plants and discuss the differences between the two. Where would you prefer to live? Why?

Turn to your Bible and summarize the reading from Isaiah. What a wonderful vision God gave the prophet: (you may want to refer back to the pictures) the desert has been changed into a land full of life, the sick are healed, and no one is hungry or afraid anymore. What a great place to live! Have a discussion about what it would be like to live in such a world. Wonder together how long it will be until we see Isaiah's dream come true. Do we see any signs of it yet?

2. Impatient waiting (James 5:7–10)

Materials: seeds in a seed packet, few pots full of soil, and a small watering can full of water

Excitedly show the seed packet and explain that you want to grow some of these plants. Ask for a few helpers to help you plant and water the seeds. Place them on a small table. Now the fun begins! Stare intently at the seeds and explain that you are waiting for the seeds to grow. Start to become very impatient that the seeds aren't growing fast enough. Pace up and down, tap your feet, complain loudly, suggest that maybe the seeds are shy and do not like to be stared at! It will not be long before the children will start to laugh at you! Encourage them to tell you why your expectations are unrealistic. The seeds will grow at the right time and we just have to be patient and wait.

Talk about waiting. When is it hard to wait? Why do we become impatient? Move into a brief discussion about the reading from James. You may wish to summarize the Bible reading from James 5:7-10. What were the people waiting for? What did James tell them to do while they were waiting? Like those Christians so long ago, we also have to wait patiently and trust that Jesus will come back at the right time. What can we do while we are waiting?

Prayer

Dear God,
thank you for your great love.
Help us to recognize the signs of your presence
all around us. Amen.

Fourth Sunday of Advent

Isaiah 7:10-16

Psalm 80:1-7, 17-19

Romans 1:1-7

Matthew 1:18-25

Joseph and the Angel

(based on Matthew 1:18-25)

(Encourage children to do the actions along with you as you tell the story.)

Joseph was a carpenter who lived in Nazareth. He built things out of wood. Joseph sawed and sanded and hammered as he built. *(Make sawing, sanding, hammering actions.)*

Joseph was going to marry a woman called Mary. He was confused about Gabriel's visit to her and God's message to Mary. Joseph wasn't sure that he still wanted to get married to Mary. *(Make wondering actions, e.g. chin cupped in hand, eyebrows raised and lowered.)* Joseph had a lot of questions about what he should do.

One night while Joseph was sleeping, he was very restless. *(Rest head to one side on folded hands. Shake head slightly and frown. Turn head from side to side.)* Joseph was feeling worried about Mary and the baby she was going to have. He wondered "What should I do? Should I still get married? And what about the baby?"

But then, in his dream, an angel appeared to him. "Do not be afraid, Joseph," said the angel. *(Relax face from frowning.)* "I have good news for you, too. Mary will have a baby boy and you will call him Jesus. This name means 'God Saves.' God wants you to be with Mary and care for her and the baby. God loves you very much." *(Arms around self for a hug.)*

When Joseph woke up he remembered what the angel said to him in his dream. Now he knew what to do! He knew that God wanted him to marry his good friend Mary. *(Place hands together as if in prayer.)* Joseph felt much better. He would be happy to serve God in this way. *(Place hands over heart.)*

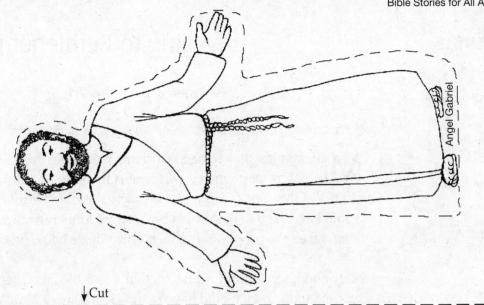

Instructions

- Cut out the angel Gabriel and glue him near Joseph.

↓Cut

Angel Gabriel

Joseph's Dream

(Matthew 1:18-25)

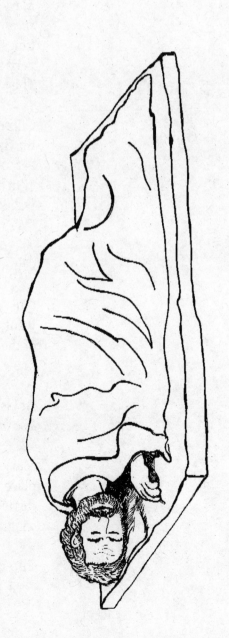

Christmas

Isaiah 9:2-7

Psalm 96

Titus 2:11-14

Luke 2:1-14 (15–20)

Travelling to Bethlehem

(based on Luke 2:1-5)

(Encourage children to do the actions along with you as you tell the story.)

Mary and Joseph had been working hard to get things ready for their new baby. One day, when it was almost time for the baby to be born, there was a knock at the door. *(knock on floor)* It was a soldier. He told Mary and Joseph they would have to go to Bethlehem because the Emperor wanted to count *(point as if counting)* all the people and write it down in his book. *(pretend to write)*

Mary and Joseph didn't want to go but it was the law. They gathered some blankets and food. They would have to travel for many days. When they were ready, Joseph helped Mary onto the donkey and they set out for Bethlehem.

Mary listened to the donkey's hooves as she rode along: clip-clop, clip-clop. *(slap knees)* Bethlehem was a long way to travel. Clip-clop, clip-clop. *(slap knees)* Sometimes Mary walked beside Joseph and sometimes she rode, but it was always very slow. Clip-clop, clip-clop. *(slap knees)* They saw many other travellers too. They walked in the day and rested at night. *(lay head on hands)*

Clip-clop, clip-clop *(slap knees)* went the donkey's hooves as Joseph led him along the dusty road. "How are you feeling?" Joseph asked Mary.

"I'm a little tired and thirsty," said Mary. "I think our baby will be born soon. Are we almost there?"
"We're very close," said Joseph.

Clip-clop, clip-clop, clip-clop, clip-clop. *(slap knees several times)*

"Just a little further," said Joseph. He picked up the donkey's reins and on they went. Clip-clop, clip-clop, *(slap knees)* Mary twisted her fingers in the rough hairs of the donkey's mane and held on as she leaned back against the blanket. She knew the baby was coming very soon!

At last they saw the gate of Bethlehem getting nearer. *(shade hand over eyes and look into distance)* Joseph said, "Look, Mary! Bethlehem! We're here at last."

Mary was so glad to hear Joseph's words. She hoped they could quickly find a place to stay. She patted the donkey's rough hair. *(pat imaginary donkey)* He had carried her safely on this long journey. She knew that Joseph would give him some food and water as soon as they were settled.

Clip-clop, clip-clop. *(slap knees)* Joseph led Mary and the donkey into Bethlehem.

Mary's Donkey

Materials
- four paper strips for each child
- four buttons or metal washers for each child

Instructions

- Cut out donkey and fold on dotted line.

- Fold 4 paper strips in accordion folds.

- Tape to donkey figure.

- Glue button or metal washer to each "hoof."

Fold

In the Stable

(based on Luke 2:1–18)

Storytelling props needed:

• wood block nativity set from page 16 or figures from page 31

Mary and Joseph finally reached Bethlehem. Joseph led the donkey down the streets until they came to a home. Joseph stopped and knocked on the door. *(everyone knock)* A man opened the door and peeked out. "I'm sorry," he said, "We have no room," *(shake head)* and started to close the door.

"Wait!" called Joseph. "Please wait! My wife is going to have a baby soon. Is there any place we can rest for the night?"

The man opened the door a little wider this time, and scratched his head. *(scratch head)* "Well," he said, "I don't know if you will want it, but there is some room in the stable. The animals are in there but it's warm and dry and the straw is clean."

Joseph looked at Mary and Mary nodded her head. *(nod head)* "Thank you," Joseph said to the man. "We will accept your offer and stay in your stable."

Mary and Joseph and the donkey followed the man to the stable. *(slap knees as if walking)*

Joseph quickly shook out their blankets and spread them over the hay to make a bed. *(shake out imaginary blankets and smooth them out)* Mary was glad to lie down in her straw bed. *(rest head on hands)*

That night Jesus was born. Mary wrapped him in soft, clean cloths. Joseph rocked him in his arms and sang softly to him. *(cradle arms)* They were so happy because Jesus was born and they were all safe.

Out on the hills some shepherds were watching their sheep. Suddenly, there was a bright light in the sky. *(shade eyes as if from bright light)* An angel appeared in front of them! They were very surprised and a little scared!

The angel said, "Do not be afraid! I have good news for you! Today, in Bethlehem, a special baby has been born. He is God's son sent to help the people. You will find him, wrapped up tight and lying in a manger. Go to Bethlehem and see him."

Suddenly the sky was filled with angels singing and praising God. When they left, the shepherds looked at one another and said, "What shall we do?"

One shepherd said, "Let's go and find the baby."

So they hurried down from the hills and went to Bethlehem. *(slap knees in running pace)* At last they found Mary and Joseph and the baby. The shepherds gathered close. Mary smiled at them and showed them the baby. The shepherds smiled at baby Jesus. They were excited and happy to see him. They left the stable and told everyone they saw about Jesus, God's son. And they praised God for all they had seen and heard.

A Crèche Scene

Instructions

- Colour figures and cut out.
- Glue the pieces onto a folded 11 x 17 piece of poster board as shown.

Folded poster board

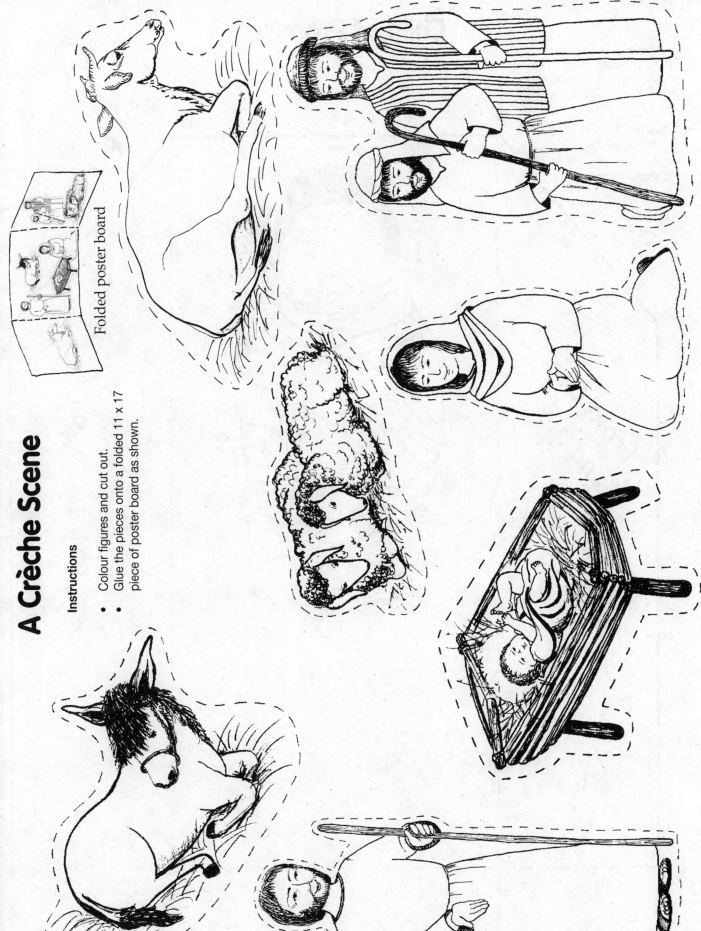

Child of Promise

Instructions

- Cut along outside solid line
- Fold bottom (1) dotted line in
- Fold again on dotted line (2)
- Fold sides in (3 & 4)
- Print title "Child of Promise" on the outside
- colour and add a ribbon to make the card look like a gift

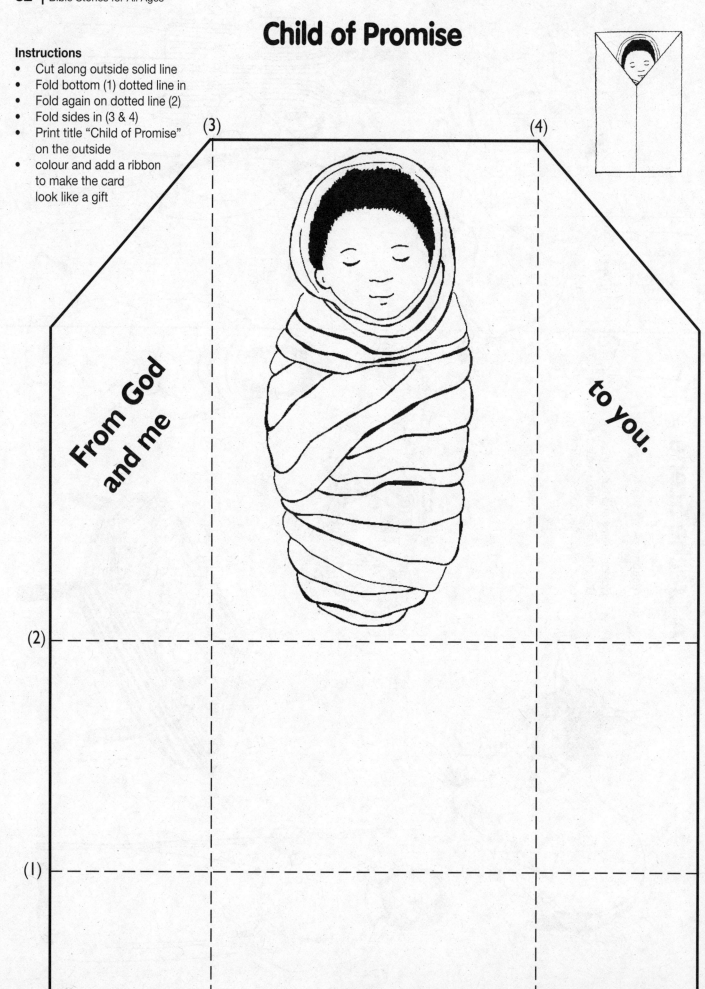

(3)   (4)

From God and me

to you.

(2)

(1)

To Egypt and Back

(based on Matthew 2:13–23)

First Sunday after Christmas Day

Isaiah 63:7-9

Psalm 148

Hebrews 2:10-18

Matthew 2:13-23

(We will use our imaginations to go on a journey with Mary and Joseph. Encourage the children to do all the actions.)

Joseph had very busy days. Joseph and Mary cared for their baby, Jesus, just as God had asked them to. They loved their baby very much.

One night Joseph, Mary, and Jesus were sleeping. *(Invite the children to pretend to sleep.)* Joseph had a dream. An angel spoke to him in his dream. *(Whisper.)* "Joseph!" said the angel. "It is not safe here for you and Mary and Jesus. Get up now! Get up and take Mary and Jesus far away to Egypt. You will be safe there."

Joseph got up right away. He woke up Mary and told her they must leave immediately. They had to take their baby to Egypt so he would be safe. Mary started to pack. She gathered clothes and blankets and food and put everything into baskets. *(Pack blankets into baskets.)* Then, Mary and Joseph began the long journey to Egypt. *(Pick up the story figures and baskets and begin walking on the spot.)* As they travelled, they looked up at the stars. They were so bright and sparkling in the sky. As Mary and Joseph looked at the stars they knew God was with them. *(Look up and imagine how many stars there are. Continue walking on the spot for awhile.)*

After a long time, Mary and Joseph stopped to rest. Joseph spread a blanket on the ground. *(Put blankets on the floor and sit on them.)* Mary set out some food for them to eat. *(Pretend to eat.)* Mary and Joseph looked around at this new place. It looked different to them. But Mary and Joseph knew that God was with them on their journey. *(Pack up again.)*

Mary and Joseph and Jesus walked on and on and on. *(Walk on the spot again.)* Finally they came to Egypt. "Here is where we will live," said Joseph. "We will be safe here." So Mary unpacked the baskets. She took out their clothes and blankets and food and put them in their new house. Mary and Joseph knew God was with them in this strange new place. *(Sit in a circle.)*

(Pause.) Mary, Joseph, and Jesus stayed in Egypt for a long time. Oh, how they missed their own country! It was hard being away from family and friends but at least they were safe. Jesus grew and grew while they lived in Egypt. *(Show with your hands how tall Jesus grew.)*

One night, while Joseph was sleeping, he had another dream. An angel spoke to him in his dream again. *(Whisper.)* "Joseph, you can go back to Israel. It is now safe for you."

So Joseph got up again. Joseph and Mary packed their clothes and blankets and food. *(Pack the baskets again and walk on the spot.)* Mary and Joseph and Jesus walked and walked. Finally, they arrived in Nazareth. They were back home at last. They would be safe now. *(sit back in a circle.)*

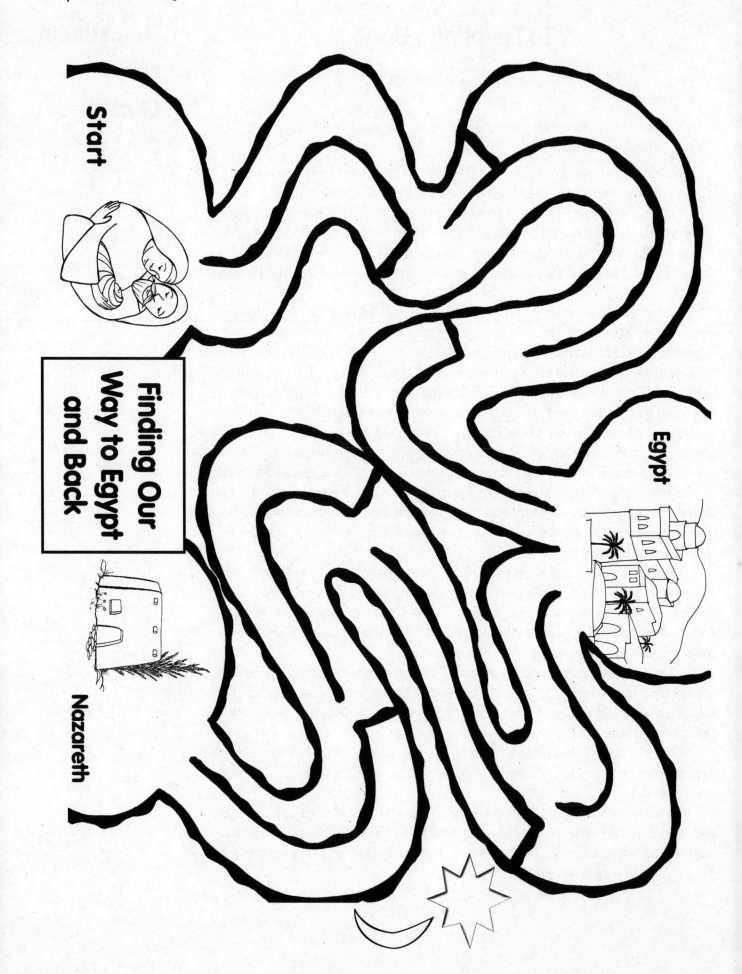

Start

Finding Our
Way to Egypt
and Back

Nazareth

Egypt

Journey to Safety

(based on Matthew 2:13-23)

(This is a guided imagination activity. As you begin, ask the children to pretend that it is night and they are sleeping. If possible, and if the children are comfortable, darken the room. When singing "The Journey," repeat each verse several times and invite the children to join in as able. If you like, everyone could move around the room and continue the story in a new spot.)

It was very late one night. Joseph, Mary, and Jesus were in their beds fast asleep. Joseph was dreaming again and he saw an angel in his dream. "Joseph!" the angel said. "It is not safe for your family to stay in Bethlehem. Get up! Get up now! King Herod is angry! He is going to look for Jesus! He doesn't want Jesus to be alive. Take Mary and Jesus and go to a place called Egypt. You will be safe there. Go now and stay there until I tell you to come back."

Sing: **"The Journey"** verse 1 *(tune "Old MacDonald")*

> In a dream the angel said
>
> run, run away.
>
> It's not safe for you to stay
>
> run, run away.

Joseph got up right away and woke Mary. They began to pack their things. *(In a whisper, say "Get up quickly! We must go to Egypt. Don't make any sound. Let's go." Sh-sh-sh.)* Mary and Joseph were on another long journey. And this time their baby was with them. They walked and they walked. Soon it was day and the sun began to get very hot *(pretend to be hot)*. They were walking across the sand and sometimes the wind blew in their faces *(huddle together from the wind)*. It was cold at night. Mary wrapped Jesus in blankets and sat close to the fire that Joseph made *(shiver and then crouch together and hold out hands to imaginary fire)*.

Sing: **"The Journey"** verse 2

> The day was hot, the night was cold
>
> walk, walk along.
>
> Soon you'll be where you belong
>
> walk, walk along.

Finally they reached Egypt and the house they would live in. Mary began to unpack their clothes and their dishes and their blankets *(pretend to unpack, shake out blankets, etc.)*. Mary, Joseph, and Jesus stayed in Egypt until the angel came to Joseph in another dream.

"It's safe now, Joseph. King Herod died. Take your family back," said the angel. "God wants you to go to Israel and live there with Mary and Jesus."

Sing: **"The Journey"** verse 3

> In a dream the angel said
>
> home, home you go.
>
> Israel is the place for you
>
> home, home you go.

Mary and Joseph packed all their things and got ready to go back home. *(pretend to pack clothes again and load the packs on a donkey)*. They travelled to Israel *(the children gently slap their legs to make the clopping sounds of a donkey's hooves)*. After a long, long journey they arrived in the town of Nazareth and found a new home. Mary said, "This is not the same as our old house but I like it. We will be comfortable here."

"Yes," said Joseph. "Jesus will be safe and happy here."

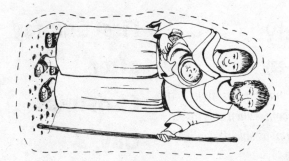

Materials
- two craft sticks for each child
- construction paper
- scissors and tape

Instructions
- Cut out Mary and Joseph on dotted line.
- Colour picture and mount on construction paper.
- Cut on "road line."
- Tape craft stick to back of people.
- Insert cutout and move back and forth.

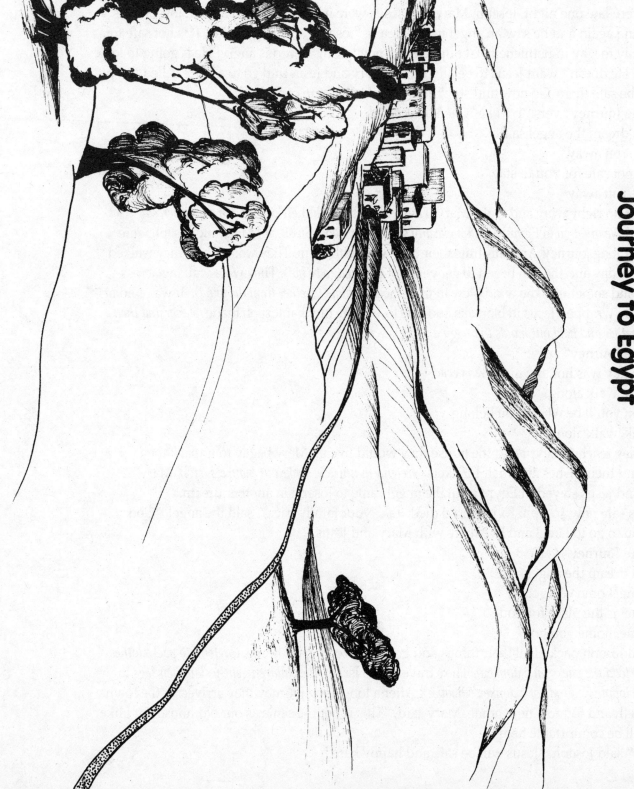

Journey to Egypt

Jesus Comes to Be Our Light

(based on John 1: [1–9], 10–18)

Second Sunday After Christmas

Jeremiah 31:7–14
or Sirach 24:1–12

Psalm 147:12–20
or Wisdom 10:15–21

Ephesians 1:3–14

John 1: (1–9), 10–18

(Encourage the children to respond to the suggestions in italics.)

There once was a man named John. John loved God very much. John knew that God was sending someone very special to the people. Someone who would teach about God's love and how to live God's way. John wanted to tell all the people about this special person. John wanted to share this good news with everyone.

One day John went for a walk very early in the morning. The sun was just beginning to peep over the horizon. He sat down on a big flat rock to think. (*Imagine you are each sitting on a rock like John.*) John wondered how he would tell the people about the special person God was sending. As John sat thinking, he began to feel the sun shining on his face. (*Raise faces to the sun.*) John looked around. He saw rocks and sand shining in the light of the sun. John saw plants and flowers begin to glow in the light of the sun. John looked at his hands. (*Stretch hands to the sun. How does it feel to be sitting in the sun?*) They were beginning to feel warm in the light of the sun. Everything looked and felt different because of the sun. Suddenly John knew how he could tell the people about the special person who was coming.

John ran to gather the people together. "Listen, everyone!" he called out. "Come and listen!"

The people gathered around John. John said to them, "Someone is coming to us from God."

"Is it you, John?" called out a woman. (*Children call out, "Is it you, John?"*)

"Are you the special person sent from God?" called out a man. (*Children call out, "Are you the special one, John?"*)

"No," said John. "It is not me. I am here to tell you all about the one who is coming. Listen, everyone." John raised his hands towards the sun. "Look at this beautiful sun," said John. "See the light. Feel the warmth. The one who is coming to us will be like this light. He will be like light for us. He will light a way for us in the world."

The people also raised their hands to the sun. (*Give each child a paper sun. Lift high above heads.*) They lifted their faces to the light from the sun.

"Thank you for this wonderful message," said the people. "Thank you, John."

Storytelling props needed:

• paper sun-shape for each child

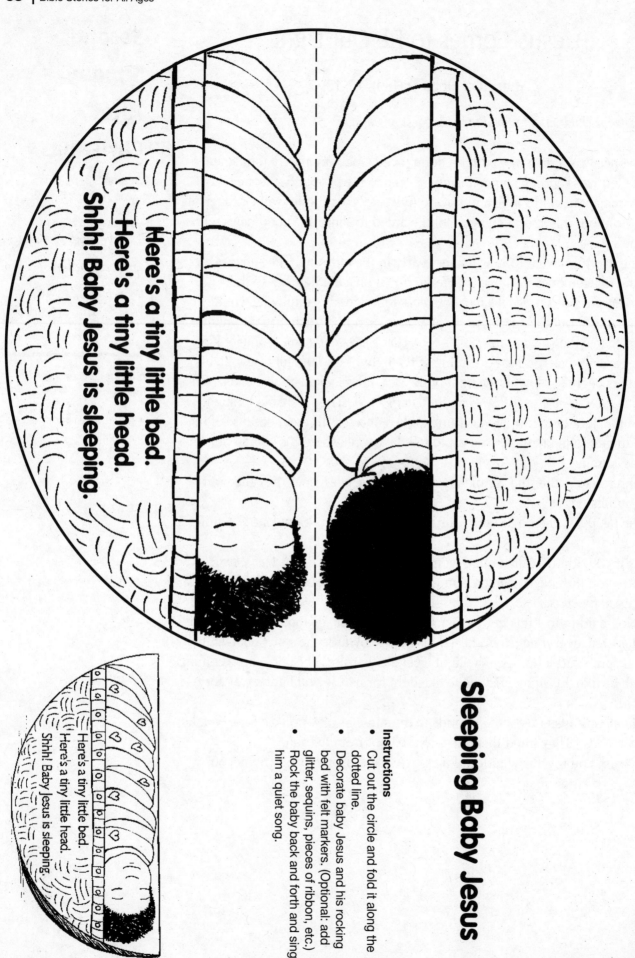

Here's a tiny little bed.
Here's a tiny little head.
Shhh! Baby Jesus is sleeping.

Sleeping Baby Jesus

Instructions

- Cut out the circle and fold it along the dotted line.
- Decorate baby Jesus and his rocking bed with felt markers. (Optional: add glitter, sequins, pieces of ribbon, etc.)
- Rock the baby back and forth and sing him a quiet song.

Here's a tiny little bed.
Here's a tiny little head.
Shhh! Baby Jesus is sleeping.

The Magi Visit Jesus

(based on Matthew 2:1-12)

Epiphany Day

Isaiah 60:1-6

Psalm 72:1-7, 10-14

Ephesians 3:1-12

Matthew 2:1-12

(Fill a beautiful box with samples of incense, spices, and perfume.)

When Jesus was a little boy he loved to help his father Joseph build things out of wood. One day, after they had been working very hard, Joseph said to Jesus, "Let's go up to the roof and look at the stars." All of the houses had flat roofs on them where the families would sit together and eat a meal or tell stories. Jesus loved to sit on the roof.

They climbed the stairs together. They spread a blanket on the roof and Jesus and Joseph lay down side by side. They looked up at all the beautiful stars spread across the sky.

"Look at all the stars!" said Jesus. "There are so many!"

"Yes, there are," said Joseph. "Would you like to hear a story about one very special star?"

"Yes," said Jesus. "Tell me the story, please."

"Well," said Joseph. "It's a story about you too."

"About me?" Jesus was amazed and excited. "A story about me and a star? Please tell me."

Joseph began. A long time ago, when you were just a tiny baby, some wise people called magi were looking at the stars. They thought that the stars were showing them that someone special had been born. They wanted to find out who it was. So they went to visit Herod, who was our king then, and said to him, "The stars tell us about a special child. Do you know where we can find him?"

Herod was angry when they told him about this special child. He was afraid this special child might try to be king instead of him. He told the Magi, "My helpers tell me that the child is in Bethlehem. Why don't you go and find him, then come back and tell me where he is. Then I will go and visit him too." But Herod didn't really want to visit the baby, he just wanted to get rid of him!

The Magi went to Bethlehem. As they travelled they saw a very bright star in the sky. "That star is leading us," they said. "Look! It has stopped moving. That must be the place where we will find him!"

"And they did find you, Jesus. They found you and gave you three wonderful gifts." Jesus and Joseph looked up as Mary came up the stairs and spoke to them. She was carrying a beautiful carved box with her.

"I have the gifts in this box. Come and look at them," she said. Mary opened the box and Jesus bent his head to look inside. Mary showed him the three gifts. There was shining gold, sweet-smelling incense, and a perfume called myrrh.

(Open the box you have brought and show the children the "gifts." Let them smell the scent of the incense, spices, and perfume. Wonder together about why the Magi brought gifts like this for a baby.)

"And that is the story about you and a star," Joseph said to Jesus.

"I like that story!" said Jesus. "And I like my gifts. Can I hear the story again some day?"

Mary and Joseph laughed. "Yes," they said, "we will tell the story again some day."

Storytelling props needed:

• beautiful box or container with samples of incense, spices, and perfume (check for scent allergies before using these items.)

Instructions
- Colour and cutout the figures of the magi and place on wood blocks or cardstock folded to stand up.

Note: see page 16 for Wood Block Nativity idea.

The Magi Travel at Night

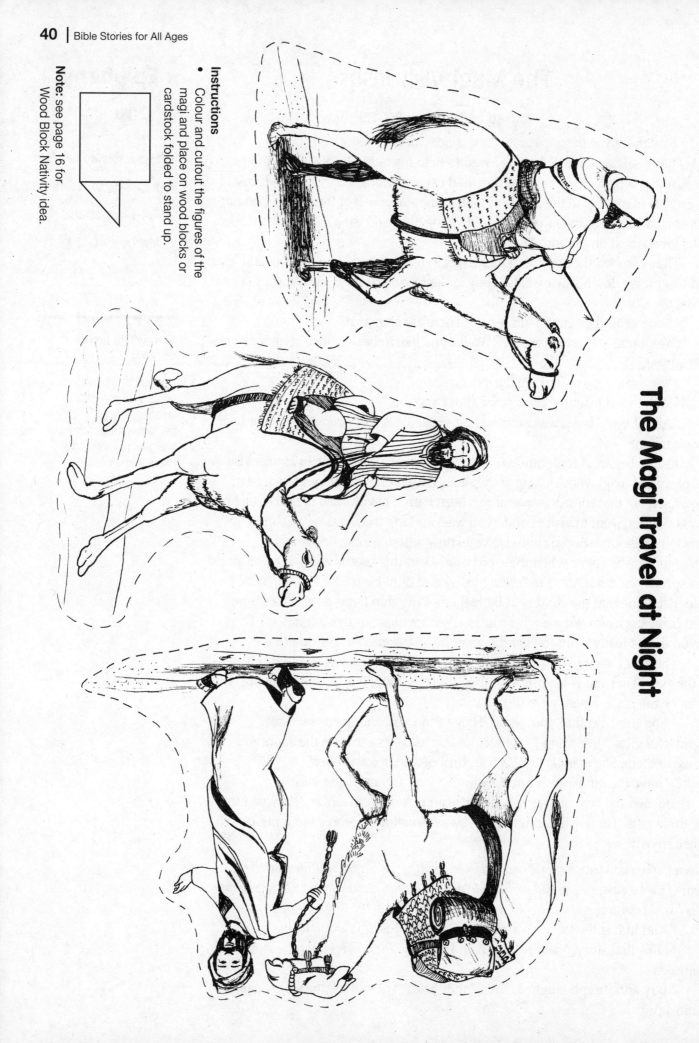

Celebrating Epiphany

1. Searching for a star

In advance: draw a large star on a piece of poster board, and cut it into six pieces. Keep one piece and hide the others in different places around the church. Note: Hide them in fairly obvious places so that the hunt will not take too long! Bring a star-shaped stamp or some star stickers.

Show the children the piece of the star you have kept and explain that this is one piece of a puzzle. Invite them to hunt for the other pieces. When all the pieces have been found, ask them to help you put the puzzle together. What have we got? Explain that stars are often mentioned in the Psalms as signs of God's creation. Tell the story of the Magi on page 39. Give every child a star sticker, or stamping a star on their hands, as a reminder of the story.

2. Twelfth Night celebrations

Epiphany is the 12th day after Christmas. The night before Epiphany is sometimes called "Twelfth Night." One of the many Twelfth Night traditions is to serve a special cake. Many people in places such as Quebec and New Orleans still make this cake. The cake is round to portray the circular route taken by the Magi to confuse Herod who was trying to follow them. In the cake is placed a dry bean to symbolize the baby Jesus. Tradition says that the person who finds the bean would be responsible for organizing the games for the night. Today children living in Quebec still get to choose a game if they find a bean in their slice of cake.

(You may wish to arrange to have a Kings Cake baked to serve after the service. A simple version can be made using any recipe for sweet yeast bread. Let the dough rise and punch it down. If you wish to have a bean in the cake, knead a dry bean into the dough. Shape the dough into an oval ring. Let it rise again. (*optional:* sprinkle glaze the top of the cake evenly with one cup of icing sugar mixed with a little water or lemon juice, and make swirls of food colouring all over the top.) Place pieces of candied fruit on the top of the cake, concentrating most of them in a narrow band all the way around to give the impression of a bejewelled crown. Set the cake on a baking sheet and bake according to the instructions for the dough recipe you use.)

Prayer

(This prayer is an adaptation of the ancient prayer of blessing used by Orthodox families at this time of year. Many Orthodox churches will be celebrating Christmas today, rather than on December 25.)

May God bring us all good fortune throughout
 the coming year.
Let us thank God for the many blessings in the past.
Christ is born. Let us glorify him. Amen.

John Baptizes Jesus

(based on Matthew 3:13–17)

First Sunday after the Epiphany (Baptism of Jesus)

Isaiah 42:1–9

Psalm 29

Acts 10:34–43

Matthew 3:13–17

Storytelling props needed:

- blue fabric
- bowl or baptismal font
- pitcher of water
- Jesus and dove figure from page 15

(Have a piece of blue fabric to represent the river and a bowl or baptismal font filled with water nearby. Or have a pitcher of water and pour the water into a bowl or baptismal font at that part of the story.)

One day, long, long ago, John went to the Jordan River. John walked into the river. The water covered his feet. The water covered his knees. John stood in the water and called out to the people who were standing beside the river.

"Come," John called to the people. "Come into the water. Come and be baptized."

Soon the people came. They came from their houses. They came from the hills and fields. The people came from everywhere. There were so many people who wanted to hear about God! They were ready to change and live God's way of love and peace. They were ready to be baptized. And so the people stood in the river with John. And one by one, John dipped them into the water and said a prayer. *(Invite the children, one by one, to dip their fingers in the water.)* "Now you are baptized," John said. "Go and live God's way." As the people left, they felt clean and new inside. It was a wonderful feeling.

Near the end of the day, John looked up and saw a man standing beside the river. The man looked very familiar. Why, it was Jesus! He was the special one sent from God. *(Show the Jesus story figure.)*

"John!" called Jesus. "Please baptize me."

"No, no!" said John. "You should baptize me instead."

"No, John," said Jesus. "This is what God wants. God wants you to baptize me."

Jesus walked out into the river. *(Place Jesus figure in the river.)* Jesus and John smiled at each other. John said a prayer to God, then dipped Jesus under the water and lifted Jesus up again.

(Whisper.) Something wonderful happened! As Jesus came out of the water, he felt God's love in a very special way. Jesus heard God's voice say, "This is my own dear child. I love him." And then, looking up, Jesus saw light all around. It looked as if a dove was gently touching him. *(Gently touch the dove figure to the Jesus figure. Invite the children to dip their fingers in the water and touch each other gently on the back of a hand and say, "God loves you.")*

John felt happy that he had baptized Jesus. John knew he had done what God wanted.

Flying Dove

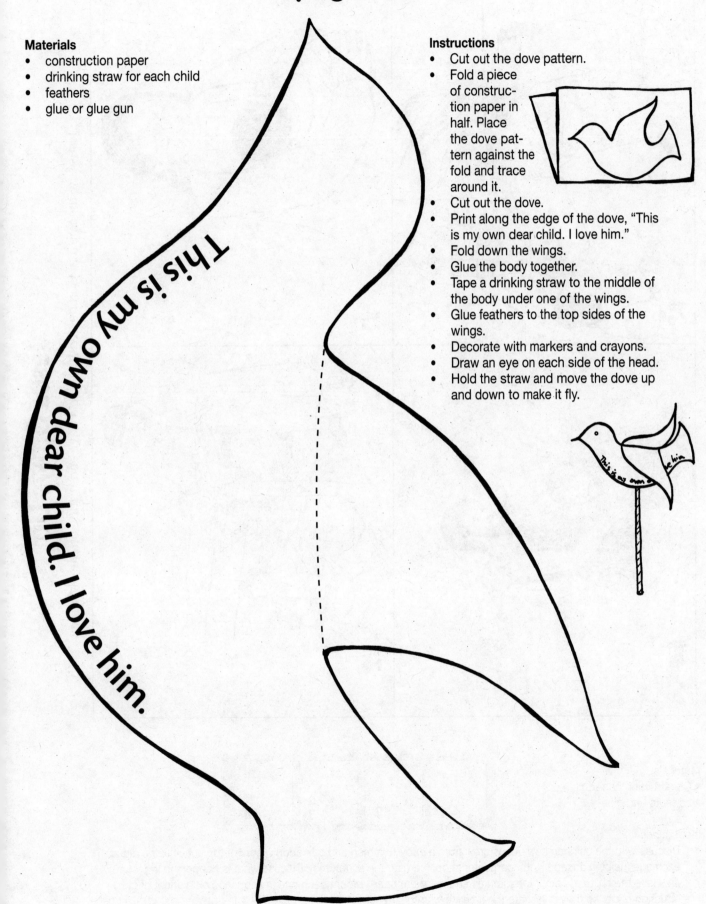

Materials
- construction paper
- drinking straw for each child
- feathers
- glue or glue gun

Instructions
- Cut out the dove pattern.
- Fold a piece of construction paper in half. Place the dove pattern against the fold and trace around it.
- Cut out the dove.
- Print along the edge of the dove, "This is my own dear child. I love him."
- Fold down the wings.
- Glue the body together.
- Tape a drinking straw to the middle of the body under one of the wings.
- Glue feathers to the top sides of the wings.
- Decorate with markers and crayons.
- Draw an eye on each side of the head.
- Hold the straw and move the dove up and down to make it fly.

This is my own dear child. I love him.

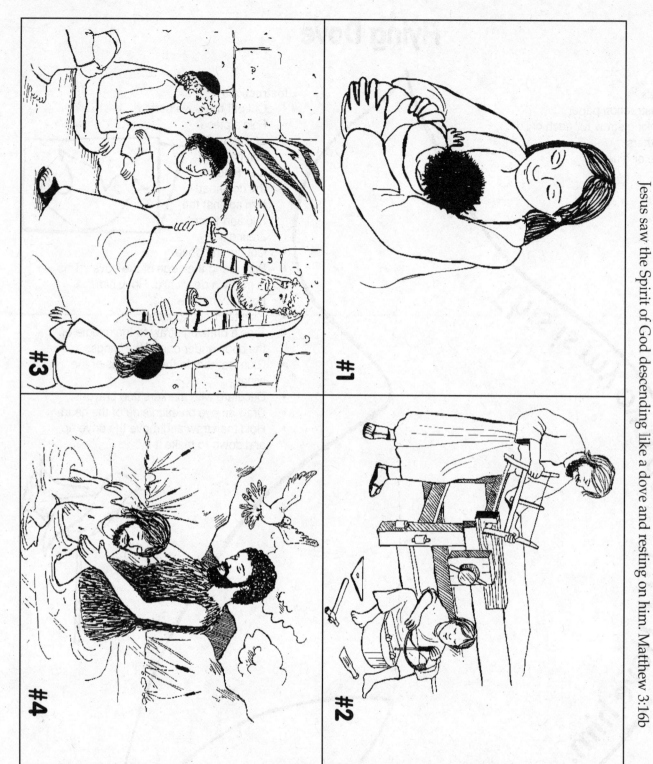

Jesus Grows Up

Jesus saw the Spirit of God descending like a dove and resting on him. Matthew 3:16b

1	2	3	4

Materials
• Construction paper
• scissors and glue

Instructions
• Discuss with the children how Jesus grew from a baby to a man and talk about some of the activities he did at each age (helping Joseph in the carpenter shop, learning the scriptures). Discuss what is happening in picture #4. Have the children colour the pictures and cut them apart. Mount each one in sequence on a sheet of construction paper so they can share the timeline with their family.

Other ideas for exploring the lectionary readings (Epiphany 1)

1. Images of God (Psalm 29)

No single image can describe God, so we use many. Ask how the children imagine God. Psalm 29 describes God as powerful and mighty, like a thunderstorm. What do you see and hear during a thunderstorm? How might these remind us of God? (The discharge of electricity through the air that creates thunder and lightning reminds us of the power of God to do other great things.) God is also described as gentle and quiet like a dove. When might we think of God in these ways?

Look for symbols or visual images of God in your worship area. What do they say God is like? You could read and discuss the words of the song "God Is Like" (on *Seasons Growing Faith CD* [#5] and *Seasons Growing Faith Songbook* or in *Rainbow Songbook* [#15]; both resources published by Wood Lake Publishing, www.woodlakebooks.com), and develop some new verses together. Use images suggested by the children. Sing the song with the congregation.

2. Learning about the sacrament of Baptism (Matthew 3:13–17)

Gather at the baptismal font or baptistry. Briefly describe your baptismal traditions. Explain that Christians are baptized (either as children or adults) as a special sign to say that we belong to God and want to follow in God's way. Jesus was baptized and Christians can follow his example. Some children may be able to tell about their own baptism or may have seen others being baptized.

In the early church, people being baptized would go to a river. They would take off their robe, leave it on the river bank, and walk into the river. A church leader would gently push them under the water and say a prayer. Then they would climb out on the other side. The members of their church would give them a new robe to remind them of their new life as a Christian. Sometimes they were even given a new name! Baptism is a very happy time for that person and for the whole church.

3. Experiencing *asperges*

Materials: bowl of water and sprig of greenery

In some churches, greenery is dipped in water and after being blessed, the water is sprinkled over the congregation. This tradition is called *asperges,* a Latin word meaning "to sprinkle." This sprinkling can be a reminder of what happens at baptism.

Show the children the water. Have a brief discussion about uses and meanings water has for us: cleaning (water reminds us that God loves us and gives us fresh starts to live in God's way); drinking (water reminds us that God's love is refreshing and gives us life).

The minister could be invited to pray over the water that will be used for the *asperges.* The children could help create a special prayer. Sprinkle some of the water over the children to demonstrate. If it is appropriate in your congregation, some children could help sprinkle the water over the congregation. Use a sprig of greenery that has significance in your area.

Prayer

Loving God,
thank you for everything
that reminds us of your love.
Amen.

Second Sunday after the Epiphany

Isaiah 49:1–7

Psalm 40:1–11

Corinthians 1:1–9

John 1:29–42

Storytelling props needed:

• blue fabric

• Jesus, John, Andrew, Simon, and another disciple figures from page 15

Meeting Jesus

(based on John 1:29–42)

(Place a blue cloth or construction paper "river" in one area. The storytelling figures of John, Andrew, and another disciple are beside the river. Place Simon in another area for later.)

Jesus was walking with some friends. *(Hold the figure of Jesus and invite all the children to walk around your space with him. Imagine what you might see and hear as you walk with Jesus. Is the sun shining? Do you hear any birds?)* Jesus smiled and said hello to all the people he passed. Soon they came to the river. "Look," said Jesus. "It's John." *(Together point to John.)* "It's John who baptized me yesterday!"

Jesus smiled and waved to John. Then they continued on their walk. *("Andrew" and "another disciple" join your walk.)* But soon Jesus noticed that two of John's helpers were following him. One of these helpers was called Andrew. These helpers remembered John telling them that Jesus was the special one sent by God.

Jesus turned around and looked at them. Then he said, "What are you looking for?"

Andrew and the other helper were a little surprised. At first, they didn't know what to say. Then Andrew spoke, "Teacher, where are you staying?'

Jesus laughed and welcomed them. "Come and see," he said.

(Continue walking and move into the taped outline of Jesus' house. What would it be like in Jesus' house? What would you want to talk about?)

Later that day, Andrew left to find his brother Simon. *(Have a child take "Andrew" and go and find "Simon.")* "Simon," called Andrew, "we have found the special one sent from God. Come and meet him."

Andrew took Simon to Jesus. "Jesus," said Andrew, "this is my brother Simon."

Jesus looked at Simon. "Welcome. Your name is Simon but I have a new name for you. Now your name is Peter. It means 'rock.' Please stay with me."

Peter and Andrew and the other disciple looked at each other. Oh, yes, they would stay! They were so happy.

Other ideas for exploring the lectionary readings (Epiphany 2)

1. God knew us and loved us before we were born (Isaiah 49:1–7)

The reading from the Hebrew Scriptures today says that God knows us and loves and cares for us before we are even born.

Talk about questions and dreams parents might have about a baby they're going to have. If you have gone through this experience yourself, you could share some of the hopes and worries you had. Will it be a boy or a girl? What kinds of things will the baby enjoy? If there is someone in your congregation who is looking forward to the birth of a child, invite them to share their thoughts.

2. Other people can see God working in our lives (1 Corinthians 1:1–9)

Ahead of time: You may wish to compliment one or two individuals in the congregation. Talk to them beforehand and arrange for them to respond by saying, "Thank you, and thank God!" (Note: In a society where an unhealthy emphasis is placed on the way we look, it is important to compliment people on their gifts or the way they act towards others rather than on their physical appearance.)

In the reading from the epistle, Paul compliments the church in Corinth by talking about the wonderful way in which God has worked in their lives. Talk about giving and receiving compliments. What is a compliment? When would you give someone a compliment? Why? When might you receive a compliment? Mention that sometimes we are embarrassed when someone compliments us because we don't like to brag. However, we can remember that when other people are complimenting us they are also complementing God, who made us. This means we can accept such compliments because we are also saying a thank you for God's good work.

3. We are the church

Have you heard that it's not buildings that are the church? If it's not buildings, what is the church made up of? People! Teach the words and actions to the song "We Are the Church." (see page 253; also on *Seasons Growing Faith CD* [#19] and *Seasons Growing Faith Songbook*; or *Rainbow Songbook* [#59]; both available from Wood Lake Publishing, www. woodlakebooks. com). Invite a discussion about the song. Conclude by singing the song together.

Prayer

Dear God,
there are so many exciting things to hear and to learn.
Be with us today as we learn more about you.
Amen.

Third Sunday after the Epiphany

Isaiah 9:1-4

Psalm 27:1, 4-9

1 Corinthians 1:10-18

Matthew 4:12-23

Storytelling props needed:

• rope or twine

**Fingerplay:
"Jesus Calls the Fishers"**

Andrew, Peter, James and John *(hold up 4 fingers)*
went fishing every day.
They rowed their boat
(cup hand like a boat)
and threw their nets *(making throwing motion)*
always the same way.

Then one day Jesus called them
"Come and follow me! *(make "follow me" motion)*
We'll show God's love to others. *(cross hands over heart)*
Teachers we will be!"

Andrew, Peter, James and John *(hold 4 fingers up)*
left their boat that day. *(cup hand like a boat)*
Now they were disciples
living in God's way. *(cross hands over heart)*

Jesus Chooses His Disciples

(based on Matthew 4:12–23)

(If there is room, create a "boat outline" with a rope or twine. Otherwise, use your imagination to create the boat.)

Peter and his brother Andrew were fishers. Each day they threw their net into the sea to catch fish. Their net was so big. Their net was so heavy! They each had to hold a side of the net and throw it as hard as they could. *(Invite the children to stand in the boat and hold an imaginary net with you. Throw it into the sea. Pretend it hasn't gone far enough and say, "Everyone use your muscles. Ready? One, two, three, let's throw the net again!" Pretend to drag in the heavy net of fish and then do it again. Do this several times and then sit down and rest.)*

Sometimes Peter and Andrew had to wait all night before they caught any fish. During their long waits they talked and told stories. Often they told stories that they had heard about the new teacher Jesus. One night, as Peter and Andrew were fishing, Jesus walked by. Jesus waved and called out. "Peter! Andrew! I need friends to help me! Come and follow me. I need helpers to live and work with me." Peter and Andrew looked at each other. Jesus was inviting them to follow him! What do you think they did? *(Listen to children's answers.)* Right away Peter and Andrew put down their nets and followed Jesus.

Then Jesus walked with Peter and Andrew down the beach to where their friends James and John were fixing their fishing nets. *(Invite the children to imagine holding a net and sewing and mending it. Show how to make big sewing motions.)* And again, Jesus called and waved to these fishers. "James! John! I need friends to help me! Come! Follow me!". What do you think James and John did? *(Listen to children's answers.)* They dropped their nets. They left their boat. They knew they wanted to follow Jesus, too.

Now Jesus had more new helpers. They were called disciples. They would travel everywhere together. And they would tell everyone about God's love.

Follow Me

(based on Matthew 4:12-23)

Instructions

• Colour the picture of Jesus calling "Follow Me." You are a disciple, too. Draw and colour your picture beside the other disciples.

Following Jesus

Instructions
- Trace a path to help each disciple follow a path to Jesus. You are a disciple, too. Draw your face and clothes on the bottom figure, add your name in the space provided, and trace your pathway to Jesus.

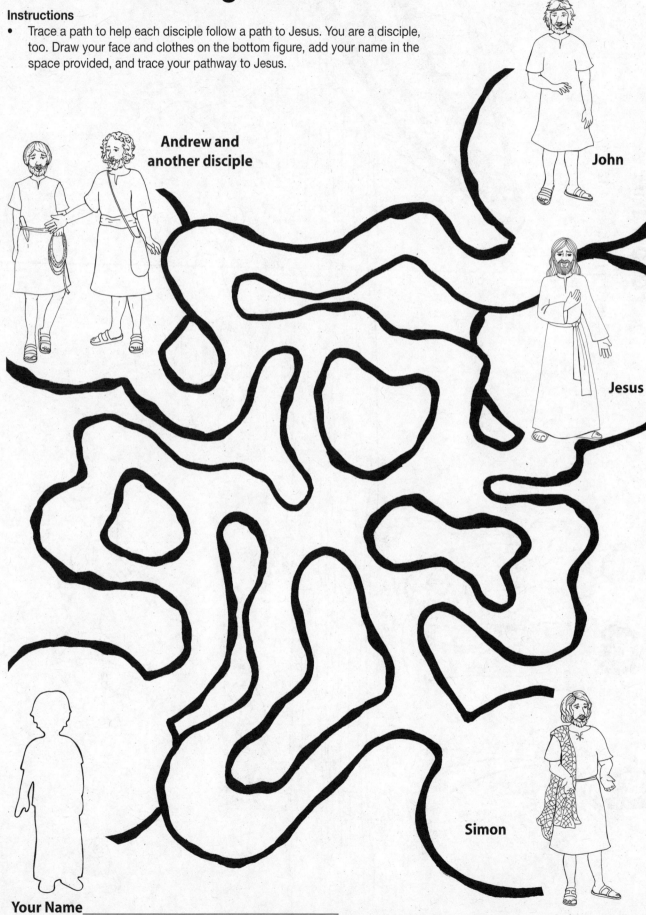

John

Andrew and another disciple

Jesus

Simon

Your Name_____

Jesus Puppet

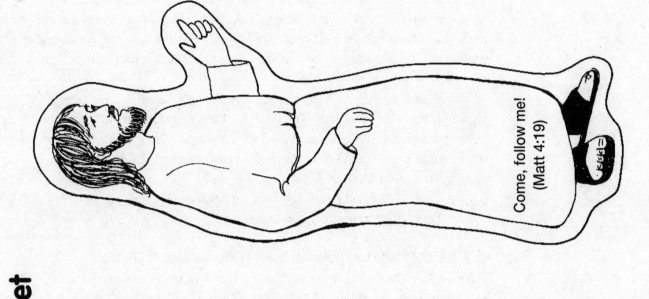

Come, follow me!
(Matt 4:19)

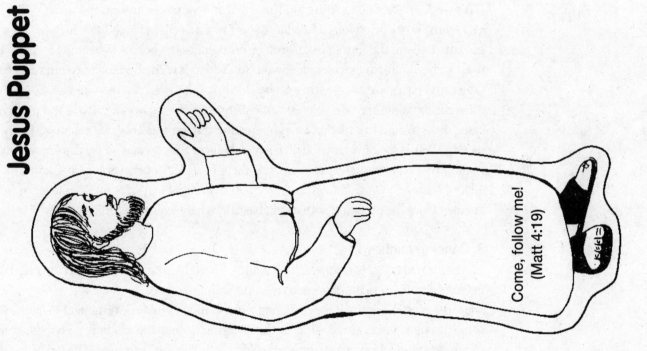

Come, follow me!
(Matt 4:19)

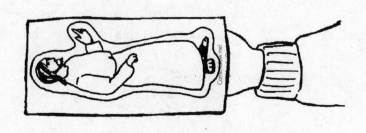

Materials
- an envelope for each child
- scissors and glue or stapler

Instructions
- Cut out Jesus figure.
- Seal an envelope and cut off one narrow edge.
- Glue or staple edges of envelope to back of Jesus (open edge down).
- Child inserts hand into envelope and moves Jesus.

Other ideas for exploring the lectionary readings (Epiphany 3)

1. God's light (Isaiah 9:1–4, Matthew 4:12–17)

Materials: non-electric sources of light, such as candles, flashlights, oil lamps

The readings from Isaiah and Matthew both speak of a great light coming to people who have been in darkness. Have you ever been in a situation when all the lights went out and you were in the dark? How did you feel? What did you do? Tell your story and encourage others to share some of their experiences with you. What might be helpful in these situations? Show and discuss the items you have brought.

There is another important light in our lives. Read the words to the chorus of "This Little Light of Mine." God's love shines on us all the time. Just as we might share a flashlight, or the light from a candle, so we can shine and share the light of God's love every day in how we treat other people. Repeat each line of the chorus and then sing the song together.

This Little Light of Mine

This little light of mine, I'm gonna let it shine (x3)
Let it shine, let it shine, let it shine.

2. Week of Prayer for Christian Unity (1 Corinthians 9:10–18)

(This week is celebrated at different times at different places around the world.)
Materials: boxes of crayons and a large sheet of paper placed on a hard surface

In Paul's letter to the church in Corinth he encourages the people to be united. Ask people to use a favourite colour crayon to help you fill the paper with all kinds of colours and patterns. (You could have several colouring groups.) While colouring, discuss what is the same and different about the crayons. Express appreciation for the variety of colours and patterns being used. Would this picture be as interesting if there was only one colour and only one pattern? Just as we can enjoy the different colours of the crayons, so we can enjoy the different traditions of other churches and celebrate them in a Week of Prayer for Christian Unity. We all love Jesus and worship God, and we do it in different ways. It's exciting to learn from one another. Place the drawing, with a suitable title, where everyone can enjoy it.

3. Dancing rainbows

Materials: cut crystal ornament, light source. Sunlight is best, but an alternate may be needed indoors. Arrange a plain surface to reflect the rainbow onto.

Show the crystal, admire it together, enjoy the sparkles. Hold the ornament to let the light shine through. Discover the rainbow that is formed. Shine the rainbow on hands, over the congregation, etc. How many different colours can you see? Why does the light turn into a rainbow?

Indicate that this crystal reminds you of your church. The light of God's love shines into our church family, and is reflected out in many different ways, just like the colours of a rainbow are reflected through the crystal. e.g. when you smile at someone, you are shining with God's love. When you sit beside someone who is sad, you are shining with God's love. Ask about other ways God's light shines through your church family.

Prayer

God of light,
we know you love us very much.
Help us to shine with your light.
Amen.

Different Disciples with Different Gifts

(based on Matthew 4:12–23)

Epiphany 3

Matthew 4:12–23

Storytelling prop needed:

• copies of disciples page 54. Colour, cut out, and mount on cardstock. Add popsicle sticks to the puppets *(optional)*.

Jesus and his new friends were travelling on a long road. Everywhere they went they taught others about God. Most of the people were happy to hear how to live in God's way. But others did not understand. They said, "These disciples don't look like special teachers. They look like ordinary fishers! Why is Jesus travelling with these people? They should be fishing in a boat, not talking about God's love."

When Jesus looked at the disciples he saw them the way God sees them. Each one of them was special in their own way. He knew they had gifts inside that they shared with others. *(Make movements as you talk about each disciple.)*

Andrew was a quiet, gentle man. He was a good listener. Andrew helped the others to feel calm and quiet too. *(Cup hand to ears or thoughtfully hold chin.)*

[Simon] Peter loved to talk. He moved his arms all around when he talked. It was exciting to listen to Peter. He had many ideas. *(Wave arms around excitedly.)*

James and John were brothers. It was fun to listen to their stories about when they were little boys. James and John liked to make people laugh. *(Pretend to laugh.)*

Jesus and the disciples walked along the road every day. They travelled from town to town. *(Have children walk on the spot.)* Everywhere they went they met different people who were all special in their own way. Some of these people wanted to follow Jesus and be disciples too.

Salome was James' and John's mother. Salome had been alive for a long time. Jesus knew she had many important stories to tell. *(Pantomime an old woman with a cane.)*

Matthew knew a lot of important leaders. His job was to collect money from the people to help the disciples care for others. Matthew's job gave Jesus lots of ideas for stories about how to live in God's way. *(Pantomime counting out money and putting it carefully in a money bag.)*

Joanna and Susanna were important women. They had many friends and lots of money. They shared their money with the disciples. *(Pantomime giving money to others.)*

Mary Magdalene was a good friend to Jesus. When some people wanted to hurt Jesus, Mary did not run away. Her love for Jesus helped him to be brave. Mary was strong inside too. *(Pantomime standing tall and putting arm caringly around someone else.)*

Thomas was a carpenter. His hands could make beautiful things. Thomas asked good questions that helped everyone understand Jesus better. Thomas loved Jesus very much. *(Pantomime someone cutting wood with a saw and hammering nails or building something beautiful.)*

Soon Jesus had many disciples. They were from many different places. They had many different gifts to share. And even though some people said, "What's so special about these people?" Jesus loved and valued each one.

Matthew

(Simon) Peter #1

Joanna

Susanna

Mary Magdalene

Jesus

Thomas

Andrew

James

John

Salome

Jesus and the Disciples

The Disciples Remember Words from Micah

(based on Micah 6:1–8)

Fourth Sunday after the Epiphany

Micah 6:1-8

Psalm 15

1 Corinthians 1:18-31

Matthew 5:1-12

Storytelling prop needed:

• a pretend campfire

(Place a pretend campfire on the floor, or imagine a campfire, and invite the children to gather around it.)

One day the disciples sat together around a fire. It was the end of the day. They had been walking with Jesus, teaching about God's love. Now it was time to rest. They held their hands out to the fire to warm them. *(Invite the children to stretch and yawn and hold out their hands to the fire.)* They gave a big yawn and settled comfortably on the blanket.

Then one disciple spoke up, "Friends, it is good that we are Jesus' helpers but I have a question. 'How do we know that we are doing what God wants? How do we know we are helping Jesus?'"

"Hmm," thought the other disciples, "that is a good question. We all want to show our love to God. How do we know what God wants?"

"I know," said another disciple. "Do you remember hearing the words of the prophet Micah? He shared some ways for us to live God's way."

The disciples thought some more.

"I remember!" said another disciple. "Micah said that God wants us to treat each other fairly." *(Invite the children to say an emphatic "Yes! We can do that!" Invite them to think of a gesture to add to the words.)*

"And Micah said that God wants us to be kind and loving to each other and to care for God's earth," called out another disciple. *(Children respond, "Yes! We can do that!")*

"And one more thing," said another disciple. "Micah said that we must think always of God." *(Children respond, "Yes! We can do that!")*

Then all the disciples looked at each other and said, "If we can do those three things, we will be worshipping God with a big heart!" And then one by one, the disciples happily settled down and fell asleep for the night. *(Children pretend to fall asleep by the campfire.)*

Puppets in a Cup

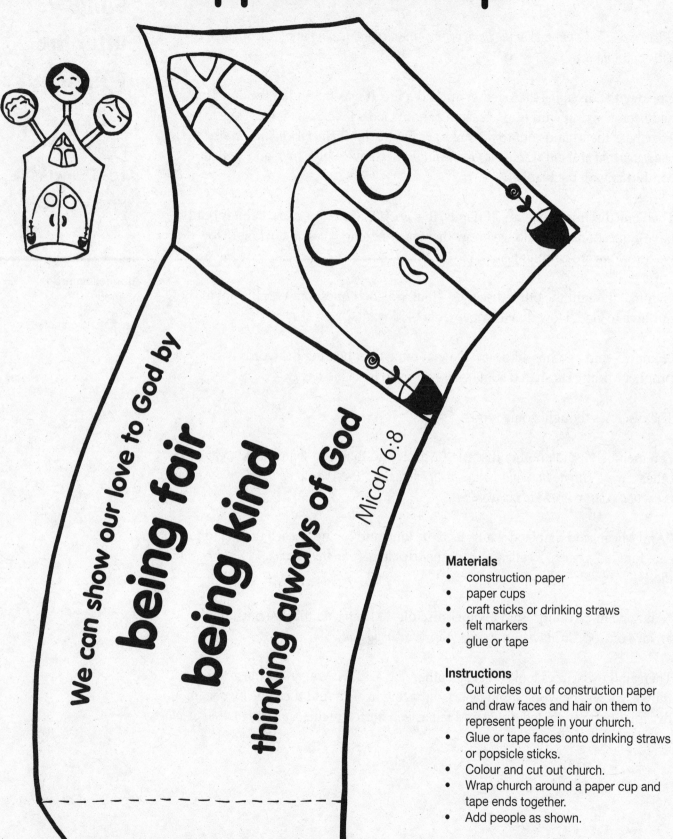

We can show our love to God by

being fair

being kind

thinking always of God

Micah 6:8

Materials

- construction paper
- paper cups
- craft sticks or drinking straws
- felt markers
- glue or tape

Instructions

- Cut circles out of construction paper and draw faces and hair on them to represent people in your church.
- Glue or tape faces onto drinking straws or popsicle sticks.
- Colour and cut out church.
- Wrap church around a paper cup and tape ends together.
- Add people as shown.

Sharing God's Blessing

What can you do to help share God's blessing?

Other ideas for exploring the lectionary readings (Epiphany 4)

1. Praying for our world (Micah 6:1–8)

Ask: If you could make the world "perfect," what things would you keep the same? What things would you change? Discuss these ideas. What do you think God would want to see changed in our world? What would the world look like if everyone lived in God's way?

We can help make the world a better place by living in God's way. We can pray about things that need to change. Generate some prayers to use in the service today. You could paraphrase Micah 6:8, today's key verse. (Record ideas on newsprint. Some ideas might include: Thank you God for... We pray for our church family... We pray for people in need... We pray for our world...)

Try to involve all. Some will offer one-word prayers and others will have a lot to share. Give those who are quieter the opportunity to share their ideas. Keep the language simple. Consider creating a short refrain, perhaps accompanied with some simple movements.

2. The mouse and the lion (Matthew 5:1–12)

Retell Aesop's fable about a mouse that was captured by a hungry lion. The mouse pleads for its life and in return promises to help the lion. The lion is amused by this idea. How could a tiny mouse possibly help him? However, the lion lets the mouse go. A few days later the lion is caught in a hunter's trap. He struggles mightily but is not able to escape. Just then the little mouse arrives. It is not strong enough to untie the ropes. What could it do to help? (It can chew through the rope and free the lion.) So the tiny mouse is able to save the mighty lion.

When Jesus taught people he often said surprising things, which helped them to see things in new ways, just like the lion and the mouse did.

3. What is true worship? (Micah 6:1–8)

Engage in a conversation about worship. What it is, where and when do we worship, etc. Our Bible readings for today speak about worship. Worship is the church service on Sundays, and we also worship God every day by living the way God wants us to. When we are kind to someone, we are worshipping God. When we share what we have, we are worshipping God. In Micah 6:8 we hear that God wants us to be fair and to be kind and to walk in God's way. Encourage the congregation to name some of the ways we can do this at home, at work, at school, and in our church.

Prayer

Dear God,
help us to walk with you in God's way.
Help us to make our world a better place. Amen.

Learning about Jesus

Fifth Sunday after the Epiphany

Isaiah 58:1-9a, (9b-12)

Psalm 112:1-9 (10)

1 Corinthians 2:1-12, (13-16)

Matthew 5:13-20

Station #1: Jesus Tells Stories

Let's pretend I am Jesus. We're walking from town to town to tell others about God. We don't have a car to ride in so we must walk for a long time. *(Walk around the room on the "pathway" a few times, imagining and acting out what it would be like to walk with Jesus.)* We're tired now. Let's stop and rest on this hillside. *(Have the children leave the "pathway" and then sit and close their eyes. Encourage them to imagine they are sitting on top of a hill. What does the ground feel like? What do we smell? What animals do we hear? What can we see from the top of the hill? etc.)* There are many new people with us now. They have followed us here. I'd like to tell them a story. Oh, look! *(Point up at the sky)* Look at the birds in the sky! It looks like fun flying from tree to tree. The birds seem to play all day. God loves them. Oh, and look at those pretty flowers! *(Point across the room.)* They seem to dance in the wind. What colour has God made those flowers? *(Encourage responses.)* God loves us just like God loves the birds and the flowers. *(Move to Station #2.)*

Station #2: Jesus Cares for Others

(Have several dolls and items to care for them set out) Invite the children to imagine that the dolls are the people we are meeting on our travels.
What can we do to show our love for these people? *(Encourage the children to use the items to show their love, e.g. put clothes on the dolls, pretend to feed them, wrap them in blankets, etc.)* Some of these people are sick and sad. What can we do to help them? *(Allow time for the children to act out their responses, e.g. tell a joke, sing a song together, play a simple game, give gentle hugs, apply bandages, say a prayer, etc. Then, move to Station #3.)*

Station #3: Jesus Shares Meals with Others

(Have buns, cheese and fruit set up on a blanket or low table.) Explain that whenever disciples are with Jesus, they learn about God's way. Even when they sit together to eat a snack, Jesus teaches them that God loves them. Jesus likes to visit. Jesus likes to eat good food with his friends. *(Say the prayer and share a snack that Jesus and his disciples might have had together.)*
Prayer: Thank you, God,
  for Jesus' gentle ways
  and thank you for this food.
  Amen. *(Children respond "Amen.")*
(Move to Station #4.)

Station #4: Jesus Learns and Teaches

Explain that Jesus goes to a special place called a synagogue. He goes there to learn the old, old stories about God's people. He helps others to understand those stories too. Jesus and the disciples also go to a huge Temple in Jerusalem to praise God. Singing was one way that they praised God.
Sing: Sing a familiar song or teach a simple song of praise.

Have the children go onto the "pathway" again and follow it around the room. Help the children take their biblical costumes off, explaining that our pretending time is over. Encourage them to talk about what it was like to travel and learn with Jesus.

Storytelling props needed:

• Create a pathway with yarn, tape, or construction paper strips

• Simple biblical costumes (optional) to be put on before the story

• several dolls or stuffed animals and items to care for them (e.g. clothes, drinking cups, food items, rattles, bandages, blankets, etc.

• buns, cheese, fruit or other snack

• choose a simple song of praise to teach or sing

Transfiguration Sunday

Exodus 24:12-18

Psalm 2

or Psalm 99

2 Peter 1:16-21

Matthew 17:1-9

Storytelling props needed:

• 5 candles

It's a Mystery!

(based on Matthew 17:1-9)

(In telling this story pay attention to voice quality. This is a place of awe and wonder. Teach the children the repeated phrase, "And then what happened?" Explain that they are to say this when they see you lighting a candle on the table. You will need 5 candles. Start with a normal tone of voice.)

One day, Jesus invited Peter, James, and John to go for a walk with him up the side of a mountain. They walked for a long time. *(light a candle)*
    And then what happened?
The men were very tired when they got to the top of the mountain.
"Whew! That was a long climb," said Peter.
"It sure was," said James. "I'm glad we're finally at the top."
"Me too!" said John. *(light a candle)*
    And then what happened?
"Look!" cried John. "Jesus is changing!" The three friends looked at Jesus. They couldn't believe their eyes! *(speak in a very quiet voice)* They saw Jesus' face begin to shine. They felt like they were looking right into the sun. His clothes became dazzling white as if he were glowing all over. Peter, James, and John were amazed! *(light a candle)*
    And then what happened?
Suddenly, they saw two people talking with Jesus.
"Who is it?" whispered James.
They looked and listened and realized that it was the prophet Elijah and the great leader Moses. They had died a long time ago!
Peter called out , "Jesus, it is good for us to be here. Let's build three little houses. One for you, one for Moses, and one for Elijah." *(light a candle)*
    And then what happened?
While Peter was still speaking, a bright cloud came all around them and they heard a voice from the cloud!
The voice said, "This is my son. I love him. Listen to him."
Peter, James, and John became very frightened. They fell to the ground. *(light a candle)*
    And then what happened?
Jesus came and touched each of his friends and gently said, "Don't be afraid. Get up."
Peter, James, and John looked up and saw Jesus looking like himself again. The cloud and the bright light was gone. They stood up and began to walk back down the mountain together. The three friends had a lot to think about. They thought they understood everything Jesus was teaching them. But today was a mystery for them. They were very glad that Jesus shared this day with them.

Jesus' face was shining like the sun.

Matthew 17:2

Instructions
- Make a copy for each child.
- Cut a construction paper frame using border area of this picture as a pattern.

Transfiguration Sunday

Exodus 24:12-18

Storytelling props needed:

• shawl or biblical headress and robe

Joshua and Moses Climb a Mountain

(based on Exodus 24:12–18)

(Place the shawl around your shoulders or put on a costume. When the children are invited to climb the mountain with you, you might consider having them sit on a table when you reach the top.)

"Hello, everyone! My name is Joshua. I've heard that you are learning how to be helpers. I've heard that you are learning how to live God's way. Is this true? What are you learning? Please, tell me all about it. *(Allow time for the children to respond.)*

"It sounds as if you are learning so much! Long ago I was a helper too. I was a helper just the same as you. I was a helper to a man named Moses. Let me tell you a story about one very special day when I was helping Moses.

"On this day, Moses received a message from God. God said to Moses, 'Come up the mountain. I want to give you something. I will give you two big stones. There will be words on the stones. The words will teach the people how to live God's way.'
"So Moses invited me to walk up the mountain with him. Let's pretend we are walking up a mountain now. Let's go, everyone! *('Climb' around the room.)*

"Moses and I walked and walked. Look up, everyone. Oh, my! This is a tall mountain! Do you think we can climb it? Moses and I did. We went up and up and up. Whew! This is a long way up. Look around, everyone. What can you see? *(Allow time for responses.)* Does it look different up here on the mountain?

"Let's sit down again and I'll tell you what happened. Moses asked me to sit down too and wait for him. I watched Moses continue to climb right to the top of the mountain. I waited for Moses just as he asked me to. And then something amazing happened! A cloud covered the top of the mountain. I couldn't see Moses anymore! Where was he? Then a brilliant light shone through the cloud. It was so bright!

Something very special was happening. I started to feel God's love all around me. It was such a wonderful feeling but, but... I couldn't understand what was happening. I sat very still and waited and waited for Moses to return. Finally, after a very long time Moses joined me.

"'Come, Joshua,' Moses said to me. 'We will walk back down the mountain now. I have something very important to tell the people. I will tell them about living God's way.'

"So Moses and I slowly walked back down the mountain. *(Children 'climb' down the mountain.)* I had a lot to think about. I was glad that Moses shared this time with me. And I'm glad you've shared this time with me, too. Thank you for listening to my story." *(Remove shawl or costume.)*

Moses and Joshua

Instructions
- make copies of the Moses and Joshua and give a set to each child to colour so they can tell the story using the figures.

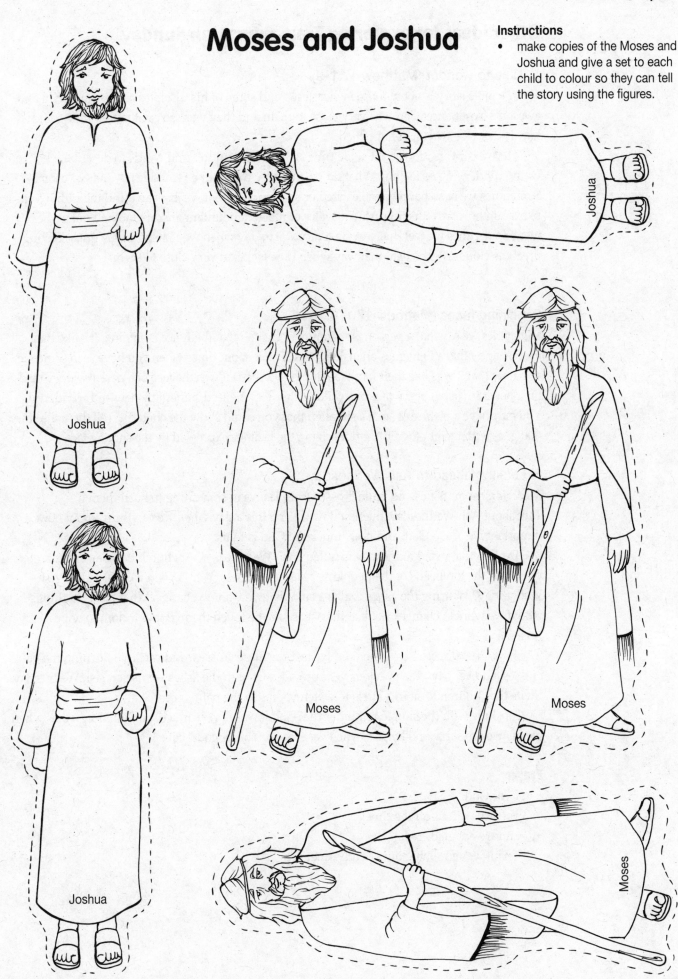

Other ideas for exploring Transfiguration Sunday

1. Time to wonder (Matthew 17:1–9)

Today's Bible story is about a time when Jesus and some of his disciples had a wonderful and awesome experience. God was very close to them and they were so excited that they could hardly describe what had happened.

Have a conversation about some times when you couldn't find words to describe what you were experiencing or feeling. What do we mean by words like "wonderful" and "awesome"? Sometimes we're so happy or so excited or so surprised that we just can't find the right words to explain how we're feeling. Maybe we've climbed a mountain and are looking out at the view. Sometimes we feel that way on a nice warm day when we're lying in the grass looking up at the clouds. People feel that way when they feel God very close to them.

2. Shining faces (Matthew 17:1–9)

Sometimes we say that a person is so happy or excited that their face is shining. It's like they are so happy that a light goes on inside them. Think about times when you have seen someone so happy that it was like their face was shining. Perhaps it was the face of a parent as they held their newborn baby, or the face of a child as they experienced something new and wonderful. You may have a picture of such a situation that you could show the children. Tell them the story that goes with the photograph, emphasizing the feelings expressed by the shining face.

3. Looking ahead to Ash Wednesday

Materials: some ashes and palm crosses from last year, something to burn them in
Talk about Ash Wednesday, the first day of Lent. It is a day when we can think about how important we are to God, and how important God is to us.

Explain that next Wednesday is called "Ash Wednesday." At church that day ashes are placed on the foreheads of the people as a sign of sadness. Why would we feel sad on Ash Wednesday? Wearing the ashes is also a sign that we want to change. What kinds of things would we want to change? Look at the ashes, maybe touch them. (Have a cloth to wipe fingers.)

Show the palm crosses. When did we last see these crosses? Indicate that burning the palm crosses left over from the previous year provides us with the ashes we use on Ash Wednesday. Invite the children to sit in a circle to watch you burn the palm crosses.

Conclude with the simple reminder that God loves us very much, and will forgive us when we say we are sorry and help us when we are sad. This is good news!

Prayer

Dear God,
you are with us all the time,
and we are glad.
Thank you for being our friend. Amen.

Lent/Easter

The Easter cycle begins with Ash Wednesday during the week after Transfiguration, and moves through the seasons of Lent, Easter to Pentecost Sunday.

Through our Lenten contemplations, like Jesus in the wilderness, we voice our need for God's love and we surrender self-will to the divine. The "Great Fifty Days" of Easter expands our conscious awareness of the power of Christ's continuing presence through the Spirit.

LENT is the 40 days (not counting six Sundays) which fall between Ash Wednesday and Holy Saturday. Sundays are not counted in the 40 days of Lent because every Sunday is considered a "little Easter." In the early church, Lent was a time of final preparation for people who were seeking to be baptized. During this period of baptismal preparation, the church community adopted a 40-day discipline of fasting, almsgiving, and prayer. Prayer was for healing souls, fasting for healing bodies, and almsgiving for sharing – which heals community. People reflected on their own way of life in light of baptismal commitments. Then at dawn on Easter morning, as the rising sun announced the resurrection of Christ, baptism was joyfully celebrated. Church members expressed common faith and commitment by renewing their baptismal promises. And the newly baptized joined the rest of the church in sharing the meal of communion.

In our day, we're re-learning the power and significance of preparing during Lent to celebrate baptism, and renewal of baptism, at Easter.

Many people in the northern hemisphere have believed that the word "Lent" comes from the same root as "length," and refers to the lengthening days of spring. Some now believe, however, that it may actually derive from the Latin word lentare which means "to bend." This understanding reinforces a sense of Lent as a time of preparation for personal and collective transformation. Having nurtured ourselves through Advent, Christmas and Epiphany, Lent becomes the time to look truthfully at our selves and make changes.

The colour used throughout Lent is violet, the colour of repentance. Some faith communities use red for Palm/Passion Sunday and through the poignant days of Holy Week. The cross may be shrouded in black for Good Friday, or stripped of all colour during the service of Tenebrae (the liturgy of shadows.)

Lent is a good time to change the mood of physical surroundings through the tone of decorations. Flowers are generally not used. Candlesticks and crosses can be made of simple wood. Vestments and banners should be stark and simple in design and material.

EASTER is the joy and celebration of the Christ-life. The stone is rolled away – the tomb is empty and hearts are full. Jesus lives!

The Easter season is "The Great Fifty Days" of revelation when all creation sings for joy, and the whole panorama of salvation through Christ unfolds before our wondering eyes. The Easter season prepares us for the great synchronicity of life in the Spirit, culminating in the fiery, windy festival of Pentecost, when the Spirit breathes new life into us. During the seven weeks of the season of Easter, we rejoice in the victory of love which is revealed in the resurrection of Jesus, in the transformation of Jesus' followers, and in the biblical vision of Christ as harmony for all of creation.

Through the season of Easter, we're transformed for sacred friendship with Christ and one another in community. The power of resurrection in peoples' lives and in communities is shown in scripture by the transformation of Christ's disciples. Week by week in Sunday worship we hear how the risen Christ came to the disciples, to help them understand how God was making things new, and to help them see the holy in new ways. We hear how the disciples received the gifts of the Spirit, and how the Spirit sent them out as "apostles" speaking languages of love. And we hear how the apostles became a close-knit community, continuing Jesus' ministry as channels of healing and as witnesses to holy love and presence.

The exuberance of Easter should be expressed both musically and visually. Textiles should be fine and elegant, and colours brilliant in contrast to Lent. The colours of Easter are white and gold, signifying purity, new life, rejoicing, and holiness. As the presence of the Spirit becomes more fully manifest through the seven weeks of Easter, tinges of red can be added to the white and gold, until red becomes the dominant colour for Pentecost – the fiery festival which concludes the Easter season.

– excerpted from *Living the Christ Life: Rediscovering the Seasons of the Christian Year*, by Louise Mangan, Nancy Wise, and Lori Farr. Copyright © Wood Lake Publishing Inc., www.woodlakebooks.com. Used by permission.

Ideas and Routines Suggested for Lent/Easter

1. Lenten Family Giving Box Pattern

Use this box to collect a special offering decided by your church.

Instructions

- Cut out pattern
- Trace onto light cardboard and cut out
- Score along dotted lines with a dull knife
- Help children fold on lines
- Glue marked areas
- Press together
- Decorate

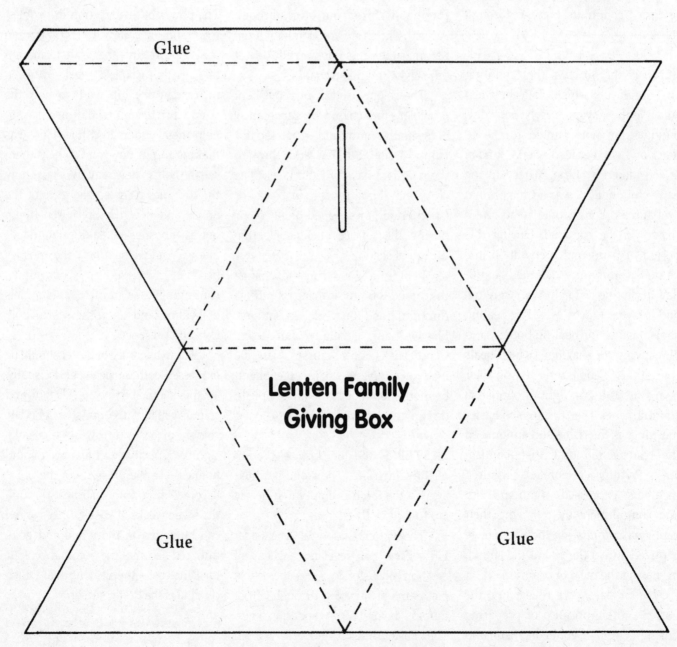

2. Family Ritual Alleluia Eggs

Did you know that in some churches the word "Alleluia" is not used during the season of Lent? The alleluias are put away so that on Easter Day, when everyone shouts "Alleluia!" it will be extra special. Today, the first day of Lent, begin hiding "alleluias" in a special place and prepare a surprise for everyone on Easter Sunday.

Materials needed for each egg: a plastic egg that opens (available from some discount stores), self-adhesive stickers, fine-line permanent markers, 40 purple and 6 gold sequins, a small and large plastic resealable bag, purple paper, 4 "alleluia strips"

Preparation for each egg: Place 40 purple sequins and 6 gold sequins in a small plastic bag. Cut apart the "alleluia" words. Cut out the letter to parents.

Instructions for the children: Decorate the eggs with stickers or markers. Mention to the children that they are getting ready for Easter. Place four "alleluia" strips into each egg. Mention that we are tucking our alleluias away during the season of Lent. Glue the letter to parents on a piece of purple paper. Place the letter, the egg, and the small bag containing the sequins into a larger plastic bag to take home.

Dear parent or caregiver,

Today is the first Sunday in the church season of Lent. During our time together, your child will hear Bible stories and participate in rituals as part of the journey through Lent. Use these items as part of a simple ritual at home with your child for the six weeks of Lent and Easter Sunday.

Prepare a comfortable, quiet place that is free from distractions at mealtime or bedtime. Place this kit in a special container, such as an Easter basket. Each day during Lent gather for this ritual.

Light a candle, repeating these words, "God is near, God is here."

Open the egg. Place one purple sequin inside it. Close it again. (Note: Sundays are considered to be "little Easters," so use a gold sequin.)

Say, "Our alleluias are tucked away. In the time of Lent, we get ready for God's good news of love."

Sing this prayer as a call and response *(tune: "Frère Jacques" or "Are You Sleeping?")*:

God is with us, God is with us.
Yes, we know. Yes, we know.
God will always love us. God will always love us.
Thank you, God. Thank you, God.
Amen.

On Easter Sunday, open the egg, share the "alleluias," and shower everyone with the sequins.

Alleluia!	Alleluia!
Alleluia!	Alleluia!

3. Family Lenten Flower Calendar (# 1)

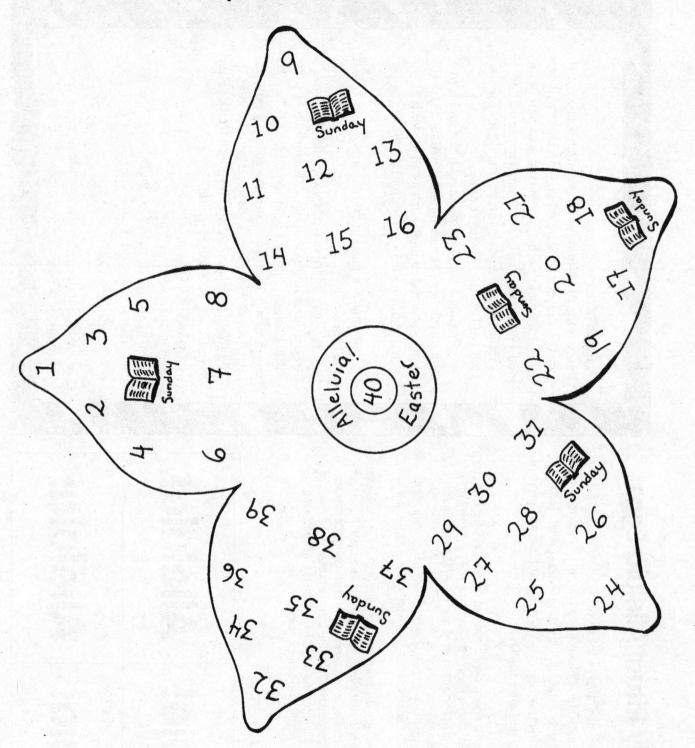

Lenten Flower Calendar

- Give each child a calendar to colour, a sealed envelope with 41 sequins (or self-adhesive stickers or tiny cut-up pieces of pretty paper) inside, and 5 more sequins. Help them glue the sequins on the numbers 1-4 and Bible for Sunday. Suggest they put the calendar on their fridge at home. Glue on a sequin each day to show how close we are to Easter.

Family Lenten Flower Calendar (# 2)

Instructions for Preparing the Family Lenten Flower Calendar

- Make a copy of activity sheet "Lenten Flower Calendar #1" for each child.
- Decide what will be used to glue over each number on the flower (e.g. large sequins, self-adhesive circle stickers, small pieces of cut up paper, etc.).
- Then, for each child, place 41 of those items into an envelope and seal it.
- Glue the instructions for the parent on the outside.
- On the first Sunday, 5 of those items will be glued onto the flower (because Lent started the previous Wednesday – Ash Wednesday).
- Altogether 46 items will be glued onto the flower (40 days plus 6 Sundays). The children might like to colour around the centre on Easter Sunday and say "Alleluia."

Dear Parent,

Lent is the 40 days of preparation for the celebration of Easter. The 6 Sundays that fall during Lent are not included in the 40 days because every Sunday is a "little Easter" – a celebration of the resurrection.

Please hang this Lenten calendar on a wall or refrigerator. Each day (including Sundays), help your child cover the next number (or Bible) with one of the items in the envelope. Help your child see how close Easter is coming. We have already glued on 5 items (because Lent started this past Wednesday – Ash Wednesday). Altogether, 46 items will be glued on the flower. On Easter Sunday invite your child to colour around the centre and say "Alleluia!" at the same time.

Dear Parent,

Lent is the 40 days of preparation for the celebration of Easter. The 6 Sundays that fall during Lent are not included in the 40 days because every Sunday is a "little Easter" – a celebration of the resurrection.

Please hang this Lenten calendar on a wall or refrigerator. Each day (including Sundays), help your child cover the next number (or Bible) with one of the items in the envelope. Help your child see how close Easter is coming. We have already glued on 5 items (because Lent started this past Wednesday – Ash Wednesday). Altogether, 46 items will be glued on the flower. On Easter Sunday invite your child to colour around the centre and say "Alleluia!" at the same time.

Dear Parent,

Lent is the 40 days of preparation for the celebration of Easter. The 6 Sundays that fall during Lent are not included in the 40 days because every Sunday is a "little Easter" – a celebration of the resurrection.

Please hang this Lenten calendar on a wall or refrigerator. Each day (including Sundays), help your child cover the next number (or Bible) with one of the items in the envelope. Help your child see how close Easter is coming. We have already glued on 5 items (because Lent started this past Wednesday – Ash Wednesday). Altogether, 46 items will be glued on the flower. On Easter Sunday invite your child to colour around the centre and say "Alleluia!" at the same time.

Storytelling figures

Instructions
   Make enough copies in order
to tell the stories (page 71,
73, 80,85, and 92)

Adam and Eve in the Garden

(based on Genesis 2:15–17; 3:1–7)

Place your story basket in front of you. Help the children identify the pieces: purple cloth, two storytelling figures: one woman and one man, ball of play dough. Place the items back in the baskets. Wait until all is quiet. Then spread the purple cloth on the floor in front of you.

A long time ago God created a beautiful place called the Garden of Eden. This garden was filled with trees and flowers, animals and birds. I wonder what kinds of animals and birds were in the garden. (*Invite responses.*)

God also created two people: a man named Adam, and a woman named Eve. (*Place the two story figures on the purple cloth.*) Adam and Eve took care of the garden. God told them to enjoy the birds and the flowers, and to eat the delicious fruit from the trees – except for one tree.

In the middle of the garden, God had planted a special tree. The fruit looked very good to Adam and Eve. But God told them they could eat the fruit from all the other trees except for this special tree.

One day, when Eve was walking in the garden, she met a snake, a snake that could talk. (*Roll out the play dough and form a snake. Place it between the two people*).

The snake said to Eve, "Did God tell you not to eat the fruit from these trees in the garden?"

Eve said, "We can eat as much fruit as we want, but we are not to eat the fruit from the special tree in the middle of the garden. We are not even to touch the fruit!" The snake said, "Don't worry, you won't be harmed. Go on, eat it!"

So Eve and Adam picked the delicious fruit and ate it. They listened to the snake and not God. (*Pause.*)

Now Adam and Eve felt very sad because they did something they were not supposed to do. They wondered what would happen to them. (*Remove Adam, Eve, and the snake and return them to the story basket.*)

But the story does not end there. God did not leave them alone. They knew that God would always be with them. And God was. (*Ask these questions thoughtfully.*)

I wonder if Adam and Eve were afraid?
I wonder how they knew God was with them?
I wonder how we know God is here?

(Reverently place each of the storytelling props back in the basket. The props may be given to the children to practice telling the story themselves.)

First Sunday in Lent

Genesis 2:15-17, 3:1-7

Psalm 32

Romans 5:12-19

Matthew 4:1-11

Storytelling props needed:

• story basket

• purple cloth

• a man and a woman storytelling figure from page 70

• small ball of play dough

Play dough recipe

60 grams (1/2 cup) flour
30 grams (1/4 cup) salt
60 mls (1/4 cup) water

Mix the flour and salt together in a bowl. Slowly add the water while mixing until the dry ingredients are uniformly moistened. Knead for several minutes. Store in a plastic bag or container.

We Make Choices

Every day we need to make choices.

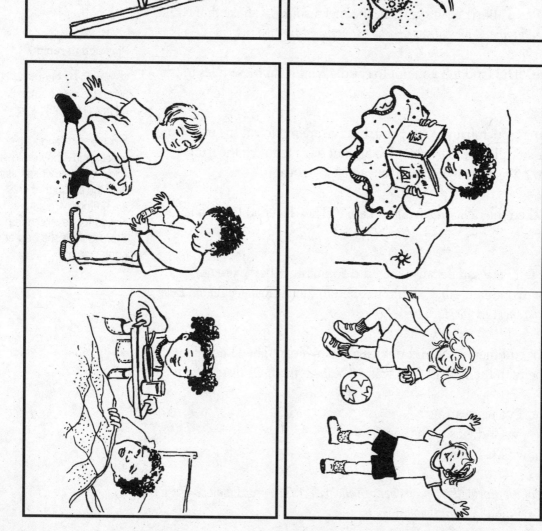

Instructions
- Look at the pairs of pictures.
- Choose one in each pair you would like to do.
- Colour your choice.

We Thank You, God

(based on Psalm 121)

Second Sunday in Lent

Genesis 12:1-4a

Psalm 121

Romans 4:1-5, 13-17

John 3:1-17

Place your story basket in front of you. Help the children identify each item: purple cloth, six story figures, yarn, streamer, paper. Place items back in the baskets. Take out the paper and crumple it into a ball. Place it on the floor and cover it with the purple cloth so that a "mountain" is created. Wait until all is quiet.)

A long, long time ago, God created the mountains and the sky (*point to the mountain*). God made the hills and the valleys and pathways ran through them. (*Using the yarn, create a winding path starting at one end of the cloth and ending at the opposite end.*)

God created girls and boys and women and men to enjoy God's beautiful world. (*Set out the story figures at the beginning of the path.*) God loved the people very much and took good care of them. The people wanted to find a way to show their love to God. So they made up songs, which were called psalms. This is one psalm they sang. (*Make up a chant to the words below. Invite the children to do what you do.*)

> Where does my help come from? (*Hold hand above eyes.*)
> My help comes from God (*Extend outstretched arms, palms up.*),
> who made heaven and earth. (*Raise right hand on "heaven," lower left hand on "earth."*)
> God is always with us! (*Pick up streamer and wave it.*)

Sometimes the people travelled to Jerusalem to worship God in the temple. On the way they would stop and thank God for caring for them. (*One at a time move the people along the path.*) Let's say a prayer right now.

> Dear God, thank you for always looking after us.
> Thank you for keeping us safe when we are at home or away.
> We love you. Amen.

Sometimes when the people came to a mountain (*move figures near the mountain*) they would sing and dance and celebrate that God was with them. (*Wave the streamers. Sing the following song to the tune "Jesus Loves Me."*)

> God is with me every night.
> God is with me every day.
> God cares for me all the time,
> when I sleep and when I play.
> Yes, God is with me.
> Yes, God is with me.
> Yes, God is with me.
> I love God very much.

After the people shared their love with God, they would continue on their way. They could trust that God was with them and caring for them. (*Move figures to the end of the path. Wave streamers again and say, "Thank you, God."*)

Storytelling props needed:

- story basket
- purple cloth
- 6 various storytelling figures from page 70
- yarn
- streamer
- paper to create a mountain

Celebrate God's Loving Presence with Musical Instruments

Children enjoy singing and making music. Through music, they can express their love for God and celebrate their joy as children of God. Follow the instructions below for simple music-makers to accompany the songs from this session.

(Note: aquarium gravel, buttons, or paper clips could be substituted for the small pebbles.)

Plastic bottle shaker

Materials: clean, plastic bottle with lid, gift wrap or construction paper, stickers or permanent markers, small pebbles

Instructions
1. Cut out gift wrap to wrap around the bottle.
2. On the paper, print the words, "Rejoice, God is with us."
3. Glue or tape the paper to the bottle.
4. Decorate the bottle with stickers or pictures using markers.
5. Fill the bottle one-quarter full with pebbles.
6. Place white glue around the inside rim of the bottle and seal closed.

Egg carton shaker

Materials: an empty egg carton, tissue paper or crepe paper squares, glue sticks, masking tape, small pebbles

Instructions
1. Put some pebbles into the carton.
2. Tape the carton closed.
3. Decorate by gluing the paper squares all over the carton.

Tambourine shaker with streamers

Materials: two reusable foil kitchen plates (approximately 12 cm/5 in), small pebbles, two strips of crepe paper or ribbon (40 cm/16 in)

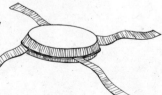

Instructions
1. Place a handful of pebbles inside one plate.
2. Form a cross with the two pieces of ribbon over the plate.
3. Place the second plate upside down on the first.
4. Staple the two plates together around the rim, being sure to staple the ribbon in place.

Balloon shaker

Materials: balloons, small pebbles, self-adhesive stickers

Instructions
1. Pour a small number of pebbles into a deflated balloon.
2. Inflate it, but not fully.
3. Decorate with self-adhesive stickers.

Paper bag shaker

Materials: a small paper bag, small pebbles, markers or crayons, stapler

Instructions
1. Decorate the bag with markers or crayons.
2. Put the pebbles into the bag.
3. Staple the top of the bag closed.
4. Hold the top of the bag and shake.

Songs That Celebrate God's Loving Care and Presence

Sing these songs with joy, using the shakers and tambourines with enthusiasm.

God Is with Me
(tune: "Jesus Loves Me")
God is with me every night.
God is with me every day.
God cares for me all the time,
when I sleep and when I play.
Yes, God is with me.
Yes, God is with me.
Yes, God is with me.
I love God very much.

God Is with Us
(tune: "Frère Jacques" or "Are You Sleeping?")
God is with us, God is with us.
Yes, we know. Yes, we know.
God will always love us. God will always love us.
Thank you, God. Thank you, God.

Abraham and Sarah's Long Journey

(based on Genesis 12:1-4a)

Lent 2

Genesis 12:1-4a

Sarah and Abraham lived very long ago in a city called Haran. *(Bring out figures of Sarah and Abraham.)* They had lived there a long time – ever since they were young – and they liked their city very much. Sarah and Abraham were quite rich. They had sheep and goats and cows and chickens and donkeys. They had a lot of servants to help them care for all their animals and things. *(Bring out figures of servants and animals.)*

One day God had a big surprise for Abraham and Sarah. God told them to move. Just like that! "Leave your home and friends behind. Just go. I'll tell you where, later." Sarah and Abraham both loved God so they listened and started to get ready to leave the city of Haran.

It was a big job! They had to pack up many tents for all the people. They had to pack food for all the family and their servants. They had to plan how to take all their animals along. Their nephew Lot was going to go with them. *(Bring out figure of Lot.)* He helped them get everything packed and ready to go.

Finally, everything was ready. Sarah and Abraham gathered with their servants for a prayer before they left. *(Group story figures together.)* They thanked God for their home and life in Haran. They asked God to travel with them and keep them safe. Then they all set out on their journey – Sarah, Abraham, Lot, the servants, and the animals.

They didn't know where they were going but each day they celebrated that God was with them.

Storytelling props needed:

• story figures of Sarah, Abraham, Lot, Servants and animals from page 76 (colour and cut out a set.)

Materials: activity sheet "Abraham and Sarah Story Figures," craft sticks, play dough (see recipe on page 71) or plasticine

In advance: make copies of the activity sheet and cut out a set of figures for each child.

Look together at a set of story figures and recall Abraham and Sarah's journey. God was with Abraham and Sarah as they travelled and God is with us. Hand out a set of figures to each child and invite them to use crayons or markers to colour the figures. Tape or glue a craft stick to the back of each figure. Place the end of the stick in a small lump of play dough to make it stand upright. Encourage the children to use their figures to tell the story to their families.

Sarah and Abraham Figures

Nicodemus Learns from Jesus

(based on John 3:1–17)

Lent 2

John 3:1–17

(Open and close the flap of the paper bag to make the Nicodemus puppet look as though he is talking.)

Storytelling props needed:

• "Nicodemus puppet" on page 78. (See the instructions on page 79.)

Hello, girls and boys. My name is Nicodemus. Ever since I was a child like you, I've wanted to know more about God. I love to learn! Sometimes I learn by looking. Sometimes I learn by listening. Sometimes I learn by touching. Often I learn by talking. That's why I was so happy to talk with Jesus.

My friends and I saw that Jesus was helping everyone he met. We knew he must have a special friendship with God. I had so many questions to ask him! So one night, I decided to go and talk with him. I was glad that he wanted to talk about God too. He listened to all my questions. Jesus told me that God's Spirit is like the wind.

(Blow so that the children can hear and feel your breath.) We can hear the wind. We can feel the wind. But we don't know where it comes from. We don't know where it will blow next. Jesus said that if I am filled with God's Spirit it will be like beginning life all over again. I didn't understand. I still had so many questions. Begin my life again? How can I do that? Jesus said that God loves me very much. If I let that love grow inside me then I will be a new kind of person!

I said goodbye to Jesus and went home. It was late at night but I couldn't sleep. I was too excited. I knew that meeting Jesus had given me a new life—a life full of God's love.

A Time for Wondering
I wonder how Nicodemus could be a grown-up man, an important teacher, and still have lots to learn?
I wonder what we learn from Jesus?

Circle Song: *(Join hands and move in a circle as everyone sings the following song. Then, go back to the first verse and continue until the children get the idea that this song circles around. Song tune: "Drunken Sailor" [traditional folk tune]).*

Song: "Learners Together"
God wants us to ask good questions *(3x)*
questions help us lea-rn.

God wants us to keep on learning *(3x)*
learning helps us gro-ow.

God wants us to keep on growing *(3x)*
grow and ask good questions!

Nicodemus Paper Bag Puppet

Puppet Instructions

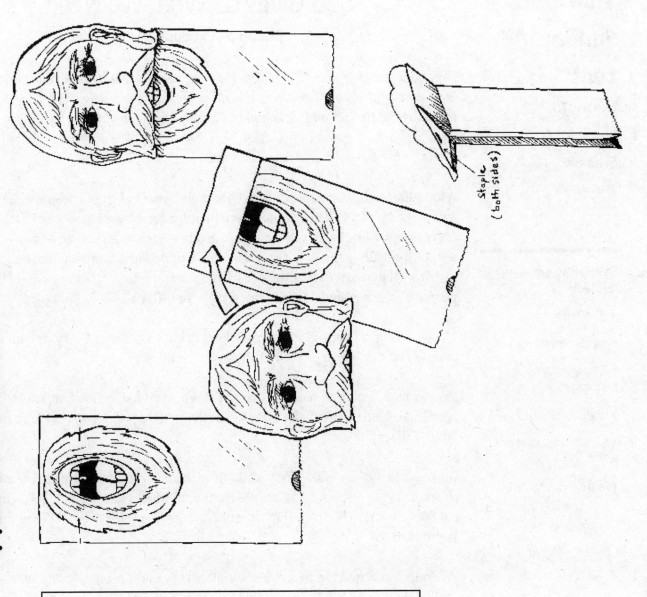

Instructions
Before

- Make a copy for each child and cut out.
- Line up the lower jaw along the edge of the folded bag bottom by using the little line on the lower jaw. Once in place, glue it down.
- Now line up the face so the upper lip or teeth just touch or slightly overlap the teeth of the lower jaw. Once in position trace the outline of the face onto the bag. Put glue inside the tracing marks and glue the face on the bag.
- Staple the edge on each side of the top flap. (This makes it easier for a small hand to move the flap without having it open.)

During

- Have children colour the face and the bag.
- Show them how to move the flap of the bag to make Nicodemus "talk."

Staple (both sides)

Third Sunday in Lent

Exodus 17:1-7

Psalm 95

Romans 5:1-11

John 4:5-42

Storytelling props needed:

• story basket

• purple cloth

• 3 storytelling figures from page 70

• large stone

• tiny closed container of water

• twig

God Gives Us What We Need

(based on Exodus 17:1–7)

Place your story basket in front of you. Help the children identify each item: purple cloth, three story figures, large stone, tiny closed container of water, twig. Place items back in the basket. Set the rock on the cloth near a corner. Tell the children that when you raise your hand to your mouth as if to drink, the children say, **"We're thirsty. We're thirsty."** *Practice a few times. Proceed when all is quiet.)*

A long time ago the people of Israel left their home in Egypt and travelled far, far away to a new land. They went where their leader, Moses, took them. (*Pick up one figure to lead. Move the figures slowly one at a time across the cloth to the middle.*) They set up camp along the way. One time they stopped at a campsite that had no water to drink. They went to their leader, Moses (*two figures face the third*), and all the people said (*raise hand*), **"We're thirsty. We're thirsty."**

Moses was upset because the people kept asking for water. Every day, all the people said (*raise hand*), **"We're thirsty. We're thirsty."**

(*Move Moses away from the other two.*) Moses prayed to God, "What am I to do? The people are going to hurt me! They keep saying to me (*raise hand*), **'We're thirsty. We're thirsty.'"**

God said to Moses, "Take your walking stick and wait for me by the big rock." (*Move figures to the rock.*) The people went with Moses to see what God would do. All the way to the big rock they complained, saying (*raise hand*), **"We're thirsty. We're thirsty."**

When they reached the rock, Moses took his stick and hit it. (*Pick up your stick and gently hit the rock.*) What do you think happened next? (*Wait for responses.*)

Suddenly water came gushing out of the rock– clean, good water for all the people to drink. (*Carefully open the container and pour the water onto the rock.*) Water from a rock! What an amazing thing! What a wonderful surprise God gave the people! The people drank and drank until they could not drink another sip of water. Then they knew that God was still with them and God would provide what they needed.

After that, the people did not have to say (*raise hand*), **"We're thirsty. We're thirsty."** Instead they could say, "Thank you, God, for giving us what we need. Thank you, God, for being with us even when we are thirsty." (*Pause before inviting reflection.*)

I wonder how the people felt when there was no water to drink?
I wonder if Moses was surprised when he hit the rock?
I wonder if God gives us what we need?

God Gives Water

Travel with Moses and God's people to find water.
Use your finger or a crayon to walk with Moses to find the water.

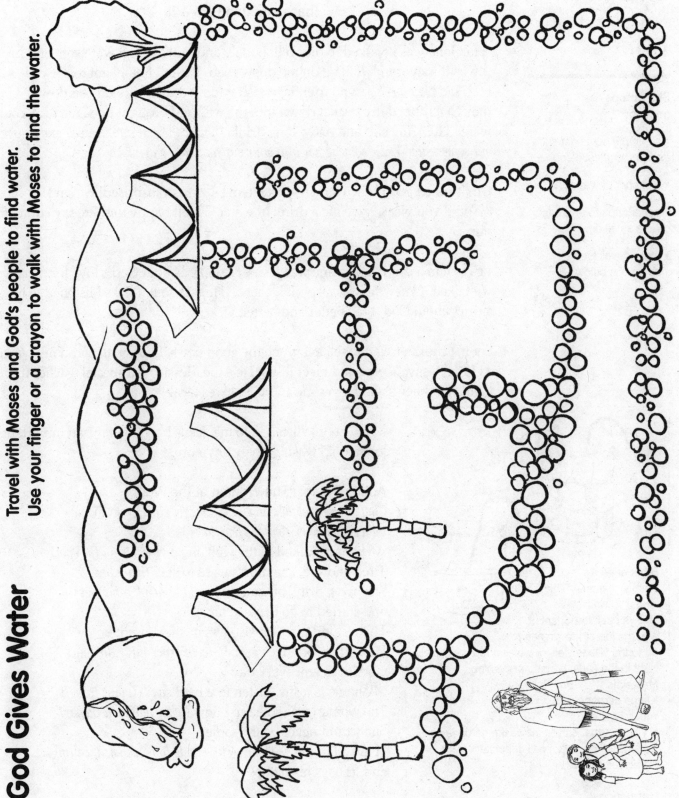

Lent 3

John 4:5–12

Good News at the Well

(based on John 4:5–12)

I felt lonely as I walked to the well. Lonely and hot! My feet were sore and I was thirsty from walking on the dusty road. When I finally got to the well, I felt sad because I had no friends to visit with. It did feel good to sit down though. I dipped my bucket down into the well and brought up some nice, cool water. I took my cup and had a long drink. (*Lower the pail into the well and bring out some water. Ladle some water into your cup and have a drink.*)

Oh, it tasted good! Then a man spoke to me. I was so surprised! He said, "Would you please give me a drink of water?" I felt happy to share my cup with him.

I gave him a drink. His name was Jesus. He talked about God's love for me. As we talked, I knew he was a special teacher. He was so kind! As I listened to his stories about God, I felt better and better.

Soon, I couldn't wait to tell everyone the good news. I forgot all about my water as I ran to say, "Come and meet Jesus! He's the Messiah – a special teacher from God. Good news! God loves me and God loves us all!"

Many people listened to me. Jesus had given me an important job to do. I wasn't lonely anymore.

Action Poem: "The Woman at the Well"
(*Say the poem slowly and encourage the children to do the italicized actions. Repeat a few times.*)
A woman walked to the well one day (*walk on the spot*)
Tired and sad, she didn't want to stay (*hang head*)
She had a drink of water (*pretend to drink from glass*)
and started to go (*walk on the spot*)
Then a kind man spoke – a man she did not know.
He said, "God loves you. (*stretch arms out, palms up*)
God loves you every day.
My name is Jesus. Listen to what I say!" (*point to self*)
The woman was so happy now (*wave hands in the air*)
She would never be the same.
"I talked to the Messiah (*cup hands to mouth as if calling*)
and Jesus is his name!"

Story props needed:

• an empty container such as a pail or plastic cup,

• a pitcher of water

• paper cups to give each child a small drink,

• make a well (see instructions below)

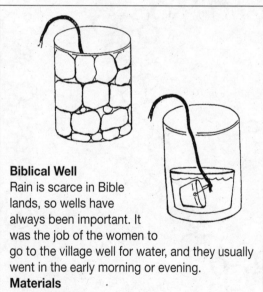

Biblical Well
Rain is scarce in Bible lands, so wells have always been important. It was the job of the women to go to the village well for water, and they usually went in the early morning or evening.

Materials
• large garbage can
• mural paper
• a bucket that can sit inside the garbage can
• a smaller ice cream pail or bucket
• a piece of rope

Instructions
Cover the garbage can with mural paper and colour or paint a stone design. Place a bucket of water inside the garbage can. Tie a rope to the small pail and lower it into the "well." Draw up a full pail of water.

Folded Paper Cup

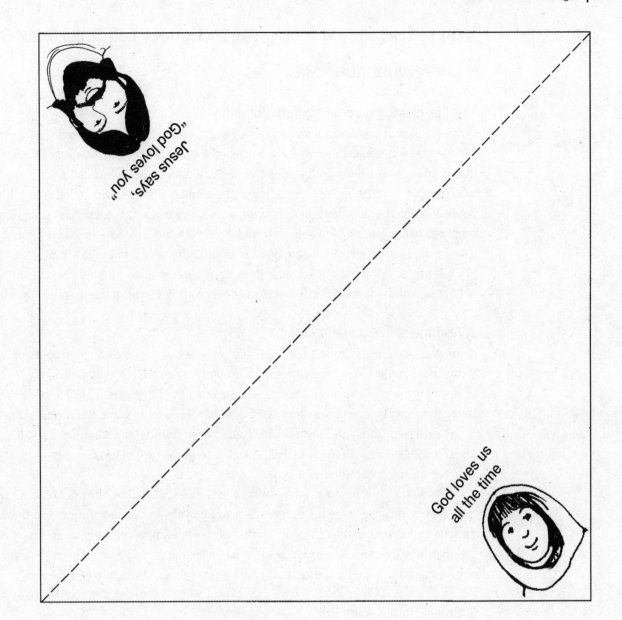

"God loves you."
Jesus says,

God loves us
all the time

Instructions

- Make copies on white paper and cut out.
- Fold paper into a triangle, with pictures at the top inside.
- Fold one bottom corner over to touch the middle of the opposite side. Repeat with the other corner.
- Fold down the small triangular pieces at the top of your cup – one over the front and one over the back.
- Decorate the cup and then pop it open.
- Give the children extra copies to take home to share the message.

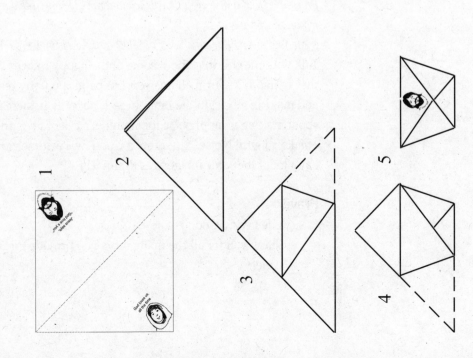

Other ideas for exploring the lectionary readings (Lent 3) – Life-giving moments

1. A life-changing conversation (John 4:5–42)

(Invite the woman who has read the part of the Samaritan women from the Gospel reading for today to come and talk with the children. Ask her to imagine what it was like to have Jesus talk with her – a woman and a social outcast.) Indicate that today you have a special guest who is going to tell us what happened when she met Jesus. Invite the woman from the well to tell the children about her feelings in the story and then encourage children to ask any questions they might have. Be prepared to ask questions to help the children get started. Her basic message should be that Jesus made her feel respected and loved even though she had made lots of mistakes in her life. She might also point out that in those days Jesus was breaking all kinds of rules by talking to her because she was a woman. Jesus invites everyone to be full participants in the church.

2. Springs of living water (John 4:5–42)

Before the conversation reflect upon the difference between two different sources of water represented by the Greek words *phrear* (a humanly made well or cistern) and *pege* (a natural source of water like a spring). The first source of water (phrear) is subject to becoming dry or losing its contents when the cistern is cracked or there is a drought; the second source of water (pege) gushes up from an inexhaustible source deep within the ground and never runs dry. Jesus' conversation with the Samaritan woman in John's gospel today is based upon playing with the meaning of these two words.

Engage the children in a conversation about different sources of water without using the Greek words. Describe the difference between a cistern and a spring-fed well. Invite the children to act out the difference with their bodies. Enjoy their offerings. End your time together with a sentence such as: "Jesus is like a spring of living water for us – never ending, always quenching, making sure that we are always moist and ready for new life."

3. Small drum (Psalm 95)

If possible, find a liturgical dancer to combine the song, the dance, and the children's participation with rythym instruments.
Materials: a small drum/shaker or other joyful noisemakers
Talk with the children about some of the happy images in Psalm 95. How do people show they're happy? Affirm all answers but be particularly responsive if a child suggests singing and making music. In the Bible, in fact, not only is there is a lot of talk about singing but also about making a joyful noise for God. Let's celebrate with noise right now! We're going to sing "Make a Joyful Noise," (by Linnea Good, www.linneagood.com) (It is based on Psalm 100 but has a lot of the same imagery as Psalm 95.)

Prayer

> Life giving God,
> thank you for all the many ways you provide for us to enjoy life.
> Amen.

Samuel Listens to God

(based on I Samuel 16:1–13)

Fourth Sunday in Lent

1 Samuel 16:1-13

Psalm 23

Ephesians 5:8-14

John 9:1-41

Place your story basket in front of you. Help the children identify each item: purple cloth, ten story figures, tiny closed container of oil and a cotton ball, smaller piece of cloth. Place items back in the baskets. Prepare for the story.

First, we prepare our story cloth. *(Set out the purple cloth.)*
Next, we put out Jesse's house. *(Place smaller cloth on purple cloth.)*

Let's put Jesse in his house. *(Place one figure in the house.)*

Now let's put his eight sons in the house. *(Count each one as they go in the house.)*

But wait! The youngest son is in the field. His name is David. He is looking after the sheep. *(Take out the smallest figure and place him near the edge of the purple cloth.)*

This is Samuel, God's leader. *(Hold the last story figure in hand as you begin the story.)*
This is a special oil that Samuel used. We will use it later. *(Hold it, then place it in the basket.)*

Samuel loved God and listened to God when he was a young child like you. He listened to God when he was a grownup, too. One day God told Samuel that it was time to find a new king. God said, "Samuel, take oil with you to Bethlehem. There you will find the new king."

So Samuel went to Jesse's house. *(Move Samuel along the cloth to the house.)* Samuel was sure that one of Jesse's sons would be the new king. Jesse told his sons to stand in a row so that Samuel could look at them. *(Place the seven story figures in a row on the cloth. Place Jesse and Samuel near the row of figures.)*

Then Jesse pointed to his oldest son. *(Children touch the first figure.)* He said to Samuel, "Is this the one who will be king?"

Samuel shook his head and said, "No, he's not the one." *(Children shake head and repeat this line.)*

Jesse pointed to his second son *(touch next figure)*. "Is this the one who will be king?"

Samuel shook his head and said, "No, he's not the one." *(Children repeat.)* *(Repeat comments and actions for the other five story figures.)*

Then Samuel said, "God has not chosen any of your sons to be the next king. Do you have more sons?" *(Wait for the children to answer.)*

Jesse answered, "Yes, my youngest boy, David, is out in the field looking after the sheep."

"You must go and bring him here," said Samuel. *(Move David from the field to the house.)*

When Samuel saw David, he knew that this was the one who would be king. He knew that God had led him to this house to find David. Samuel was happy that he had listened to God. Then Samuel took his oil and anointed David to be the next leader. *(Carefully open the canister, take out the cotton ball and dab it on the head of David.)* David became a great king because, like Samuel, he listened to God.

Storytelling props needed:

• purple cloth

• 10 story figures from page 70

• tiny closed container of oil and a cotton ball

• smaller piece of cloth

Samuel Anoints David

(based on 1 Samuel 16:1-13)

Draw a line from the face on the side to the same face in the picture. Decorate the picture using crayons or markers. Dab a cotton ball in oil and use it to anoint David's head. Take the picture home and remember to trust and follow God as Samuel and David did.

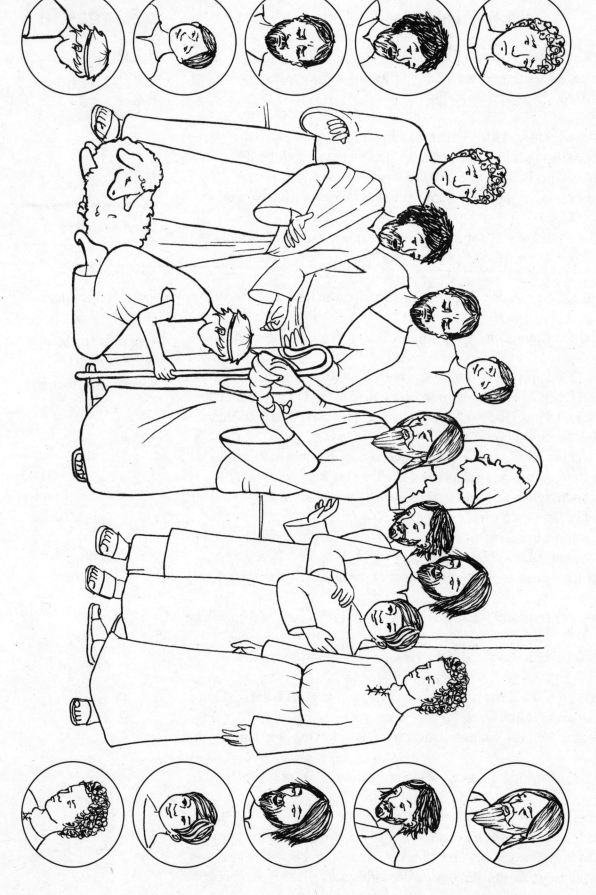

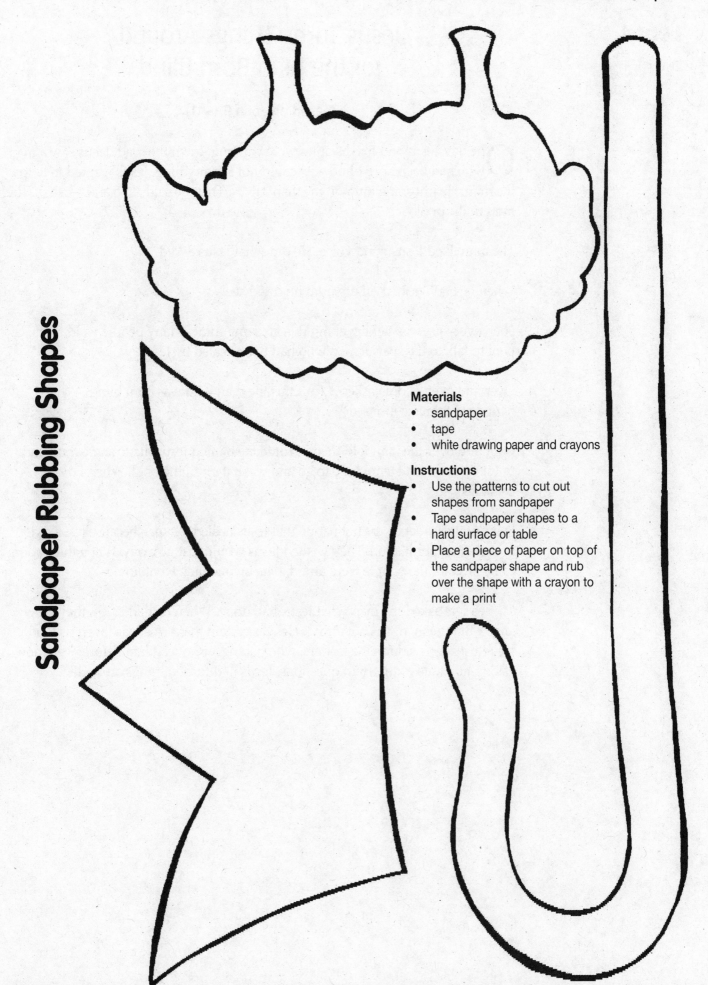

Sandpaper Rubbing Shapes

Materials
- sandpaper
- tape
- white drawing paper and crayons

Instructions
- Use the patterns to cut out shapes from sandpaper
- Tape sandpaper shapes to a hard surface or table
- Place a piece of paper on top of the sandpaper shape and rub over the shape with a crayon to make a print

Jesus Turns Things Around
for the Man Born Blind

(based on John 9:1–41)

One day, Jesus and his disciples were walking down the road. Jesus saw a man who had been born blind – he could not see anything. Jesus wanted to help the man. He put some mud on the man's eyes. Then he said, "Go and wash off the mud in the pool."

The man liked Jesus' kind voice. He did what Jesus asked.

When he had washed off the mud he could see!

Soon everyone was talking about this amazing thing. Many people went to the pool to talk to the special man who had been healed by Jesus.

Over and over, people asked, "Isn't this the man who was born blind? What happened to make him see?"

Over and over the man told them, "Someone named Jesus made some mud and put it on my eyes. He told me to go and wash it off in the pool. When I did, I could see!"

Some of the leaders were not happy that Jesus healed the man because Jesus did not ask their permission. They wished Jesus would just go away. When the leaders came around, the people were afraid. One by one they went home.

The leaders asked the man what Jesus had done. When he told them, they grew angry. But the man was not afraid. He was certain that Jesus was loved by God. He felt strong inside as the leaders, who had never noticed him before, were now asking him many important questions. Jesus had turned things around!

Jesus turns things around for the man born blind

fold

fold

Jesus teaches us to see in new ways

Jesus teaches us to see in new ways

Instructions

- Cut one strip and fold in half (pictures facing out).
- Color both pictures.
- Tape a pencil, straw, or dowel to the inside.
- Tape the sides together.
- To set the Blind Man in motion, revolve the pencil back and forth between your palms.

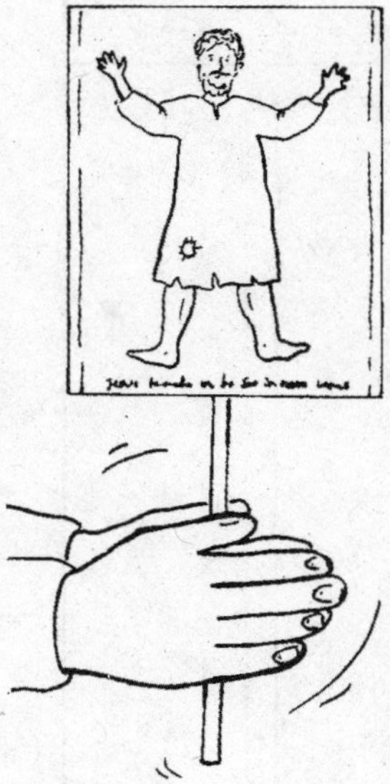

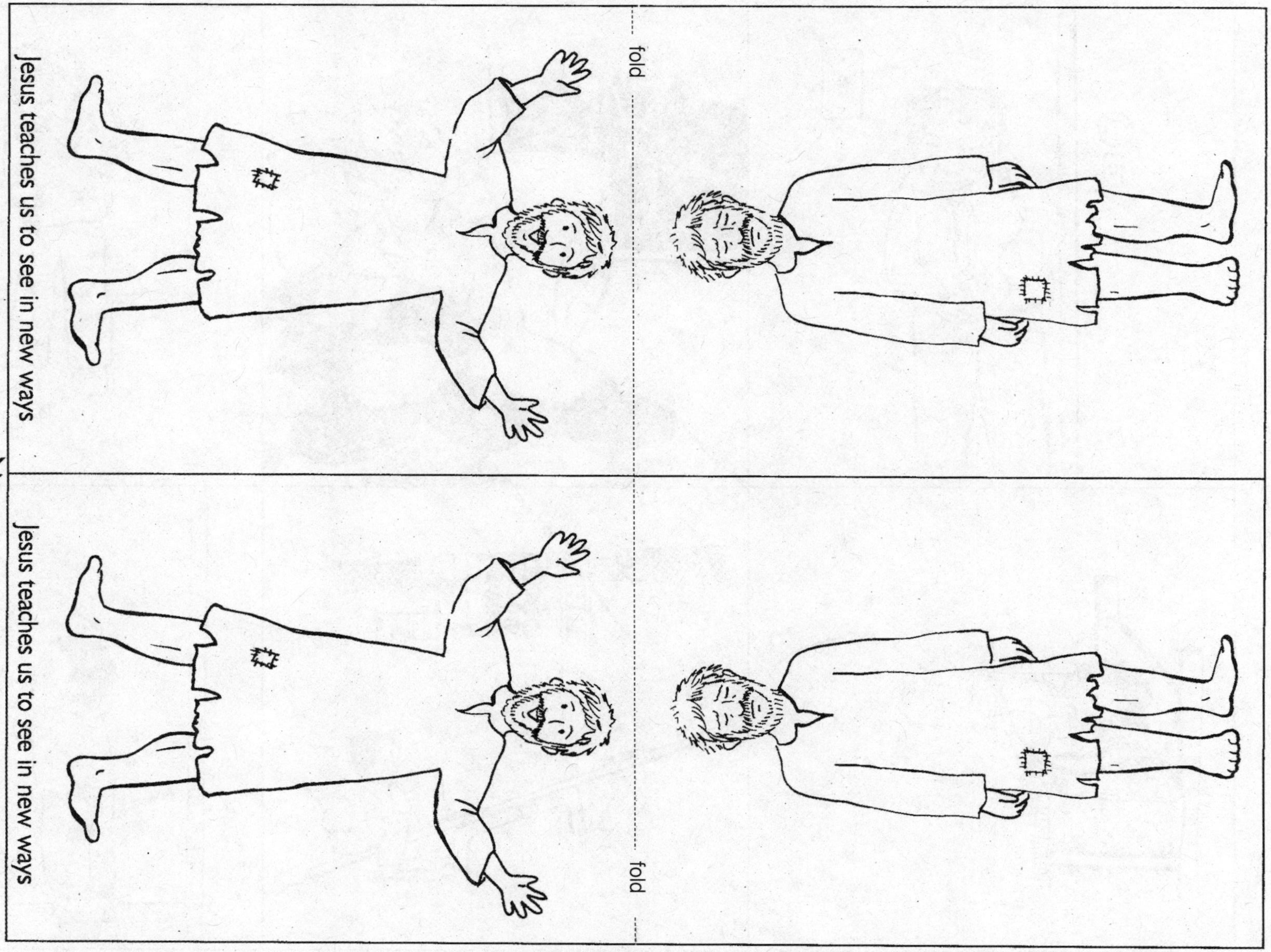

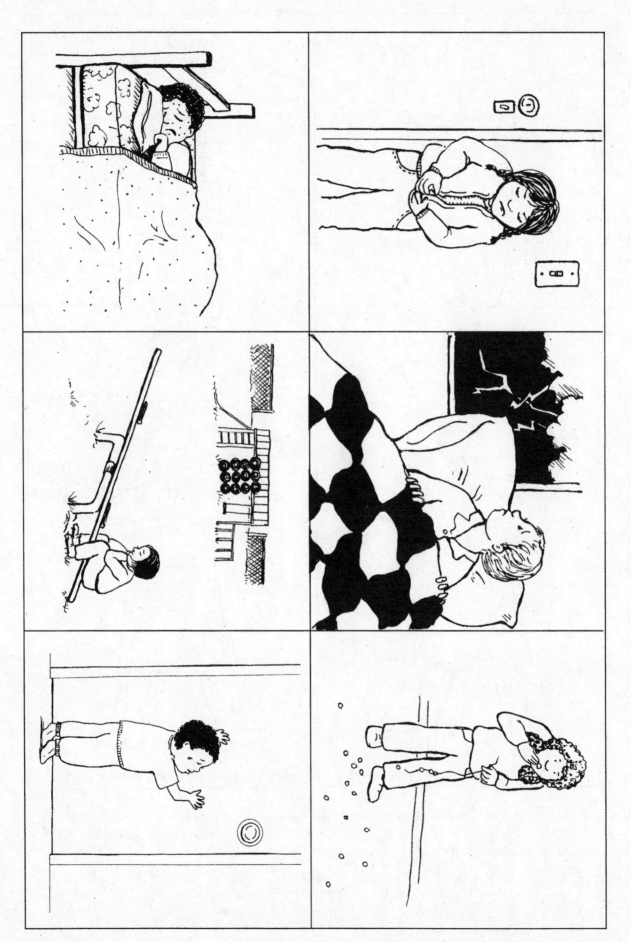

Our Love Can Turn Things Around

How could you turn things around for the people in these pictures?

Other ideas for exploring the lectionary readings (Lent 4)

1. God sees things differently

Materials: an assortment of seeing aids such as a magnifying glass, binoculars, dragon's eye, kaleidoscope, rose-coloured glasses

Use the seeing objects to demonstrate seeing differently. Talk about how many of the stories in the Bible show us the way God sees things. Sometimes, especially when we're having difficulty with something or someone, it can really help to stop and look again "through God's eyes." Think of some examples together, such as changing our opinion about someone because we look again through God's eyes. In your groups today you're going to hear a story about the way God sees things.

2. The light in the chapel

Materials: one tealight candle for every child

Tell the true story of a church that was built in the mountains of Switzerland. It was a beautiful church that had been built with great care, but there was something important missing. There were no lights in the church, not one. Everyone was shocked. How could they have forgotten the lights?

When the time came for the first service the people realized that they would have to bring their own lights. The little church started to fill with light, and as more and more people arrived with their lanterns the light became brighter and brighter. Suddenly the people understood they didn't need lights in the church, they could bring the light with them. For many it was a reminder that God's light was with them and in them. The only time the little church was lit up was when the people were there. That's when it truly became a church.

Talk about how God's light lives in us and shines through all of us. Use examples the children may experience in their own lives. When we use kind words we shine with God's love. When we share with others we shine with God's love. Sometimes God's light shines through us not because we do anything special but just because we are ourselves. Today you will be hearing a story about a boy whose heart shone brightly with the light of God.

Hand out the tealights, and encourage the children to place them at the front of the church. These candles can be lit during a song about light, such as "This Little Light of Mine" *(see below).*

3. This Little Light of Mine

Materials: a flashlight with a fresh battery

Talk about how everything is different when seen in the light of God's love. God's light shows things that no other light can see. When God's light shines on us and through us, we become light and we shine too. Jesus shone with God's light. He wants us to remember that we shine with God's light too. Sing "This Little Light of Mine" with actions. *(See suggestions below or make up your own to share with the children.)*

Song   This little light of mine, I'm gonna let it shine (x3) *(pretend to hold a candle in hands and then wave the candle around)*

Let it shine, let it shine, let it shine. *(cup hands and then open up arms three times)*

Hide it under a bushel. No! I'm gonna let it shine (x3) *(cover one hand with the other hand and then open up your arms 3 times)*

Let it shine, let it shine, let it shine. *(cup hands and then open up arms three times)*

Fifth Sunday in Lent

Ezekiel 37:1-14

Psalm 130

Romans 8:6-11

John 11:1-45

Story props needed:

- purple cloth
- a pitcher of water and
- 4 story figures from page 70
- white cloth strip
- disposable cup
- gray paper to represent stone

A Sad Time for Jesus and His Friends

(based on John 11:1–45)

Place your story basket in front of you. Help the children identify each item: purple cloth, four story figures, white cloth strip, disposable cup, grey paper "stone." Place items back in the basket.

(Place the purple cloth in front of you.)
To get ready for this story, we must make a grave. In Bible times, when people died, they were put in a cave. *(Use one corner of the purple cloth to tuck in and around the cup to form a cave. Wait until all is quiet before you begin.)*

Jesus had many friends. He liked to visit them in their homes and eat with them. Lazarus and his sisters, Martha and Mary, were special friends of Jesus. *(Place three story figures on the edge of the cloth opposite the cave.)* Mary and Martha and their brother spent lots of time together.

One day Lazarus became very, very sick. *(Lay one figure down.)* Mary and Martha sent a message for their dear friend Jesus to come and help. They waited and waited. But Lazarus got sicker. Mary and Martha still waited and waited for Jesus. "Where is Jesus?" they wondered. "Why is he taking so long?" Soon their brother died. Everyone cried. Their friends helped to wrap Lazarus in a clean white cloth. *(Wrap white cloth strip around the figure, covering it completely.)* Then they put him in the cave. That is how they buried people a long time ago. *(Gently place Lazarus in the cup cave.)* They covered the opening to the cave with a large stone. *(Place paper "stone" across open end of cup.)* Still Mary and Martha waited for Jesus.

Finally Jesus arrived. *(Place fourth figure near Mary and Martha.)* Jesus felt very sad, too. He put his arms around Martha and Mary and cried with them. It felt good to cry together. Then Jesus did a surprising thing. He went to the cave where Lazarus was buried. *(Move figures to the cave.)* He said to some people standing there, "Open up the grave." Slowly the stone was removed. *(Remove stone.)* Jesus prayed, "Please, God, hear me." And then Jesus called out, "Lazarus, come out!" *(Pause.)* And Lazarus walked out! He was alive again! *(Unwrap the figure slowly. Place Lazarus beside the other figures.)*

Everyone cried again. But this time it was tears of joy. They were so happy to be together again. Martha called out to everyone, "I knew we were right to have hope in Jesus. I knew Jesus would help us!" *(Pause before inviting reflection.)*

I wonder how Martha and Mary felt when Jesus came and cried with them?
I wonder how God helps me feel better when I feel sad inside?
I wonder how I can help my friends when they feel sad inside?

"Jesus Is Our Friend" Locket

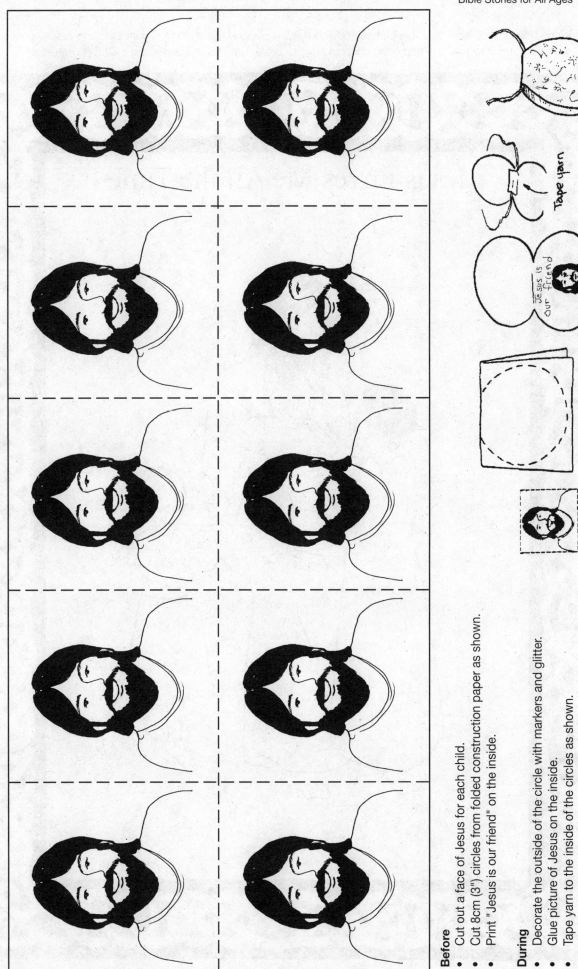

Before
- Cut out a face of Jesus for each child.
- Cut 8cm (3") circles from folded construction paper as shown.
- Print "Jesus is our friend" on the inside.

During
- Decorate the outside of the circle with markers and glitter.
- Glue picture of Jesus on the inside.
- Tape yarn to the inside of the circles as shown.

Tape yarn

Jesus is our friend

Instructions Have the children olour the picture and add eyes, nose, and mouth to the figure touching Jesus' sleeve. Invite the children to draw themself and other children around Jesus. Cut out and frame and mount on cardstock.

Jesus Loves Me All the Time

Ezekiel's Dream

(based on Ezekiel 37:1-14)

Create "marionette bones" by gluing or taping string to popsicle sticks and tying them to a dowel or twig. The popsicle sticks should be close enough together to click when shaken. Add faces to one side of the sticks as shown. Place the marionette bones face down with blank sides showing.

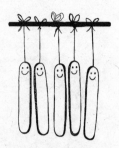

Long, long ago the people of Israel felt very sad. *(Everyone make a sad face.)* The temple where they had gone to worship God had been destroyed. There had been a lot of fighting and the people had to leave their homes and live in a faraway land. They felt very lonely. They felt very sad. They felt like everything they wanted was gone. *(Big sigh and sad faces.)* But God had not gone away. God was there. They couldn't see God but God was with them.

One day God spoke to a man named Ezekiel in a dream. *(Have children close their eyes while you start to describe the dream.)* In his dream, God showed Ezekiel a valley full of bones. Bones. That's all he could see. Bones. Bones were everywhere. And they were very, very dry. Then God said to Ezekiel, "Talk to these bones. Tell them I will breathe on them and make them alive again." *(Have children open their eyes.)*

So, Ezekiel spoke to the bones and told them what God had said. As he spoke he heard a rattley, clacky sound. *(Begin to rattle the marionette bones slightly.)* Ezekiel looked at the bones and couldn't believe his eyes! The bones were moving and coming alive. They were dancing! *(Continue to move the marionette bones faster and faster – have them click against each other. Invite the children to blow on them and make them dance.)* Ezekiel was amazed. Look what God had done! The breath of God had made the bones new again. The bones became people and more people. All sorts of people, alive and breathing.

After the dream, Ezekiel went back to the Israelite people and said to them, "Don't be sad. I have seen what God can do. God will blow new breath into you, and you will be happy again. Some day soon you will return to your homes and rebuild the temple." The people listened and weren't sad anymore. *(Everyone make a happy face.)* God's Spirit would always be with them. God is with us too, wherever we are.

Story props needed:

To make "marionette bones"

• popsicle sticks

• string (tape or glue (optional)

• felt marker

Bones in the Valley

Instructions

- Draw a pile of bones dancing or cut bones out of construction paper and glue them on the page under Ezekiel's arm. Or glue toothpicks in joyful shapes to represent the bones dancing.

Ezekiel told the dry bones God would breathe new life into them. God gives us new life too.

Other ideas for exploring the lectionary readings (Lent 5)

1. Life giving Spirit (Ezekiel 37:1–14)

Materials: blue steamers or ribbons about 86 cm (34 in.) long, toys that require wind or breath to make them work, e.g. pinwheels, kites, whistles, bubbles

In the reading from the Hebrew Scriptures today we see the Spirit of God bringing hope and new life in a wonderful and dramatic way. The Spirit is described as a life-giving wind. Using the image of breath or wind, talk about the Spirit. *(Show the toys you have brought.)* These toys do not do what they are created to do unless there is wind or breath present. In the same way God's Spirit brings life.

Handing out the streamers explain that we are going to act out being the wind or breath of God's Spirit, bringing new life and hope. Ask people to think of ways to make the streamers move that will suggest the movement of the wind. *(Be prepared to demonstrate!)* Encourage them to move around the church, bringing new life everywhere. The use of music would greatly enhance this worship experience.

2. Bumblebee (Ezekiel 37:1–14)

Materials: a picture, puppet, or model of a bumblebee

Show the picture, model, or puppet and have a brief conversation about bumblebees. Have you ever seen one? What are they usually doing? After talking for a little while about this, mention that scientists who have studied bumblebees have said that these insects should not be able to fly. They have the wrong body shape and their wings are too small to lift them up. The trouble is no one told the bumblebee, who figured that they have wings and therefore they can fly. So they do!

Indicate that there are times when something looks impossible, but in fact it is possible. Just like the bumblebee being able to fly. There are also times when something should be impossible, but God's power makes it possible. Sometimes God will ask us to do something that seems impossible, and we have to trust that God will make it possible. This trust in God is what we call faith.

Prayer

Great Spirit,
we thank you for all the new life you bring to impossible situations.
Amen.

**Palm/
Passion
Sunday
Liturgy of
the Palms**

Matthew 21:1–11

Psalm 118:1–2, 19–29

**Liturgy of
the Passion**

Isaiah 50:4–9a

Psalm 31:9–16

Philippians 2:5–11

Matthew 26:14 – 27:66

or Matthew 27:11–54

Holy Week Stories

(based on Matthew 21:1–11; 26:14 – 27:66)

*This Holy Week story station option could be used as an intergenerational event.
Note the storytelling props in each section that need to be gathered ahead of time.*

Move to the first station. Sit down. Tell the story with people participating as much as possible. When moving on to the next station, take the purple cloth with you and repeat the chant.

1 A Parade for Jesus

Purple cloth *Lay it on the floor. People line up on both sides of the cloth.*

Props *paper palms (see page 100) and shawls, pieces of clothing, or towels for spreading on the ground*

**Chant
We're travelling with Jesus, along the way.
We're travelling with Jesus, every day.
Step by step. Step by step.**

Special Instructions *Invite one person to be Jesus. Other people hold palm branches.*

Story One day Jesus and his friends were walking to the city of Jerusalem for a special meal called the Passover. When they were almost there, Jesus said, "Go into the city and find a donkey for me to ride." Soon his friends found a donkey and its colt and they brought it to Jesus. (*Jesus begins to walk along the cloth.*) When the people saw Jesus coming they ran to greet him. They put their coats down in front of him. (*Some people lay shawls or clothing on the cloth.*) They waved palm branches over their heads. (*People wave branches.*) They shouted, "Hosanna! Hosanna!" (*People shout.*) Soon Jesus and his friends moved on and the people went home.

Moving on *Fold purple cloth, say the chant, and move on.*

2 Supper with Jesus

Purple cloth *Spread cloth on a low table.*

Props *a plate with crackers, paper napkins, cups, a pitcher with water or juice*

Story As Jesus and his friends walked along, Jesus said, "Let's go to this house where a special Passover meal will be ready for us." (*Gather around table. Distribute napkins and cups to everyone.*) Soon everyone was sitting down to a delicious meal. Then Jesus took some bread, prayed, broke it into pieces, and gave it to his friends. He said, "When you eat this bread, remember me." (*Bow heads, say the prayer, then share the crackers.*)

Dear God, thank you for the food you give us. Amen.

Then Jesus took a cup, prayed, and gave a drink to his friends. "Drink this and remember me," he said. (*Say the prayer, then share the drink.*)

Dear God, thank you for refreshing drinks that you provide for us. Amen.

Moving on *Fold purple cloth, say the chant, and move on.*

3 Jesus in the Garden

Purple cloth *Later in this part of the story, the cloth will be placed around a group of the peoples's shoulders.*

Props *potted plants*

Special Instructions *If possible, dim lights. Gather around the plants and sit in a tight huddle. Invite someone to be Jesus.*

Story After eating together, Jesus and his friends went to a beautiful garden to pray. It was dark and everyone was tired. *(People yawn and stretch.)* Jesus was tired, too. He was also sad because he knew that some people wanted to hurt him. He said to his friends, "Wait here and stay awake while I pray." And then Jesus walked away from them. He found a quiet spot and then he prayed to God. He wanted God to help him do the right thing. He prayed for a long time. Finally when Jesus returned to his friends, they were asleep! *(People sleep.)* "Wake up. Wake up," he said. *(Pause, then use the purple cloth to cover the group as a prayer mantle. Ask the people,)* "When you are afraid or sad or lonely, what would you like to tell God?" *(Wait for responses, then include them in a prayer, ending with this prayer:)*

Dear God, we know that you are always with us. Thank you for being our friend. Amen.

Moving on *Fold purple cloth, say the chant, and move on.*

4 Trouble for Jesus

Purple cloth *Later in the story, the cloth will be placed on Jesus' shoulders.*

Props *grapevine wreath or paper crown of thorns, quiet music*

Special Instructions *Invite a someone to be Jesus.*

Story Jesus was talking to his sleepy friends in the garden when suddenly a group of angry soldiers came running toward them. They took Jesus away to their leaders. Jesus' friends were scared and they ran away and hid. *(Crouch down as if to hide.)* The leaders asked Jesus questions but they did not like his answers. The leaders wanted to hurt him. Some soldiers put a robe on Jesus and a crown made with branches on his head. *(Place purple cloth around Jesus. Put on the crown.)* They teased him and called him names. Then the soldiers took off the robe and took Jesus away. *(Remove cloth.)* Jesus' friends didn't know what to do to help Jesus. They were afraid they would be hurt, too. So they followed quietly and watched. They wanted to know what would happen next. *(Gather in a circle holding onto the cloth and being quiet. Play quiet music.)*

Moving on *Fold purple cloth, say the chant quietly, and move on.*

5 Jesus Died

Purple cloth *Later in the story, the cloth will be placed in the cave.*
Props *cardboard box to fit under worship table, large dark cloth to cover box, today's large stone and past week's stones (if used)*
Special Instructions *Place open cardboard box on its side under worship table. (When making cave, all items presently on the worship table will be set aside.)*

Story Many people were very sad because Jesus died. Some of Jesus' friends wrapped his body in soft cloth and laid him in a cave in a garden. (*Help children gently fold the purple cloth and place in open box. Cover entire worship table and legs with the dark cloth. Have cloth touch floor.*) Then they pushed a big rock across the opening of the cave. (*Place large stone on cloth in front of cave. Pile other stones around the entrance.*) Some of Jesus' friends stayed nearby, watching and waiting. They cried together because they were so sad. Finally, they went home because there was nothing else to do.

Moving on *Say the chant quietly as you take a longer walk. Return to this station again.*

6 What will happen next?

Purple cloth *The cloth has stayed behind in the cave.*
Story A few days later, two friends of Jesus, both named Mary, went back to the cave. They were so sad that their friend Jesus died and they wanted to be close by. Suddenly something so amazing happened that they didn't know what to think. I wonder what it was. (*Invite responses.*) I'm not going to tell you today. We will wait until next Sunday to find out what amazing, wonderful surprise God gave to the people! What can we do while we wait? (*Invite responses.*) Sometimes people place candles in the window as a reminder that God is with us when we are sad or afraid. Come, let's leave our story now and make a candle to take home.

Moving on *Say the chant one more time as you move to the craft area to make a candle.*

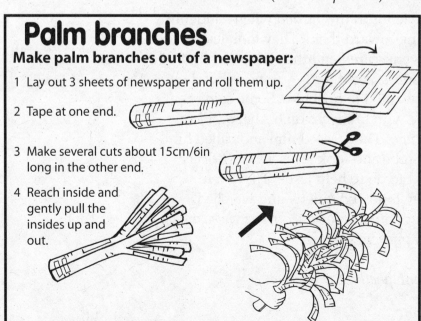

Palm branches
Make palm branches out of a newspaper:

1 Lay out 3 sheets of newspaper and roll them up.

2 Tape at one end.

3 Make several cuts about 15cm/6in long in the other end.

4 Reach inside and gently pull the insides up and out.

Instructions Use bright colours to show the joyful crowd on Palm Sunday and Jesus riding into Jerusalem

The Palm Parade

(based on Matthew 21:1-11)

Other ideas for exploring Palm Sunday

Preparation and Materials Needed

In order to share about ways of welcome in other cultures, you will need people who can share and demonstrate their traditional and/or modern customs, or you can share these or other ways of welcome yourself. Bring a small potted palm.

We just had a wonderful welcome to Jesus as he entered Jerusalem. What were some of the things we did to welcome Jesus? *(We sang, we spread our coats down, we waved palm branches, we paraded.)* Those are ways of welcome that happened in Jesus' time. We do them now in our Palm Sunday worship to remember how it happened then. We do it as a way of welcoming Jesus into our own hearts now.

There are many, many ways to welcome a very special person who comes to visit us. What if a special guest came to visit you in your home? What would you and your family do to welcome that person? *(You may want to give an example to think through, such as a grandparent you hadn't seen for a long time. Respond to the ideas given, which could include hugs and kisses, making a special meal, having a party, making a welcome card, etc.)*

Today, we're going to hear from *(name the people who will share)* about some other ways of welcome. *(Introduce each person and have them explain and demonstrate their customary way of special welcome. If you don't have guests present, elicit/explain/demonstrate how we might welcome some of the following: a member of royalty, e.g. with a motorcade, bowing, presenting flowers, and singing the country's national anthem; a new baby, e.g. with hugs, chocolates, toys, showing the world, and baptism; and a visitor in your church or church school. You might also share a welcome you're familiar with from another culture, such as the Hawaiian lei or the Maori nose rub, or the kiss on both cheeks used in many cultures.)*

There are many, many ways to welcome someone special. It doesn't really matter how it's done. What really matters are the feelings behind the welcome: feelings of love, and feelings of belonging. This is how Jesus really wants us to welcome him – not just with palm branches and songs and hurrahs, but also with love in our hearts, for God and for one another. It's how Jesus welcomes us, with arms wide open, with a feeling of everyone belonging together as part of God's family.

Materials

- construction paper
- scissors and glue
- felt markers and crayons
- yarn

Instructions

1. Copy story pages for each child. Have the children colour the pictures.
2. Fold 2 pieces of construction paper in half and put them inside each other to make a booklet.
3. Write the title "Our Easter Story" on the front
4. Glue story pages in order into the booklet
5. Tie a piece of yarn around the pages and tie at the outside to hold the booklet pages together.

Our Easter Story Booklet

(Page 1 of 3)

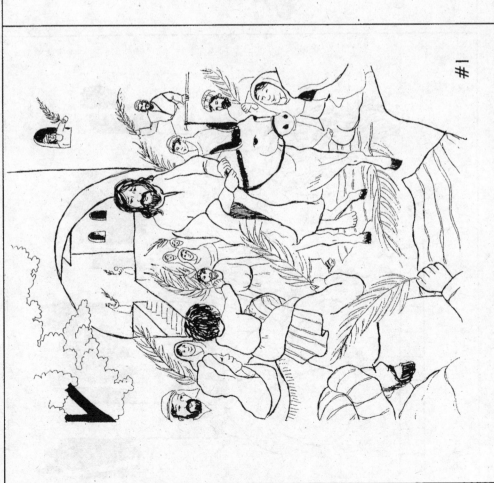

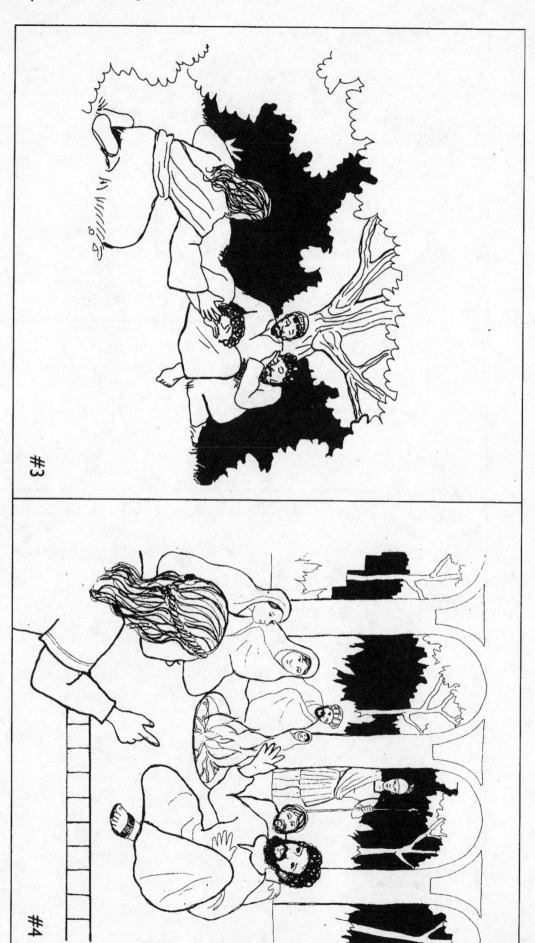

#3

#4

Our Easter Story Booklet

(Page 3 of 3)

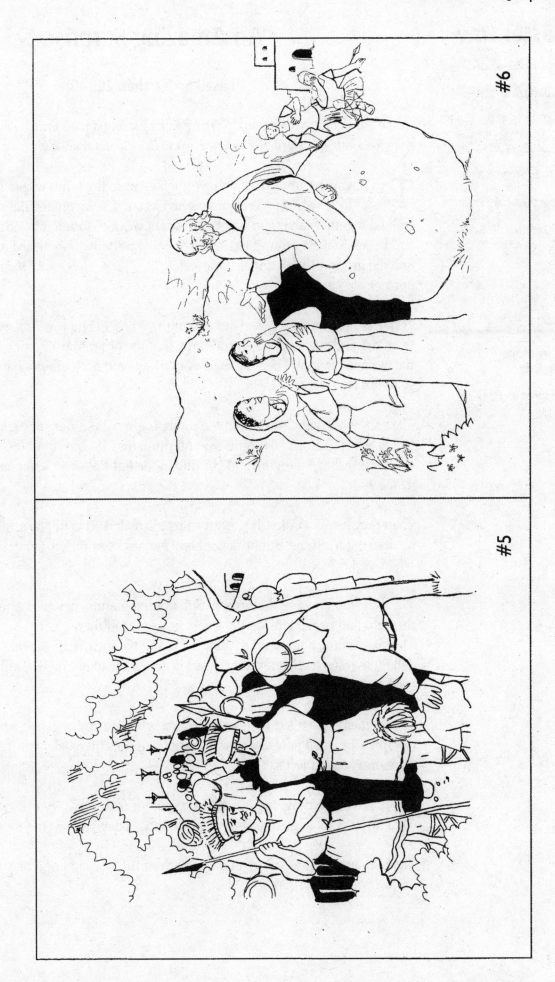

Story props needed:

• rhythm instruments

An Amazing Surprise

(based on Matthew 28:1-10)

(Hand out rhythm instruments. Practice making a sound with them. Allow the children to really celebrate this story. Encourage them to make a joyful noise.)

Two days after Jesus died, two women went to the tomb where Jesus' body was laid. These women were both named Mary. They were feeling very sad and walked together talking in quiet voices. They came close to the side of the tomb and began to walk around to the other side. Suddenly they heard a rumbling sound and the ground shook under their feet. *(Clang the pot lids, shake the shakers, bang the drums.)*

"What is happening!" called out one of the women. She was first around the side of the tomb and she stopped so suddenly that the other Mary bumped into her. Both of the women could not believe their eyes. They held each other's hand tightly as they stared in amazement.

The rock was rolled away from the tomb. Light was shining and glowing from inside. The light was so bright! Do you think they had to cover their eyes? They could see a shape glowing and shifting in the light. *Wonder about how the women were feeling.)*

Then they heard a voice. It was an angel from God. "Do not be afraid. I know you are looking for Jesus. But he is not here! He has been raised. Come and see the place where he lay."

The two women were astonished! Still holding hands they took a few steps towards the light and peeked inside the tomb. Jesus wasn't there!
The voice of the angel said to them, "Go and tell the disciples what you have seen. Tell them Jesus has been raised. Jesus is going ahead of you to Galilee and you will see him there."

The women were filled with joy! *(Everyone cheer!)* They began to run to tell the disciples the good news. And suddenly, Jesus was there! He was there beside them! "Greetings," said Jesus.

The two women came to Jesus and knelt at his feet. They were so happy!
"Tell my friends to go to Galilee," Jesus said. "They will see me there."

The two women jumped up and began to run. They had good news to share! *(Play the instruments in celebration.)*

Easter Morning

Help the two Marys find their way to the tomb

Jesus Lives Again

(based on Matthew 28:1–10)

*(Each time people hear the words **"whish, whish, whish"** in the story, encourage them to rub the palms of their hands together to make whishing sounds. When they hear "**rumbledy-rumbledy-bump,"** each person slaps one fist, loudly, on the other hand.)*

Whish, whish, whish. Early one morning two women, both named Mary, were walking in a garden. They were walking to the cave tomb where Jesus' body had been laid after he died.

Whish, whish, whish. It was so quiet. They could hear their footsteps as they walked slowly across the grass to the cave. They were feeling very sad because their dear friend, Jesus, had been killed.

Whish, whish, whish. Slowly, slowly they kept walking. They wanted to put sweet-smelling spices in the tomb with Jesus' body. But they didn't know how they would move the big stone. And they didn't know what the guards would say.

Rumbledy-rumbledy-bump. Rumbledy-rumbledy-bump. Suddenly there was a loud rumbling noise. The ground shook under their feet. The two Marys were afraid and held onto each other.

Rumbledy-rumbledy-bump. Rumbledy-rumbledy-bump. What was happening? They looked. And then they looked again. Something amazing had happened. They watched as an angel as bright as the sun rolled away the huge stone and then sat on it. Now the women were really afraid.

Whish, whish, whish. Then they heard a voice. It was an angel from God. "Don't be afraid. I know you are looking for Jesus. Jesus is alive again! Look, he's not here any more. Go, tell your friends what you have seen. Tell them that Jesus is alive again in a new way."

Whish, whish, whish. Quickly, the two Marys ran out of the garden. They must tell everyone what they had just seen.

Whish, whish, whish. But suddenly, they stopped in amazement. There was Jesus. There was Jesus standing right beside them! And then Jesus smiled and said, "Peace. Go and tell your friends to wait for me in Galilee." The two women knelt at Jesus' feet. They were so happy!

Whish, whish, whish. They were full to the top of their heads with joy. And as quickly as they could, they rushed off to tell their friends God's surprising good news. Alleluia! Alleluia! Alleluia!

A Dramatic Conversation for Two Women

(based on Matthew 28:1–10)

Learn the lines as much by heart as possible so that you can keep eye contact with the people. Don't worry about getting every sentence exactly as it is printed. What is important is that you get to know the feelings of the woman that you are playing and try to be that person.

One: Thank you very much for inviting us to join you today. I am Mary Magdalene and I am one of Jesus' closest friends. After Jesus healed me of a terrible disease I started following him everywhere. There were a whole group of us that used to go with him from place to place, and some of us got to know him really well. This is my friend Mary, who was part of our group too.

Two: It's confusing, isn't it? We both have the same name. You get used to it after a while, but sometimes it's hard when people forget who you are, or think you're somebody else.

One: But we came to tell you about Easter, not just to get you confused about our names. Look, I brought a rock to show you. It's not *the* rock, of course. But it's still a rock. Feel how heavy it is. *(Pass the rock among the people.)*

Two: The rock they used at the tomb was an awful lot heavier than that. It was just one stone but it filled the whole entry into the tomb!

One: I thought my heart had turned to stone the day I watched Joseph seal off the tomb. I felt so bad that I didn't think I would ever feel anything else again.

Two: *(to Mary)* I know what you mean. *(to the people)* Joseph was a friend of ours too. Was he ever brave! After Jesus died he actually went to the Romans and asked for Jesus' body so that he could be buried properly.

One: He could have been killed too – asking for the body of somebody who had been crucified.

Two: Yes, but he wasn't killed. He was able to get Jesus' body from the Romans. Then he wrapped Jesus' body in fine linen cloth and then placed it gently in a tomb that he had set aside for his own body in case of his death.

One: *(to Mary)* Do you remember the look on Joseph's face as he tried to roll that stone into the opening?

Two: *(to Mary)* I just remember the soldiers standing around making rude jokes. *(to the people)* You see even though Jesus was dead the soldiers had been ordered to stand guard over his body to make sure that nobody stole it.

One: All the other disciples had run away. We were the only two at the tomb. Those Romans just didn't understand how much we loved Jesus.

Two: Those soldiers sealed the tomb and then they set guard over it. When I left that day I was sure that everything was over.

One: I don't know how it works in your country, but in Palestine where we're from, people used to go visit the places where people were buried to remember them, and to grieve, and try to get used to the idea that they were dead. So after the Sabbath was over, Mary and I decided to go back to the tomb.

Two: At first it didn't look all that different. The guards were still there. The stone still sealed the hole, just as it had on Friday night.

One: And then all of a sudden there was this incredible earthquake. The earth shook; there was an incredible sound; and there was an angel there! His clothes were all white and light shone from his face. It was amazing!

Two: The guards just fainted. Right then and there. Seasoned Roman soldiers they were, but they'd never seen anything like this before.

One: I was scared too, but I didn't faint. Neither did Mary. The angel rolled the stone out of the way. Then he sat on it. He showed us how the tomb was empty, and he told us to go and tell the rest of the disciples that Jesus was no longer there lying dead in the tomb. God had given Jesus new life.

Two: Can you imagine! We didn't know what to make of it. I was scared and excited and confused all at the same time. But we did as he said. We started back to find the rest of the disciples and then something even more wonderful happened.

One: Jesus was suddenly there with us on the road. He greeted us with a blessing of peace and I felt so very warm inside, I just wanted to hug him and never let him go.

Two: Jesus told us that we were to give the message to all the disciples that he would come to see them very soon.

One: Then, just as suddenly as he had come, he disappeared.

Two: So we hurried on, wondering what the disciples would think when we told them what had happened.

One: In those days people didn't trust women with important messages. But Jesus was different. He always listened carefully to us and now he had given us a very, very important message to tell others.

Two: Our deep sadness had turned to great joy.

One: Well, today is Easter Day and we have to hurry on and tell other people our story. We want to share the good news we know about Jesus. Will you help us? Will you pass on the Easter message that God has given Jesus new life? (*Wait for the people to respond, then exit.*)

A Time for Wondering

I wonder what the frightened soldiers did after the women left?
I wonder how the disciples felt when the 2 Marys told them what had happened?
I wonder what will happen next?
I wonder if you have any questions about Easter?

Our Easter Story

1. Cut along dark line.

2. Trim and fold along dotted lines.

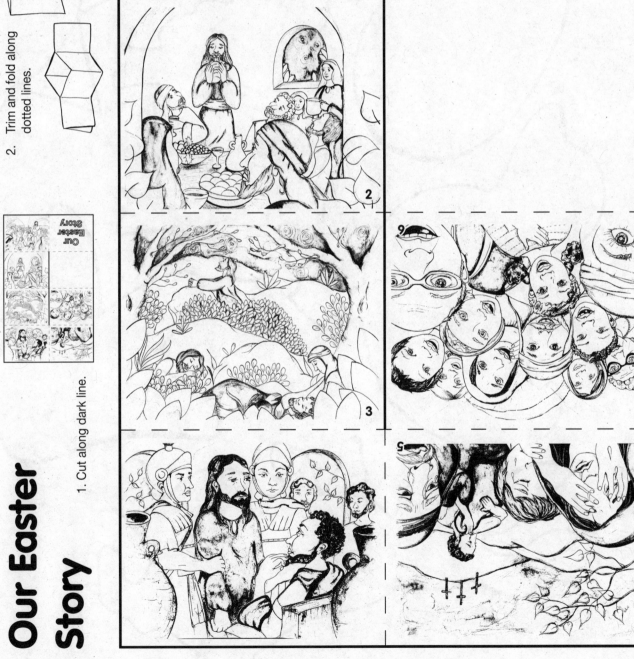

Materials
- construction paper
- glue
- felt markers,
  Easter stickers or
  other decorations

Instructions
- Cut out the picture symbols.
  Glue them onto construction
  paper egg shapes and
  decorate with bright colours.

Symbols of New Life

Other ideas for exploring Easter

1. Stone Surprises

Materials: purple cloth, yellow/gold cloth, various size rocks with the messages "Happy Easter" and "He is Risen" written with felt pen directly on each rock or written on strips of paper and taped to the bottom of each.

Invite children to look at the various rocks sitting on the purple cloth. Purple is the colour of Lent – of the time leading up to Easter. These are plain rocks like the big rock that was in front of the cave or tomb where Jesus was buried on Good Friday. But today is Easter and that first Easter Day was full of surprises for Jesus' followers. Ask the children to each choose a rock and then turn it over to find a special Easter surprise message. When all the children have a rock, set the white or yellow/gold cloth over top of the purple cloth. Ask the class, one by one, to share their message and then set their rock, message side up, on the white/gold material.

2. Easter Egg Hunt

Eggs can also remind us of new life that God gives. God gave Jesus new life and he came out of the tomb, like a baby chick breaks out of an egg.

Before beginning the hunt ask the children to tell you again what Easter eggs remind us of in the Easter story. In the true spirit of Jesus' followers try to encourage those who find a lot to share with those who have only a few.

3. Easter Lily

Materials: white, yellow, and green paper, pencils, pipe cleaner, tape, felt markers

Show children the sample that you have made. Talk about how the lily is shaped like a trumpet. Trumpets were used to announce the entrance of a king or to call people's attention to an important message. So Easter lilies appear to be announcing the news that Jesus has risen. Have each child trace their hand (with fingers spread apart) onto white paper. Take a small rectangle of yellow paper (that fits into the palm of the traced hand as shown) and cut it like grass. (See illustration.) Glue it onto the hand. Then curl each finger around a pencil away from the yellow paper. Roll hand shape at the wrist to form a lily-shaped flower. Attach to pipe cleaner with tape. Cut out green leaves and tape to the stem. Print an Easter message such as "Alleluia" or "He is risen" on the leaf. Give the lily to someone as a special Easter present.

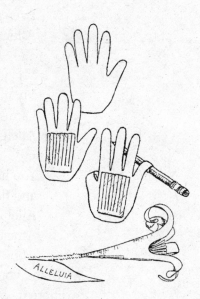

Prayer

Dear God,
we thank you for the gift of new life.
Alleluia! Amen.

Second Sunday of Easter

Acts 2:14a, 22–32

Psalm 16

1 Peter 1:3–9

John 20:19–31

I Praise You, God

(based on Psalm 16)

Step, step, up the stairs went the people. Step, step, step. They went all the way up, up, up to the roof of the house. The roof was flat. It was a good place to look at the stars. It was a good place to sit together and sing thank you to God. The people were so happy that Jesus was still with them.

"What song shall we sing?" asked one of the women.

"I know," said a young boy. "Let's sing a song that was written a long, long time ago. A song written by David."

"Yes, that's a good idea," said a man sitting nearby. "David wrote so many beautiful songs that help us to say thank you to God. Which song did you want us to sing?" Everyone turned to the young boy again. They waited to hear which of David's songs he would choose. And then the people listened as the young boy said these words… (*Invite the children to follow your actions.*)

I praise you, God. (*Extend both arms toward the front.*)
You show the way. (*Open both arms to the side.*)
Even at night you are with me. (*Fold hands under head.*)
Alleluia! (*Raise both arms over head, wriggling fingers.*)

My heart is happy. (*Place hands over heart.*)
My mouth sings for joy. (*Touch mouth.*)
I am safe with you. (*Hug self.*)
Alleluia! (*Raise both arms over head, wriggling fingers.*)

You help me find my way (*Walk fingers up the opposite arm.*),
and fill me with joy. (*Bring arms slowly upward along your sides.*)
Alleluia! (*Raise both arms over head, wriggling fingers.*)
Amen. (*Fold hands in prayer.*)

"Thank you," they said to the young boy who had suggested the song. "How many different ways can we say this thank you song to God?" (*Encourage the children to suggest ways such as using a whispering voice, using a joyful voice, using a different body position… and then repeat the psalm again using those suggestions.*)

Instructions

- Colour the pictures. Cut out the strip of pictures and slide through slits to show times that God is with us. Can you think of other times? Encourage children to draw, on a blank stip of paper, other times when they can praise God and say, "Alleluia!."

Jesus Visits the Disciples

(based on John 20:19–31)

(Speak in a quiet voice.)

The disciples were feeling afraid. They had lost their friend
Jesus and they knew that soldiers might be looking for
them. Now it was almost night time and the disciples, except Thomas, were meeting
together in a small locked room. They worried and wondered what would happen to
them. They all began talking at once.

Suddenly, Jesus was standing right there with them. Everyone glanced at the doors
and windows. They were still locked. How could this be? They became even more
frightened. And then Jesus said four little words. He said, "Peace be with you."
*(Encourage the children to repeat **"Peace be with you."** Invite them to say this phrase each
time it is repeated in the story.)*

Peter stopped talking and heard Jesus say, **"Peace be with you."**
James stopped talking and heard Jesus say, **"Peace be with you."**
John stopped talking and heard Jesus say, **"Peace be with you."**
One by one, all the disciples stopped and heard Jesus say, **"Peace be with you."**

The disciples began to feel more calm. They began to feel more peaceful. Their whole
body felt good. They knew that Jesus loved them. They began to breathe more easily.
They began to hope again. And then suddenly Jesus disappeared.

Later the disciples told Thomas, "We saw Jesus! Jesus is alive again in a new way!"

Thomas did not believe them. "I won't believe Jesus was here until I can see him
myself," he said.

A week went by – Monday, Tuesday, Wednesday, Thursday, Friday, Saturday, Sunday.
All the disciples, even Thomas, were gathered in the same room. Suddenly Jesus was
with them again. And again he said, **"Peace be with you."**

Thomas looked at Jesus. It really was Jesus! He reached out to Jesus and said, "It's
really you! My teacher and my God. I believe."

And Jesus said to Thomas, "I am with you even when you can't see me. Always
remember that." And then Jesus disappeared again.

Jesus Appears to the Disciples

(based on John 20:19-31)

- Give each child a folded copy of the activity sheet. Invite them to open up the folds (doors) and look inside. Notice the gathered disciples. Do they look surprised? Do they look excited? They were feeling worried and afraid until Jesus came to them. Sometimes we feel that way too. It can help us to remember Jesus is with us. Invite the children to colour their picture using markers or crayons. Fold the doors closed again and seal them with a reusable sticker. Encourage the children to open the doors and tell their family why the disciples were behind the closed doors.

Other ideas for exploring the lectionary readings (Easter 2)

1. Starting to grow (John 20:19–31)

In advance: bring the seeds that were planted a week ago so that they have started to germinate and some extra seed packages.

Talk about the plants. What has happened to the seeds? What signs of new life and growth are showing? Do you think the plant is feeling very strong? If you have the seed packet look at the picture on the front. Do the seedlings look like these plants? Why not? Mention that these little plants remind us of the disciples just after Jesus came back to life. They knew Jesus was alive and they were very happy, but they were not feeling very strong yet. Like these seedlings, they were just starting to grow and change.

Bring some seeds that you planted a few days ago:

Talk about what is happening to the seeds. What do you think is happening? Why don't we see anything yet? Mention that these seeds remind us of the disciples just after Jesus came back to life. They knew Jesus was alive and they were very happy, but they were still scared and were hiding. However, like these seeds, the disciples were changing and starting to grow, it just didn't show yet.

Don't forget to keep your plants watered. You may want to show them again at Pentecost (page 147).

2. Thomas' journey (John 20:19–31)

Materials: a world globe or world map.

In our gospel reading today we see the disciples gathered together behind locked doors, because they were afraid of the Roman soldiers and the religious leaders. What a remarkable transformation occurs once the disciples have met the risen Christ and have received the gift of the Holy Spirit. The disciples took the gospel message to many different places, often showing extraordinary bravery. This option gives you the opportunity to talk about the journey of the apostle Thomas. According to tradition, Christianity was first brought to Kerala, the southern state of India, by Thomas.

Talk about the missionary journeys of Jesus' disciples. Explain that the disciples were so excited about the things Jesus had said and done that they wanted to share the story with everybody. What do you think the disciples would tell people about Jesus? You may wish to invite the children to tell you their favourite story about Jesus.

Tell the children that many Christians in Kerala *(indicate this region on the map)* believe that the apostle Thomas travelled all the way to India to bring the good news about Jesus to their country. Have a brief conversation about Thomas' journey. Show them where Thomas would have started and how he may have travelled to India. Emphasize the bravery and courage that would have been required to undertake such a journey. Indicate that after the disciples discovered that Jesus was alive, they did many brave and courageous things.

Prayer

Dear God,
we thank you and praise you
for the gift of new life.
Jesus is alive in a new way.

On the Road to Emmaus

(based on Luke 24:13-35)

Third Sunday of Easter

Acts 2:14a, 36-41

Psalm 116:1-4, 12-19

1 Peter 1:17-23

Luke 24:13-35

Storytelling props needed:

• a strip of paper for each child

(Give each child a strip of paper to put in front of them. This will be a road. As the story is told, invite the children to use their two "walking fingers" on each hand and "walk" along this road.)

Two disciples were walking down a road. *(Walk fingers.)* As they walked along, they talked about their friend Jesus who had died. They missed him very much. While they were talking, Jesus came along and joined them, but they didn't know who he was. *(Walk fingers again.)*

Jesus asked, "What are you talking about? Why are you so sad?"

The disciples said, "Haven't you heard? Don't you know what happened in Jerusalem?"

Jesus shook his head and asked, "What happened in Jerusalem?" *(Invite the children to answer the question.)*

They talked some more as they walked along the road. *(Walk fingers.)* "We had hoped he was God's special leader but now he's gone. A woman told us Jesus is alive – but where is he now?" asked one of the disciples.

When the disciples arrived home, they asked Jesus to stay with them. *(Walk fingers and then sit – close fists.)* They still didn't know who he was.

When they sat down to eat, Jesus said a prayer to thank God for the good food. Then he broke the bread into pieces and shared it with the friends. Suddenly, the two disciples knew it was their dear friend Jesus sitting with them! And just as suddenly Jesus disappeared.

The disciples looked at each other. And one said, "I should have known on the road it was Jesus. I felt so good being with him."

The two friends quickly got up from the table and went to find the others. They ran out of their house and down the road. *(Run fingers.)* They shouted "Jesus is alive! We've seen him. We knew it was Jesus as soon as he broke the bread to share with us!" *(Run fingers again and everyone shout "Good News! Jesus is alive!")*

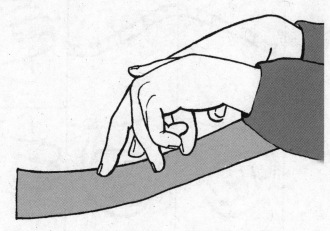

Happy Disciple Puppet

Materials

- crayons or felt markers
- tape and hole punch
- yarn

Instructions

- Cut along solid lines.
- Decorate each piece with crayons or felt markers.
- Tape the puppet legs and arms onto the puppet body.
- Use a hole punch to make a hole in the top of each puppet.
- Thread yarn through the hole and tie the ends of the yarn together to make a handle.
- Jiggle the puppet up and down to make the puppet move.

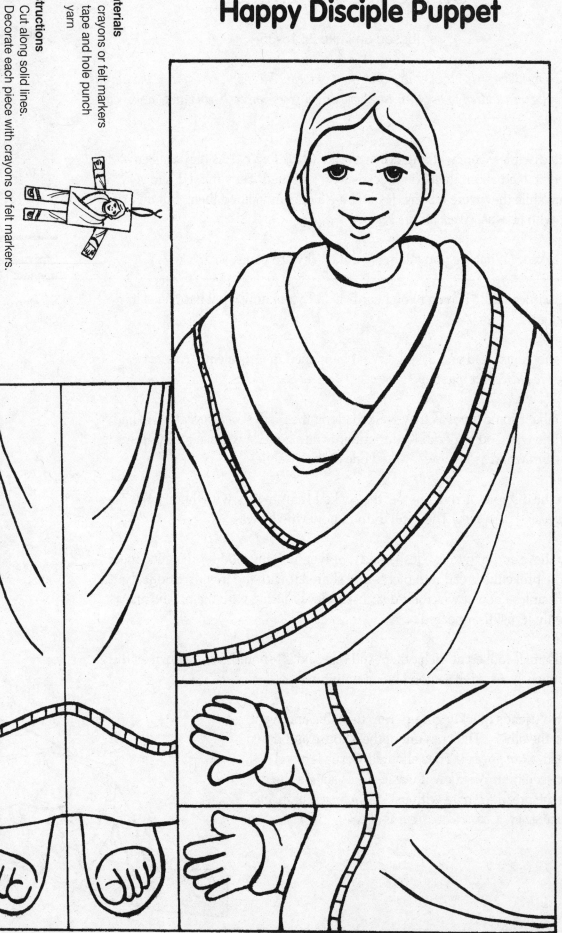

Who Could This Be?

(based on Luke 24:13–35)

(Together practice the phrase "Who could this be?" Use a strong questioning voice and make an exaggerated gesture with arms each time it is said. In the story, make that exaggerated gesture to indicate to the children when to repeat the phrase.)

Clatter, clatter. Clippity-clop, clippity-clop. Step, step. Along the dirt road came the people – some with carts, some riding donkeys, and some walking.

Along this dirt road walked two friends. They were on their way to a little town called Emmaus. They were very sad because their dear friend Jesus had died and they missed him very much. Soon they heard someone walking behind them. **Who could this be?** They each stepped to one side to let the person pass. But he did not pass. He stopped and said, "Hello. May I walk with you?" **Who could this be?**

The two friends nodded their heads and said, "Yes, please join us."

As the three people walked together, the man asked "What makes you so sad?" **Who could this be?**

The two friends said, "Haven't you heard? Don't you know what happened in Jerusalem?"

The man shook his head. **Who could this be?** Then he asked, "Please tell me. What happened in Jerusalem?" *(Invite the children to answer the question.)*

Clatter, clatter. Clippity-clop, clippity-clop. Step, step. It was getting dark. There were still many people on the road. And still the three people walked together, talked together and enjoyed being with each other. The man told the two friends many stories about God. But **who could this be?** When they arrived in Emmaus the two friends said, "Please come and stay the night with us. We would like to talk to you more. We could eat together." They still didn't know **who could this be.**

When they all sat down to eat, the man said a prayer to thank God for the good food. **Who could this be?** Then he broke the bread into pieces and shared it with the friends. Suddenly the two friends knew who this could be. It was their dear friend Jesus! As soon as this man broke the bread to share with them, they recognized him! It was Jesus!

The two friends were so excited, they shouted with joy. "We must tell everyone. We must tell everyone." They jumped up from the table, went out the door, and all the way back to Jerusalem. They didn't walk; they ran! "Alleluia! Alleluia! Jesus is still with us!"

The Road to Emmaus

(based on Luke 24:13–35)

Can you tell the story of the two friends who walked to Emmaus?

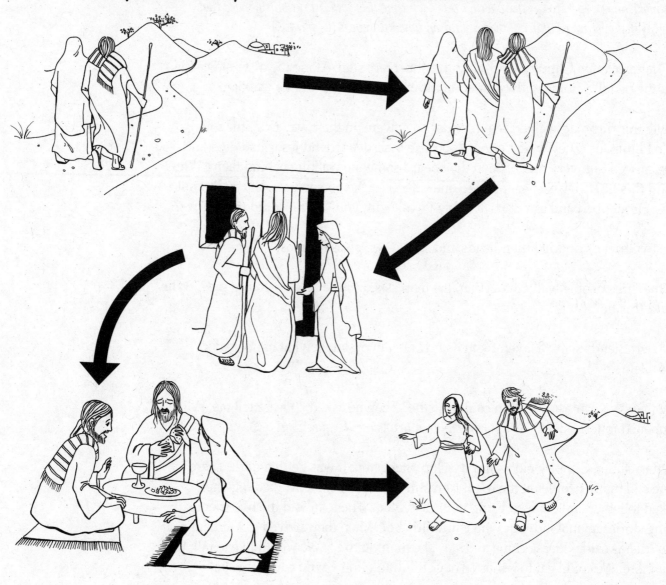

Join the dots and shout out loud.

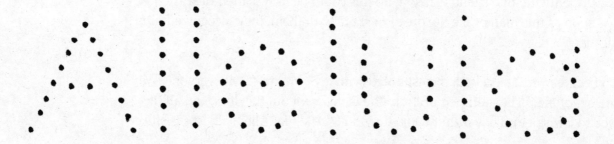

Other ideas for exploring the lectionary readings (Easter 3)

1. Lost and Found (Luke 24:13–35)
Have you ever spent ages looking for something and when you finally found it, you discovered it was right in front of you! You looked right through it. Perhaps the item had been put down somewhere it didn't belong. You couldn't see it because you were not expecting to see it there. Share your experience with everyone and invite them to share their stories.

Indicate that something like this happened to the disciples that first Easter. The disciples had seen Jesus die and they were not expecting to see him alive again. So when they did meet him, they did not recognize him at first.

2. Polaroid® moments! (Luke 24:13–35)
Materials: a Polaroid® camera and some film. Take a picture of the children. If you have a large group you may prefer to take a picture of something in the church. Let the children watch the picture slowly appear. Ask them to describe how the photograph develops. When the picture starts to form is it clear? What happens? If you have a large group you may have to do this several times so everyone gets a chance to watch as the picture comes into focus. Consider asking one of the older children to time how long it takes for the picture to become clear.

Indicate that sometimes our life can be like this photograph. Something can happen that is difficult to understand. It seems very fuzzy and confusing. Gradually the understanding comes and suddenly everything becomes very clear. *Note:* This might be a difficult concept for younger concrete thinkers to grasp. It may be helpful to give some examples that the children would experience in their own lives. Sometimes when you get a new toy or game, the instructions can seem very difficult and hard to understand. However, if you play with the toy for a while the instructions will suddenly become very clear and easy to follow. The toy and the instructions haven't changed but your understanding has.

Mention that the story they will be hearing in their groups later today is about two of Jesus' disciples who had an experience that they didn't understand at first. Their whole life seemed confused and hard to understand. Jesus helped to change their understanding.

3. Jesus turned our sorrows into dancing
Teach the song "Jesus Put This Song into Our Hearts" (*#26 in the Rainbow Songbook,* available from Wood Lake Publishing, www.woodlakebooks.com). Have a conversation about the song, especially the last verse. What does it mean to have our sorrow turned into dancing? Have you or your family ever had this experience? Indicate that this is how the disciples must have felt when they met Jesus and realized he was alive. You may wish to hand out rhythm instruments and streamers to the children (and congregation). Invite everyone to sing and dance around the church. Christ is risen!

Prayer
"God is with us, Alleluia." Invite children to touch their hearts and say, "God is with us, Alleluia."

> Dear God,
> thank you for your love.
> Help us to love in your way.
> Amen.

Fourth Sunday of Easter

Acts 2:42-47

Psalm 23

1 Peter 2:19-25

John 10:1-10

———

Story props needed:

• flannelboard or some other way to use the story figures (see page 14)

• figures from pages 125-126 prepared for storytelling method chosen

The Good Shepherd

(based on Psalm 23)

(Read the psalm once without stopping. Then hand out the biblical figures (from pages 125-126) to the children. Allow time for them to talk about their figure. Read the psalm a second time and help the children place their figure on the flannelboard as it is mentioned in italics.)

God, you are like a good shepherd.
(Put Shepherd on the board.)

You love and care for your sheep.
(Add Sheep #1.)

You give them everything they need!
When they are tired you give them soft, green grass to lie on.
(Add Sheep #2.)

When they are hot and thirsty you take them to a quiet pond for a cool drink.
(Add Pond with Sheep #3 nearby.)

You give your sheep sweet grass to eat.
(Add Sheep #4.)

Your sheep love you. You love your sheep.
(Put Sheep #5 on the shepherd's shoulders.)

You keep them safe in your arms always.
(Put Sheep #6 in the shepherd's arms.)

The disciples loved this song very much. They learned it when they were young children like you. After a while, they thought of Jesus as the Good Shepherd. Jesus cares for us just like the Good Shepherd cares for the sheep.

A Time for Wondering

I wonder who else God cares for?

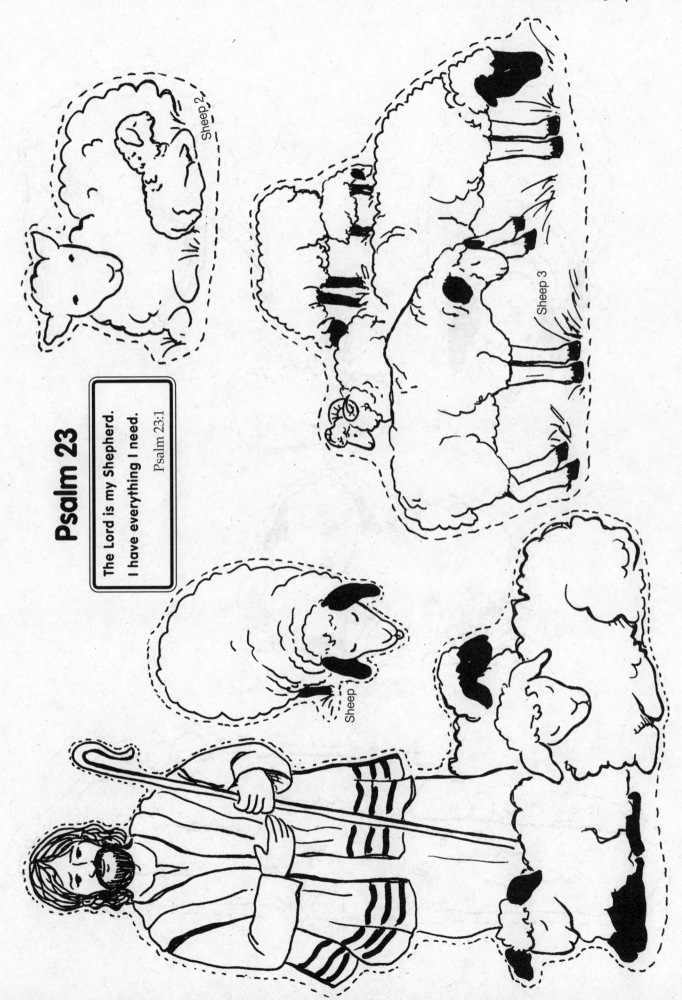

Sheep 2

Sheep 3

Sheep

Psalm 23

The Lord is my Shepherd. I have everything I need.

Psalm 23:1

Part of the Community

(based on Acts 2:42-47)

Jesus' friends loved spending time together. They would gather in one of their houses. They shared food together. If someone needed a new coat another person would give them one. Jesus' friends knew they were living just as Jesus wanted them to live. They were caring for each other and sharing all things.

They worshipped together in the Temple and told stories about God and about Jesus. They reminded each other of all the things Jesus taught them. They served meals to each other in their homes. They celebrated being together. Jesus' friends were very happy to be part of such a loving community.

Every day, as the disciples were gathered, others would come to the door and ask if they could join the community. And the disciples greeted new people with love and invited them to come in and share some food.

And the community of Jesus' friends grew and grew. It got bigger every day.

This Follower of Jesus

This follower of Jesus liked to praise and pray.
(Hold up one finger on one hand.)
This follower of Jesus learned more every day.
(Hold up two fingers on one hand.)
This follower of Jesus liked to meet and sing.
(Hold up three fingers on one hand.)
This follower of Jesus gave thanks for everything.
(Hold up four fingers on one hand.)
This follower of Jesus met with friends to eat.
(Hold up five fingers on one hand.)
Loving,
(Hold up one finger on the other hand.)
Sharing,
(Hold up two fingers on the other hand.)
Helping,
(Hold up three fingers on the other hand.)
Caring,
(Hold up four fingers on the other hand.)
When they came to meet.
(Clasp hands together with fingers interlaced.)

From *Don't Just Sit There* by Joyce Riffe © 1997 Abingdon Press. Used by permission.

Signs of Community

In Our Time

In Jesus' Time

Materials

- construction paper
- glue, scissors, and crayons or felt markers

Instructions

- Colour the pictures and cut out
- On one side of a sheet of construction paper glue the pictures which show community in Jesus' time and on the other side glue the pictures that show community in our time. If you like, draw pictures of your own to add to the sheets. Glue the titles in the rectangles to each side.

CLOTHING DRIVE

This Is Our Church

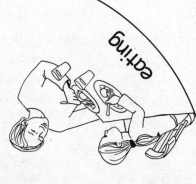

praying

eating

singing

caring

Materials

- construction paper
- glue and crayons or felt markers
- hole punch and scissors
- paper fasteners

Instructions

- Photocopy and enlarge the circles.
- Glue the circles onto construction paper to give a firmer backing.
- Cut out the circles.
- Decorate the pictures with crayons or markers.
- Print the child's name and congregation on the second partial circle. Decorate it.
- Place the second circle over the first with printing facing upward.
- Insert the brass fastener in the middle (use a pointed scissors or hole punch).
- Gently turn the top circle to reveal the pictures underneath.

paper
fastener

This is our church

This is our church

Other ideas for exploring the lectionary readings (Easter 4)

1. The gate for the sheep (John 10:1–10)

Materials: a simple shepherd's headdress

In advance: make a sheepfold with a circle of chairs. Leave a gap in the circle so the sheep can go in and out. Gather the children together in the sheepfold. You might ask the children what a shepherd does. What responsibilities do shepherds have? Why do you think people might have described God as being like a shepherd?

Jesus told a story about some sheep and a shepherd. You may want to read from John 10:1-7. Invite the children to help you act out the story so that we can understand it better. Encourage them to pretend to be sheep. Explain that the sheep knew which voice belonged to their shepherd and they would follow that voice. Put on the headdress to become the shepherd and call the sheep to follow you. Move around the church talking about the life of the shepherd and the sheep. (See #2 for more information.)

Indicate that night is almost here and you need to get the sheep into the sheepfold for safety. Herd the children into the sheepfold. Point out that there is no gate. How can the shepherd keep the sheep safe if there is no gate? Affirm all the children's suggestions and draw the conversation to a close by explaining that the shepherd became the gate. Lie down across the gap. Indicate that this was a dangerous place for the shepherd to stay. If wild animals attacked the sheep they would attack the shepherd first. However a good shepherd would take this risk to make sure the sheep were safe.

2. A shepherd comes to visit

Recruit a volunteer to dress up as a shepherd from the time of Jesus. Invite the shepherd to come and talk to the children about looking after sheep. Some important jobs a shepherd had would be:

* to find good pasture. The shepherd would need to check for poisonous plants before letting the sheep eat.
* the sheep would often get cut or scraped, so the shepherd needed to check them often to make sure they were healthy. There were also lots of bugs/insects that would hurt the sheep. So the shepherd put oil on the sheep's head to protect them .
* many wild animals would try to eat the sheep. The shepherd had to protect the flock from lions, wolves and bears. Sheep have to be watched very carefully because they wander off and get lost. The shepherd would go and look for any lost sheep.
* water was very scarce. The shepherd had to make sure that the sheep were taken regularly to the well. Sometimes there would be more than one flock at the well. The sheep would get mixed in together. The rule was you were allowed to keep whichever sheep followed the sound of your voice.
* you had to make sure all your sheep knew your voice, or you could lose all your sheep. The shepherd would sing songs to the sheep and talk to them from the time they were born. The sheep learned their shepherd's voice from a very young age.

Prayer

Dear God,
we are so glad that you look after us,
just as a good shepherd looks after the sheep.
Thank you. Amen.

Stephen, Faithful Helper

(based on Acts 7:55–60)

Fifth Sunday of Easter

Acts 7:55-60

Psalm 31:1-5, 15-16

1 Peter 2:2-10

John 14:1-14

Place a shawl over your head and shoulders as you prepare to be Deborah.

Welcome to my home and our house church. This is where my friends come to sing and pray and learn to follow the way Jesus taught. Please let me get you a drink of water before we worship together. It looks like you walked a long way to get here.

Oh, I am so happy that you are here! We have had many, many people come to be with us. We always worship together. We share everything we have. We care about each other and more and more people come to join our new community.

We decided that we would need to choose some helpers. We needed people who would help to make sure everyone was treated fairly. Let me tell you about one special person we chose. His name was Stephen. Come, sit around this bag and I will show you what Stephen did. *(Place the cloth bag of items in the middle of the circle.)*

Stephen became a church helper. He wanted to share God's love by helping people who were sad or hungry or sick. He was a good helper and he spread God's love wherever he went. These are some of the things that Stephen might have taken with him to help people.

Storytelling props needed:

• shawl

• a cloth or leather bag containing bread, clothing, money bag, bandage or cloth bandage, a container of water or a wet cloth.

Activity Open the bag and spread out the items on the cloth. As you ask each question, encourage the children to choose which item may have been given to assist that person.

If someone was hungry, what might Stephen do? *(give bread)*

If someone was cold, what might Stephen do? *(give clothing)*

If someone had no money, what might Stephen do? *(give money)*

If someone had a cut, what might Stephen do? *(wrap cloth around cut)*

If someone had a fever or a high temperature, what might Stephen do? *(apply a cloth to forehead)*

If someone didn't know about God's love, what might Stephen do? *(say, "God loves you")*

If someone wanted to know more about Jesus, what might Stephen do? *(tell stories)*

We will always remember Stephen. He was a loving kind helper who told everyone about God and God's love for them. Oh, how I miss him! *(pause)* Before you leave my home, I would like to share a snack with you. Are you hungry?

Activity Bring out a bowl of dried fruit. Pray together. Share the fruit.

Thank you for coming to visit me again. You will always be welcome with love!

Please receive this blessing. *(Invite the children, including Deborah, to place their hands on top of each other.)*

Pray Dear God,
may these hands help to share your love. Amen.

Stephen Is a Loving Helper

bread

clothing

money

bandage

love

pocket

tape

Materials
- construction paper or heavier paper
- tape

Instructions
- Cut out Stephen and the things he shares to help others.
- Glue Stephen to construction or other heavier paper.
- Tape a small piece of construction paper to the back of his bag to make a pocket.
- Carefully tuck the items into the pocket.

Other ideas for exploring the lectionary readings (Easter 5)

1. You will do even greater things (John 14:1–14)

Have a brief conversation about Jesus' ministry when he was here on earth. Work cooperatively to make a list of the kinds of things Jesus did. Indicate that in the gospel reading for today Jesus said something amazing. Read John 14:12. What did Jesus promise? What do you think he meant? Look at the list you made. Wonder together about the kinds of things we could do as a church with this promise. (Children often demonstrate great faith. Accept their suggestions enthusiastically and don't limit their imaginations!) After talking about this for a while invite the children and the congregation to identify things we are doing that are similar to what Jesus did. Affirm the children's answers and be open to their suggestions and insights. This is a challenging question, but it is a good one for the whole congregation to wrestle with.

Finish your time together with the simple affirmation that Jesus doesn't expect us to continue his work alone. Jesus promised that he would send the Holy Spirit to help us. Hallelujah!

2. We are the Church (1 Peter 2:2–10)

Materials: a picture of the cornerstone of your church. A photograph of the laying of the cornerstone or any other memorabilia of that occasion would also be helpful. Have a brief conversation about cornerstones and their importance. If you have any pictures or memorabilia show them to the children. Talk together about your church building. Does it look like other churches? In what ways is it different? The same? Consider bringing some pictures of different churches.

What do you think is the most important part of any church? If our building wasn't here, would we still have a church? Indicate that one of the readings today answers that question. Holding your Bible in your hand paraphrase 1 Peter 2:4-6. Who is the church? Who is the cornerstone? What do you think it means to be a living stone? Look at the song "We Are the Church" (see page 253; also on *Seasons Growing Faith CD [#19]* and *Seasons Growing Faith Songbook*; and *Rainbow Songbook [#59]*; both available from Wood Lake Publishing, www.woodlakebooks.com). What does this song tell us about the church? Teach the children (and the congregation) the actions and sing the song together.

Prayer

Loving God,
every one of us is different and special.
Thank you that you bring us all together
to make your church.
You are a good builder, God. Amen.

Sixth Sunday of Easter

Acts 17:22-31

Psalm 66:8-20

1 Peter 3:13-22

John 14:15-21

Storytelling props needed:

• basket of letters in envelopes (papers folded in three with the words "Hear the Good News and pass it on.")

Hear the Good News

(based on Acts 17:22-31)

(Teach the refrain: "Hear the Good News and pass it on." During the story, there will be times when a child will open a letter and bring out this message. Each time, invite all the children to say the message. They might use a different voice each time – loud voice, soft voice, singing voice, squeaky voice, etc.)

There were so many Christians now. They spent time talking about Jesus and passing on the good news. They shared stories about Jesus and all the things he taught them. Sometimes they wrote letters to each other to help spread the news. *(Show the basket of letters.)* They invited other people to come and be a part of their community. They invited everyone to pass on the Good News.

There was a man named Paul who was a follower of Jesus and one of the first Christian missionaries. He lived a very long time ago. A missionary is someone who does a very special job. Paul's special job was to spread the Good News about Jesus to many different places. *(Have a child choose a letter from the basket and open it. Everyone says…)*
"Hear the Good News and pass it on."

There was a man named Philip who was a great storyteller. He loved to tell stories about Jesus. Philip had a lot of Good News to pass on to other people. *(Have another child choose a letter from the basket and open it. Everyone says…)*
"Hear the Good News and pass it on."

There was a woman called Lydia who loved God very much. She worshipped with her friends beside a river because they had no church where she lived. One day, Lydia met Paul and heard all about Jesus. Lydia was very excited. "What good news!" she said. "We are all part of God's family. I want to tell everyone." Lydia asked Paul to baptize her and then invited him to stay at her house. Many other people came to visit and hear about Jesus. And Lydia became the leader of a brand new house church. *(Have another child choose a letter from the basket and open it. Everyone says…)*
"Hear the Good News and pass it on."

There was a woman called Priscilla and a man called Aquila who were friends of Paul. They worked together to make tents. When they learned about Jesus they wanted to tell others. They passed on the Good News. *(Have another child choose a letter from the basket and open it. Everyone says…)*
"Hear the Good News and pass it on."

(Have the children stand up) There were more and more people all the time who knew about and loved Jesus. All of them passed on the Good News. We pass it on too when we tell others about Jesus. *(Have another child choose a letter from the basket and open it. Everyone says…)*
"Hear the Good News and pass it on."

Instructions
- Have fun colouring this poster to hang in your room or to give to someone to brighten their day.

Easter 6

John 14:15-21

Storytelling props needed:

• shawl

• scroll made by attaching paper to two dowels. Roll it up and tie together with a leather shoe lace. Inside is written "Jesus says, 'I will never leave you. I will always love you.'"

• jug of water and small cups

Jesus' Comforting Words

(based on John 14:15–21)

(Place a shawl over your head and shoulders as you prepare to be Deborah.

Good morning, everyone. You came back to visit me again. I am so happy to welcome you to my home and our house church. Remember that I will always welcome you with love. *(Pause and look around at the children.)* It looks like you had another long walk to get here. Let me get you a drink of water. I have just brought back a large jug of water from the well.

Activity Pour water into cups and distribute them. When finished, collect the cups and put them aside.

Today, I want to share something that is very important to us. In fact it is so important, we had it written down so that we could look at it often. Come, let's huddle together and I will tell you. *(Sit very close together and use a quiet voice.)*

Sometimes when we gathered in our house church, we felt sad and alone. Then we remembered that Jesus promised that God would always be with us. God's Spirit would help us to do God's work, and we would feel close to God. When we meet together we read stories that help us remember all the things Jesus had taught us. What stories of Jesus do you remember? *(Help children remember that Jesus talked about loving and caring and sharing.)* Now, I want to share with you these important words. One time, John , a person who loved Jesus very much, wrote this down and we don't ever want to forget it!

Activity Have a child carry the scroll over to you. Open it and read the words "Jesus says, 'I will never leave you. I will always love you.'" Ask if there are any children who would like to "read" this important message from John. They might take turns standing, holding the scroll, and using important voices, pretend to "read" the message.

Before you leave our house church and begin your journey again, you must share a snack with me. I don't want you to leave hungry!

Activity Sit in a circle and in the middle place a large tray of food (or several trays if there are many children). Pray together and share the food. Encourage the children to help clear away the remaining food.

Go well on your journey. May God be with you this week. And remember, you will always be welcome with love in our house church!

Prayer Pocket

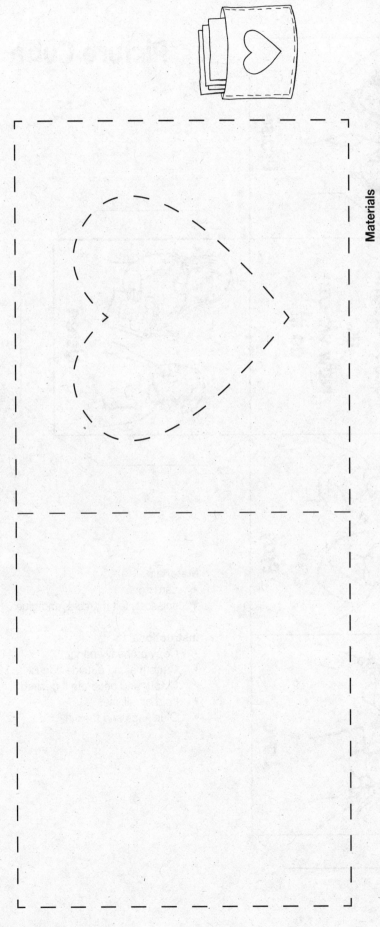

Materials

- felt pieces, scissors, needles and thread
- pockets from old jeans (optional)
- red felt for hearts
- glue and felt markers

Instructions

- Use the pattern to cut out a pocket from felt. Sew together, leaving the top end open. (Or use a pocket from an old pair of jeans.)
- Use the heart pattern to cut out a red heart from felt.
- Glue the heart to the pocket.
- Use fabric markers or a pen to print the child's name.
- Separate the prayers and place them in the pocket.

morning prayer	mealtime prayer	playtime prayer	bedtime prayer
Dear God, thank you for a brand new day. Show me how to live God's way. Amen.	Thank you, God, for food to eat, for vegetables, fruit, and meat. Amen.	Dear God, bless my friends and family, too. Help me to share your love so true. Amen.	Dear God, thank you for another day. Stay close beside me, this I pray. Amen.

Picture Cube

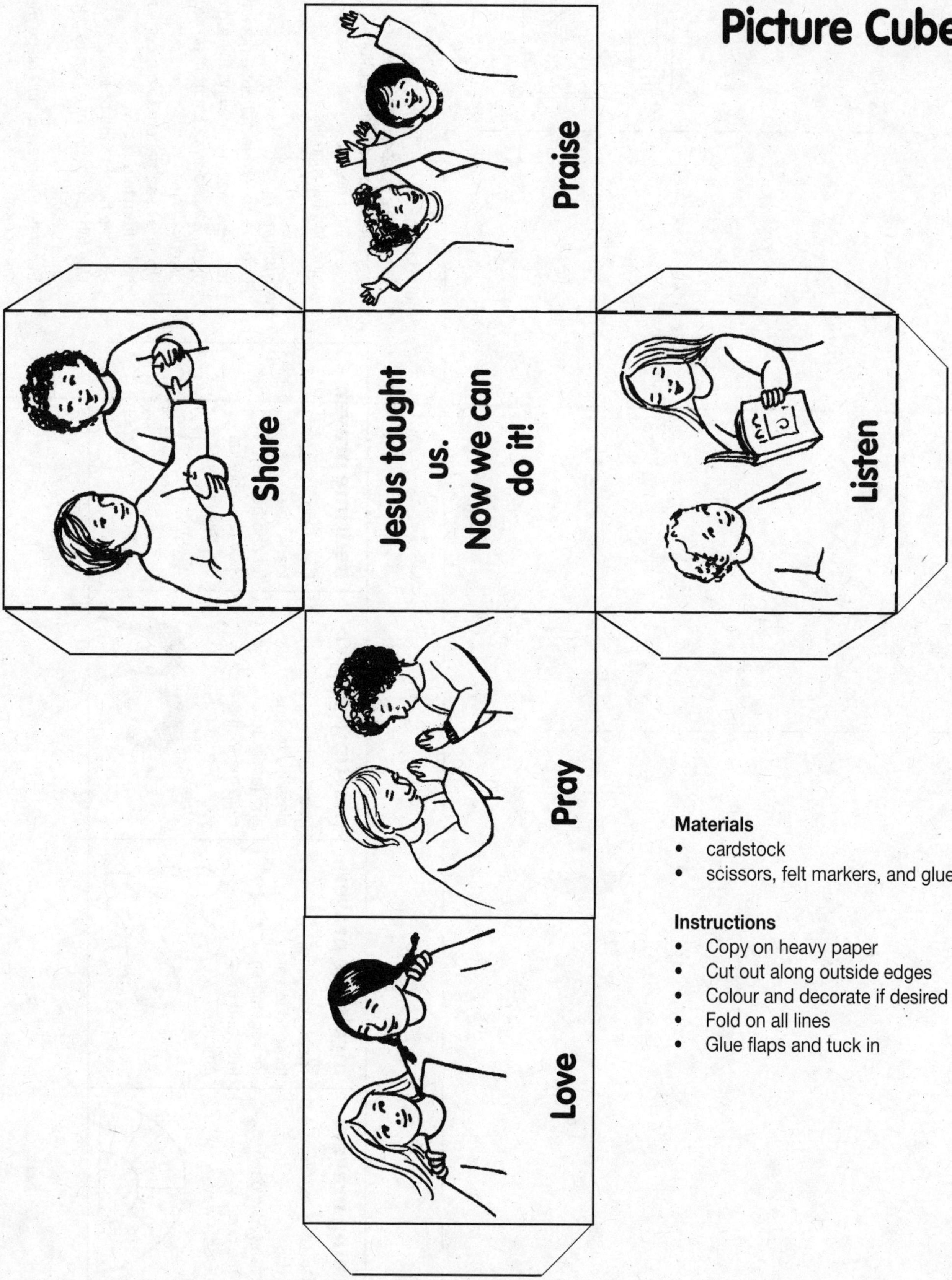

Praise

Share

Jesus taught us. Now we can do it!

Listen

Pray

Love

Materials
- cardstock
- scissors, felt markers, and glue

Instructions
- Copy on heavy paper
- Cut out along outside edges
- Colour and decorate if desired
- Fold on all lines
- Glue flaps and tuck in

Waiting and Praying

(based on Acts 1:6–14)

Seventh Sunday of Easter

Acts 1:6-14

Psalm 68:1-10, 32-35

1 Peter 4:12-14; 5:6-11

John 17:1-11

The disciples were gathered together. *(Have children place their figures in a circle.)* Jesus was with them again in a new way. They were so happy because they had a lot of questions.

(Point or pick up one figure each time a question is asked.)
"What do you want us to do now, Jesus?" asked one of the disciples.

"Do you think we are ready?"

"Should we stay in this town or should we travel to another town?"

"Is this the special time God promised for us?"

They all had so many questions! Jesus smiled at his friends. He walked around and touched each person lightly on the head or shoulder. *(Touch each figure and child.)*

"Don't worry, my friends," Jesus said gently. "I will never leave you alone. Go to Jerusalem. I want you to wait for God's Spirit. God's Spirit will be with you always. You will be able to tell everyone in the world about me."

And then something quite mysterious happened. Jesus disappeared. The disciples did not see him anymore. *(Pause.)* Everyone wondered what had happened. Everyone wondered what would happen next. *(Have children hold their figures again.)*

And so, together, the disciples went back to Jerusalem. They gathered in an upstairs room and waited. They prayed and waited. They waited and prayed. What would happen next?
(Have children pick up their figures and say, "What will happen next?")

The disciples knew that Jesus was counting on them to do God's work of helping people.

"Jesus taught us so many things," said one of the disciples. "He knows that we are ready to go and spread the good news about him. Jesus knows we can do this work now!"

So the disciples continued to pray together. And all the time they kept wondering…
(Have children pick up their figures and say, "What will happen next?")

Storytelling props needed:

• figures prepared from page 140. Enough for each child.

Story Figures

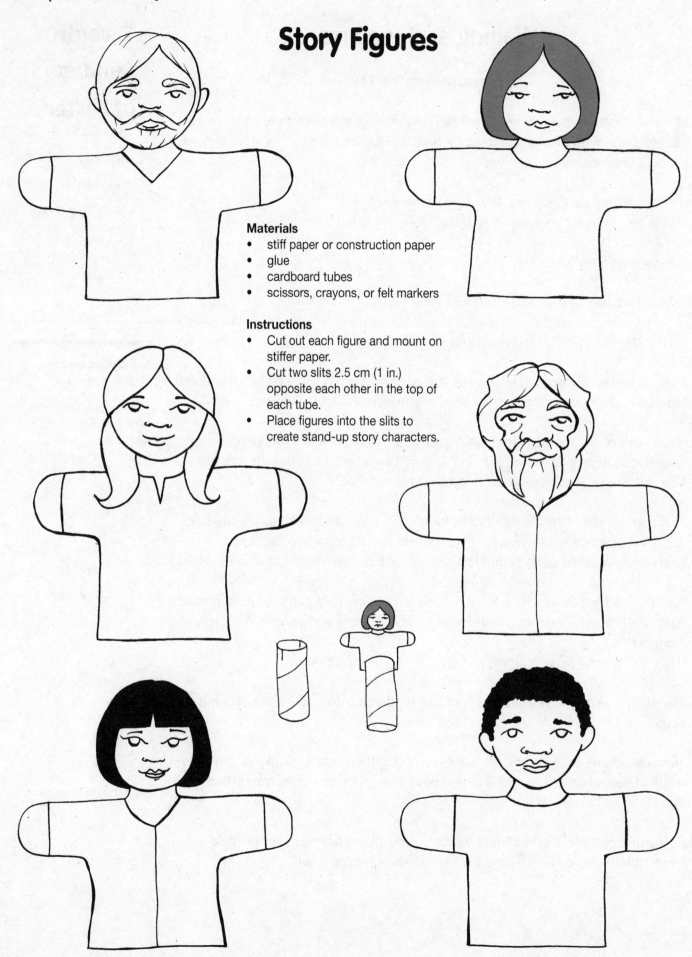

Materials
- stiff paper or construction paper
- glue
- cardboard tubes
- scissors, crayons, or felt markers

Instructions
- Cut out each figure and mount on stiffer paper.
- Cut two slits 2.5 cm (1 in.) opposite each other in the top of each tube.
- Place figures into the slits to create stand-up story characters.

Jesus Goes to Be with God

(based on Acts 1:6-14)

Easter 7

Acts 1:6-14

The disciples knew that Jesus had died and then was alive in a new way. Many of them had seen Jesus; they had touched him and eaten with him. Still, there were times when they felt alone and afraid.

They remembered that Jesus had told them, "I will never leave you alone. God's Spirit will be with you always." The disciples knew that God's Spirit was helping them to be loving and strong. God's Spirit was helping them to care for others the way Jesus had taught them.

Then one day, Jesus told them about God's Spirit for the last time. He said, "The Holy Spirit is always with you. You will be able to tell everyone in the world about me." Then Jesus was taken up into a cloud and disappeared just like the smoke of our candle. The disciples looked and looked but they could not see Jesus anymore.

Suddenly, there were two men dressed in white clothes standing there. The men asked, "Why are you standing here looking at the sky? Jesus has gone to be with God."

(Pantomime each of the italicized emotions and have the children mimic your actions.)
Some people were *happy* that Jesus was with God. Some people felt *alone and sad.* Some were *crying.* Others were *wondering* what happened to Jesus behind that cloud. Some people were *afraid.* Everyone knew that something mysterious had happened to Jesus. They wondered about it together. They wondered what would happen next.

A time for wondering
I wonder how Jesus went up into the cloud?
I wonder why everyone had different feelings?
I wonder how each of you is feeling right now?

Other ideas for exploring the lectionary readings (Easter 7)

1. It's a mystery (Acts 1:6–14)

Materials: a candle in a candleholder, and matches or a lighter

Invite the children to sit in a circle. Place the candle in the middle of the circle and light it. Watch the flame together. Ask for a volunteer to blow the candle out. Draw the children's attention to the smoke. Where does the smoke go? It's a mystery! Watch it disappear. You may wish to repeat the procedure a few times.

The world God made for us is full of mysteries. God likes us to wonder about mysteries; to ask questions and think about them. It's the way God made us. What are some mysteries you wonder about? What questions do you have about creation? What do you wonder about God? Have you found answers to some of your questions? Share your wondering questions with the children and invite them to share theirs. (Be careful to avoid connecting the idea of finding answers with losing the sense of wonder!)

2. Giving your worries to God (1 Peter 5:6–11)

Materials: a very small pebble for each child, and a ceramic bowl to put them in

Have you ever had a pebble in your shoe? You try to ignore it, but it is so uncomfortable that you have to stop and shake it out. When you do so you find that the pebble is really quite tiny. Talk about this. Most people will have had such an experience. Make the point that worries can be like a pebble in your shoe. They may not be very big, but they can make life very uncomfortable.

Indicate that God does not want us to carry worries around with us. God knows that they make us uncomfortable. Mention that the key verse for today talks about this. Read the key verse. Explain that anxiety is another word for worries.

Create a very simple prayer. "God we have some worries that are making our lives uncomfortable. We would like to give you our concerns about_____. Amen." Invite the children to place their worry pebbles into the ceramic bowl during the prayer. Place the bowl on the Communion table when you have finished.

3. Give glory to God (Psalm 66:1–10, 32–35)

The psalm for today encourages us to proclaim God's glory. Have some conversation about this. Indicate that "to give glory" means "to make known." Therefore to give glory to God means to make God known. How can we do this? What have we done in church today that would give glory to God? What about God would we like to share with others?

Look at the song "Give Glory to God" (On page 252. Also from the *Rainbow Songbook #11*, available from Wood Lake Publishing, www.woodlakebooks.com.) Talk about each verse. How does singing songs of praise give glory to God? What about speaking out for justice? Sing the song together.

Prayer

Loving God,
the whole world is in your hands.
We are glad that you care for us.
We want to tell everyone how great you are. Amen.

The Coming of God's Spirit

(based on Acts 2:1–21)

Pentecost Sunday

Acts 2:1–21 or
   Numbers 11:24–30

Psalm 104:24–34, 35b

1 Corinthians 12:3b–13 or
   Acts 2:1–21

John 20:19–23 or
   John 7:37–39

**Storytelling props
needed:**

• figures from page 140

• red, yellow, and orange
streamers or ribbon – one
for each child

(Hand out the story figures from page 140 and remind the children that these are some of the people who love Jesus very much. Encourage them to give their figures names. (Name one figure Peter.) Distribute to each child a long red, orange, or yellow streamer or ribbon and invite them to stand and use their whole bodies as they wave the streamers. Then, each time they hear the words "Whooo. Whooo. Whooo," in the story they repeat that action. Practice several times and then sit in a tight circle. Wait until everyone is quiet.)

Jesus' friends were gathered together in an upstairs room in Jerusalem. *(Have children place their figures together in a little huddle.)* They were waiting and praying. They were praying and waiting. And they were talking quietly to each other.

(Point or pick up one figure each time a question or statement is said. Whisper.)
"I miss Jesus. I feel afraid without him."

"I miss him, too. I don't know how to do God's work or show God's love, like Jesus did."

"Jesus taught us so many things but I don't think I can do those things by myself."

And then Peter said, "Remember what Jesus told us about God's Spirit coming to help us? I wonder when we will know?"

Suddenly everyone stopped whispering. They felt something happening from the top of their heads to the tip of their toes.

Whooo. Whooo. Whooo. It was like the wind blowing.
Whooo. Whooo. Whooo. It was coming through the room!
Whooo. Whooo. Whooo. It was all around them.

Everyone started talking at once.
Whooo. Whooo. Whooo. "God is with us," shouted Peter.
Whooo. Whooo. Whooo. "Yes, yes. We can feel God's love!" shouted the other friends.
Whooo. Whooo. Whooo. "We are not alone. We can feel God's Spirit! God is with us!" shouted Peter again.

Everyone became very excited. They rushed out into the streets of Jerusalem. *(Children disperse the story figures.)*

"Listen, listen," Peter called out to the people on the streets. "We cannot keep from speaking about what we have seen and heard. God is with us." And then Peter told the people all about Jesus.

(Children pick up their figures and one by one call out "Good news! Good news!")
Many people believed the good news about God's love. Many people became followers of Jesus. It was an exciting wonderful time!

Spreading the Message
How are we going to tell people about God's love?

Instructions
- Cut out mouth expressions and mount on heavier paper
- Cut slits in face.
- Insert mouth expressions in slits on face and pull through

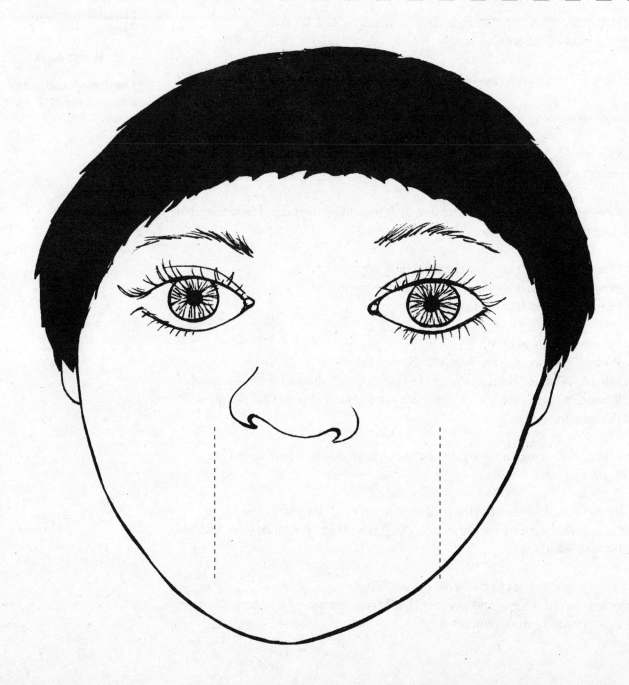

Peter's Pentecost Story

(based on Acts 2:1-21)

Pentecost Sunday

Acts 2:1-41

(Have an adult or youth volunteer to be Peter and practice Peter's words in advance so there can be some eye contact with the audience. Optional: Dress in biblical costume.)

Shalom! Hello! I'm Peter, one of Jesus' disciples. That Pentecost Day so long ago was wonderful because we experienced the Holy Spirit in a new way. Today I'd like to tell you the story of what happened. And I'd like you to help me. Whenever you hear the word "wind," blow and make noises like the wind. Let's try that: "wind." *(Practice once or twice, encouraging an enthusiastic response.)* That's terrific. Whenever you hear the word "fire," wave your streamers and whenever you hear the word "Spirit," stand up and sit down saying "Alleluia." *(Practice each of these once or twice.)* Now let me begin. *(Pauses indicate participants' responses.)*

Storytelling props needed:

• a crate or box strong enough to stand on

• streamers for each child

That Pentecost Day so long ago, we disciples were waiting. But we didn't really know what we were waiting for. Jesus had died, and risen, and appeared to us many times, and ascended to heaven. We were waiting to experience the gift of the Spirit Jesus had promised. *(pause)* But how would this happen? *(In a loud voice)* Would it be like a strong wind? *(pause)* *(In a quiet voice)* Would it be like a soft breeze? *(In a loud voice)* Would it be like a strong blazing fire? *(pause)* *(In a quiet voice)* Would it be like a candle's flame? We really didn't know.

That Pentecost Day so long ago, we followers of Jesus were all together in Jerusalem, along with crowds of people from many, many lands. Suddenly, we heard a noise like the rush of a violent wind! *(pause)* It filled the whole place where we were gathered. Then, we saw what looked like tongues resting on each one of us, like a raging fire! *(pause)* All of us were filled with the Spirit. *(pause)* Then an amazing thing happened – we started talking in languages we didn't even know as we experienced the Spirit. *(pause)* What a commotion we made!

Now word of our experience of the Spirit *(pause)* spread like wildfire *(pause)* fanned by the wind *(pause)*. People visiting Jerusalem from other countries heard us and they were amazed and confused to hear their own languages spoken.

"What does this mean?" they all wanted to know. Some people laughed at us, saying, "They must be drunk."

That's when I stood up with the other eleven apostles and spoke to the crowd. *(Stand on the crate or box.)* "We're not drunk," I told them. "After all, it's only nine o'clock in the morning." Then I told them the whole story about Jesus – about his miracles and his teachings and about his death and Resurrection. "God raised him from death," I said. "And we saw the risen Christ many times. We know he was the Messiah, the promised one from God. What you have just heard was a gift of God, the gift of the Holy Spirit.*(pause)* It has come to us this day like a wind *(pause)* and like a fire. *(pause.)*

(Step down from the crate and while walking to the back of the space, say loudly:) How exciting it was – right then and there about 3,000 people decided to follow Jesus! The church was born that day, that Pentecost Day, so long ago when we experienced the joyous gift of the Spirit! *(pause)*

place this line along fold of construction paper

Materials

Fire Spinners
- orange, red, or yellow construction paper
- orange, red, or yellow ribbons or streamers
- stapler, tape, and scissors
- a straw for each child
- felt markers

Fire Flames
- orange, red, or yellow construction paper
- orange, red, or yellow cellophane
- flashlight
- scissors and tape
- felt markers

Wrist Streamers
- tissue rolls
- felt markers
- orange, red, or yellow ribbons or streamers
- scissors and tape

1. **Fire Spinners:** Fold construction paper in half. Draw a flaming fire using this pattern as a template. Cut out. Open up and tape pieces of ribbon or streamers to the points. Fold spinner in half and staple to a straw. Print "Spirit" words on each side (e.g. peace, love, unity, togetherness, wind, fire, listen, Jesus). Rub the straw between your hands to make the flames dance.

2. **Fire Flames:** Fold construction paper in half. Draw template on one half and cut out to make one large shape and 3 small shapes. Cut small shapes along folds and tape to back edge of large one. Tape pieces of cellophane over the "windows" of the large shape. Print "Spirit" words on front (e.g. peace, love, unity, disciple, wind, fire, listen, Jesus). Shine a flashlight or sunlight through cellophane.

3. **Wrist Streamers:** Cut tissue rolls into "bangles" about 2.5cm (1in.) wide. Cut across them to make opening for wrists. Draw on colourful designs. Tape on lengths of streamers and ribbons. Put "bangles" on wrists and wave arms to create a dance of fire.

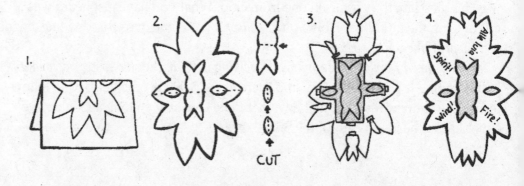

Other ideas for exploring the lectionary readings
(Pentecost Sunday)

1. Growing and changing (1 Corinthians 12:13b–13)

Materials: the plant that has grown from the seeds planted on Easter day (see page 118)
Look at the plant together. How has the seed changed? Bring some seeds to compare with the plant. You could measure it to see how much growth has occurred. The seed needed water to grow. Mention that one of the images for the Holy Spirit is water. Read 1 Corinthians 12: 13. Just as the seed needs water – we need the Holy Spirit in our lives to help us to grow and to change.

Discuss briefly the changes that we have seen in the disciples over the Easter season. How were the disciples feeling just after Jesus died? How did they change and grow once they met Jesus and received the Holy Spirit? You might bring some of the teaching pictures the younger groups have used during this season to act as visual reminders.

2. God's playfulness (Psalm 104:4–34, 35b)

Today's psalm gives us an insight into the playful aspect of God's character. Talk with the children about playing. What games do you like? What is your favourite toy? Indicate that God created us to enjoy playing. Read Psalm 104:24-26. Does anyone know what a Leviathan is? Why did God create such large creatures? You might want to mention that in some translations of the Bible it says that God made Leviathans for the fun of it. God likes to play too!

Encourage the children to create a simple prayer, thanking God for fun and laughter.

3. Overflowing love (Acts 1:1–21)

Materials: a bowl with some baking soda/bicarb in it, some vinegar, and something to catch the overflow. As the liturgical colour for Pentecost is red, consider using red vinegar. Try this experiment at home first.
Talk about the changes we have seen in the lives of the disciples since the start of the Easter season. You could highlight the differences that we have seen in Peter's life. On the night Jesus was arrested Peter was so scared that he said he didn't know Jesus. In our reading today Peter is proclaiming the story of Jesus to everyone who will listen. What happened to Peter? What made the difference?

Show the children the bowl with the baking soda/bicarb. Indicate that this is like the disciples before they received the Holy Spirit. They knew that Jesus was alive, and they had seen Jesus leave to go back to heaven. Now they were waiting in Jerusalem for the Holy Spirit to come. When the Holy Spirit came something amazing happened *(pour the vinegar onto the baking soda/bicarb)*. Suddenly God's love and joy bubbled up inside the disciples. They could not keep it in. Jesus' followers were filled with the power and love of God. Now they weren't scared anymore.

Today is Pentecost Sunday. Churches all over the world are celebrating the new life the Holy Spirit brings. Invite the children, and the congregation, to join this celebration with the whole people of God.

Prayer

Holy Spirit,
today we celebrate the power and new life you bring.
Help us to grow as we learn to walk in God's way.
Amen.

Pentecost Activity Centres

1. Pentecost tablecloth
Materials: roll of paper, stampers, stamp pads.
In advance: cut newsprint into the size you need. Print "The Spirit Comes" in large letters across the paper.

In preparing to receive guests, the children could decorate a tablecloth together. Have the children sit around the cloth and use the stampers, crayons, and markers to create their designs. When completed, put the cloth on the table to be used for serving food to guests.

2. Growing in Pentecost
Materials: large sheets of construction paper, liquid tempera paint, paper towels, shallow pans, bucket of warm, soapy water for cleanup
In advance: draw a vine or tree on each sheet of construction paper. Print "We grow in faith in Pentecost" on each paper. Fold paper towels and place in shallow pans. Pour a different colour of paint into each pan.

Give each child a piece of paper. Read the words together. Invite the children to place their hands, palms down, in the paint and then press onto their paper to form leaves on the vine or tree.

3. Pentecost flame hats
Materials: red, yellow, and orange construction paper
In advance: cut construction paper into wide strips for headbands.
Cut flames out of red, yellow, or orange construction paper.

Give each child a headband. Print the words "Come, Spirit, Come" on each headband. Encourage the children to glue the flames onto their headband. Form into a crown for each child and tape the ends together.

4. Pentecost batons
Materials: red, yellow, and orange crepe streamers, long cardboard tubes, self-adhesive stickers.
In advance: print "God's Spirit is with us" on each tube.

Make a baton to wave in celebration and remember that God's Spirit is with us. Give each child a tube and read the words to them. Help the children attach several streamers onto one end of the tube. Decorate with markers and self-adhesive stickers.

5. Our church community
Materials: activity sheet "God's Church Family (page 149)," if possible, a camera with instant developing film (Polaroid™ or digital), construction paper
In advance: make copies of activity sheet. Prepare a church for each child (and make some extras).

Give each child a prepared church. Invite them to colour it with crayons and markers. Open the doors and draw many happy faces inside. (***Option:*** *invite each child to take a photograph of people in the room who are enjoying this celebration together. Then, glue this photograph inside the doors of the church.*)

6. Party food
Materials: prepared cupcakes or cookies/biscuits, icing, sugar trims, spreading knives, serving plates, napkins

Invite the children to ice and decorate prepared cupcakes or cookies/biscuits and arrange them on a plate. Share these with each other or with their guests. (Check for allergies.)

God's Church Family

Materials
- construction paper
- scissors and glue
- felt markers or cryaons

Instructions:
- Make copies of activity sheet.
- Cut out church.
- Cut door on solid lines. Fold back on dotted lines.
- Mount church on a full sheet of construction paper.
- Colour the church with markers or crayons.
- Open the doors and draw happy faces inside. *(Option: have the children take a photo of people in the room who are enjoying the Pentecost celebration together. Then, glue this photograph inside the doors.)*

God's church family

God's church family

The Season after Pentecost

The season of Pentecost is also known as "ordinary time." However, nothing is ordinary for those Jesus sends to the world. Nothing is ordinary about letting God's healing breath blow us at will along the path to wholeness and community. Nothing is ordinary about letting the Spirit inflame our hearts with passion for mending the world that God loves. In fact, everything's extraordinary when we let the Holy Spirit breathe into each and every moment.

THE PENTECOST SEASON begins with Trinity Sunday (first Sunday after the festival of Pentecost) and lasts through to Reign of Christ (or Christ the King) Sunday which falls between November 20 and November 26 – the last Sunday before the start of Advent. Some traditions call this the "Kingdom-tide" season because we focus on making intentional contributions to the reign of holy love in the world. Other people call this "the season of the church," when we share what Jesus taught us and show our love for God by loving others.

In this season, we follow the followers of Jesus as they become the church. It seems the full significance of the ministry of Jesus was revealed to his friends only when his bodily presence was gone. In the fire and wind of Pentecost, the Spirit came among them as irrepressible life, and suddenly their experience with Jesus was inspired with new meaning – Jesus' mission was their mission! They were the hands and feet of Christ. Now they were to go to the world as apostles, a title which means "those sent out."

Jesus' followers were filled with burning passion and joy as they dashed out to share their wondrous tale. They said Jesus was "Christ," the long-awaited "Messiah," through whom a new creation would be born. They told how Jesus taught them to live every moment attentive to loving God and humankind. They told how Jesus suffered unjust violence and crucifixion but continued to love through it all. They told how Christ came to them after his death, and how the Spirit filled their hearts with holy abundance and sent them out to love as Christ loves.

All followers of Christ are part of God's creative unfolding through the power of the Spirit. As we journey together, our lives are marked by experiences of wonder and inspiration which serve as signs in our wilderness times. We start to see how the Spirit draws us out of captivity into our freedom to love. We come to know the Spirit as our source of excitement, confidence, connectedness, and insight. And we realize that, like the original apostles, we are receiving the Spirit so the transforming power of Christ will be revealed. As God sent Jesus Christ, so Christ sends us out to share, to heal, and to build true community.

For the season of Pentecost – fired by the Spirit – we focus on living the Christ-life together in ways that express God's yearning for the transformation of human lives and societies. We dream of joy and Christ invites us to service. Then the blessing we find in serving is joy.

In this season of Pentecost, we focus on being the presence of Christ in a yearning world. By God's Grace we grow and heal, as individuals and communities, making whole what was broken or divided.

In this spirit of growth-to-wholeness, in ordinary time, the central colour is green for banners and vestments. Some may choose to use red for the weeks immediately following the festival of Pentecost, in order to break the length of the season. White or gold can be used for All Saints' Sunday, and for the last Sunday of the season, Reign of Christ Sunday.

The tone of ordinary time is vibrant, communal, and active. Colours and textures could reflect this.

Symbols can include all the symbols for the Holy Spirit used to celebrate the festival of Pentecost which marks the end of Eastertide. As the Pentecost season moves through spring into summer and fall, images and decorations can reflect the many changes in nature's seasons. Growing flowers, bubbles, wind-socks, kites, and dandelion fluff are all appropriate to help us to understand the vibrant beauty and active spirit of the season of Pentecost.

God Makes the World for Us

(based on Genesis 1:1 — 2:4a)

Trinity Sunday

Genesis 1:1 — 2:4a

Psalm 8

2 Corinthians 13:11–13

Matthew 28:16–20

Sit in a circle. Give a short streamer to each child. Teach the cue and response words:
Cue: *"And God looked around…"*
Response: "That's good!"
Have the large paper circle and creation pictures nearby.

Long, long ago it was dark. The dark was everywhere. A wind from God blew over the darkness. (*Wave the streamers.*) God saw the darkness. On the first day God said, "Let there be light!" And there was light on the first day. "And God looked around… **That's good!"**

On the second day, God said, "Let the water be together in one place and let the dry land appear." And it was so. God called the dry land earth and the waters seas. (*Place large paper circle in the middle. Invite the children to place their streamers around the edge of the paper circle.*)
"And God looked around… **That's good!"**

On the third day, God said, "Now I'll make trees and plants and flowers to grow on the earth." And it was so. (*Invite a child to wave and then place picture of trees and flowers inside the paper circle.*)
"And God looked around… **That's good!"**

On the fourth day, God said, "Let there be lights in the sky." And it was so. God made two big lights. The sun for day. The moon for night. God made lots of little lights called stars, too. (*Invite children to wave and place pictures of sun, moon, and stars in the paper circle.*)
"And God looked around… **That's good!"**

On the fifth day, God said, "I want birds and fish and animals!" And it was so. The earth was filled with animals. The seas were filled with fish. The skies were filled with birds. (*Invite children to wave and place pictures in the paper circle.*)
"And God looked around… **That's good!"**

On the sixth day, God said, "Only one thing is missing. Now I will make people for the earth. And it was so. (*Invite children to place one or both hands just inside the paper circle. Go around the circle and name each child. "God made ___."*)
"And God looked around… **That's good!"**

Then God said to the people, "I made all these beautiful things for you. Please care for the plants. Please care for the fish and the birds and the animals."
"And God looked around… **That's good!"**

God had started the work of creation. God counted the days, 1..2..3..4..5..6. (*Lightly touch each picture in the circle as you count.*) Now it was the seventh day. God was very happy, 1..2..3..4..5..6..7. God blessed the seventh day. Then God rested. God rested on this special day.

Storytelling props needed:

• large paper circle

• streamers for everyone to wave

• pictures from magazines or drawings of land, water and clouds; trees, plants and flowers; sun, moon, and stars; fish, birds, and animals; people; or enlarge pictures from the activity sheet on page 152.

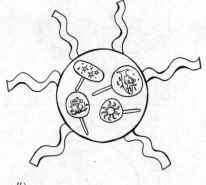

That's Good!

Dear family,

Today your child heard the story of creation. God's generous offering of light and dark, land and seas, sun, moon, and stars, all growing things and living creatures, and, of course, humankind. During the story there were many opportunities to say together, "That's good!" in response to hearing that God looked around and saw everything that God made. You will find a copy of the story in the bag your child brings home.

As a way to reinforce the story and begin to understand that God took some time to complete this awesome creation, your child has brought home a strip calendar marked into seven squares with a corresponding cut-out square to attach each day. We added the first square during our session today. You may wish to help your child retell a part of the story each day as you add a square. You may want to use words such as: "And on the second day God made the land and the waters." (Attach the square.) "And God looked around...That's good!" These last two phrases are the ones we used in our story. The squares for the next days are as follows:

Third day: trees, plants, and flowers
Fourth day: sun, moon, and stars
Fifth day: fish, birds, and animals
Sixth day: people
Seventh day: the work is done, God rested

You may want to take some time outdoors this week with your child discovering and marvelling at the wonders of God's creation. Perhaps you might search each day for signs of the particular item you are adding to the calendar that day. Say together as you spot each beautiful thing, "That's good!"

Enjoy your creation week together!

God's Creation

1	2	3	4	5	6	7

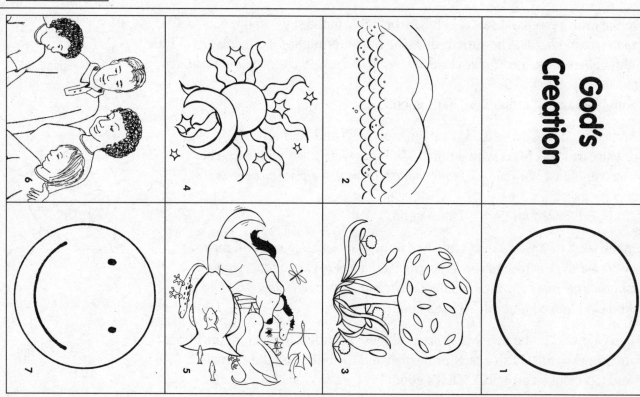

Material
- construction paper rectangle
- felt markers or crayons
- scissors and glue
- paper bag for each child

Instructions
- children colour and cut apart each square in "God's Creation" sheet
- together glue the title on the construction paper strip. Read the creation story on page 154 that corresponds with #1 and #2 squares. Together say, "That's good." Children glue these squares as shown. Place letter, construction paper, and the rest of the pictures in their bag to take home to complete with their family.

A Wonderful Promise

(based on Matthew 28:20)

God made a promise to us at the very beginning. Jesus made the same promise to us.

Material
- felt markers or crayons
- hole punch, scissors,
- ribbon for each child

Instructions
- Colour in the spaces with the letters C, J, K, M, P, Q, R, V, X, and Z.
- Read the promise in the remaining letters.
- Cut out along the solid line to make a winding spiral.
- Hole punch where indicated and attach a ribbon.
- Give thanks for this wonderful promise!

Other ideas for exploring the lectionary readings (Trinity Sunday)

1. God's care in all of creation (Psalm 8)

In advance: locate a large poster of creation, or make a montage of creation. Bring an ink pad, fine line markers, paper wipes for cleaning fingers.

Show your creation poster and talk about God in creation. In one of today's readings a psalmist wonders about creation and our place in creation, and discovers that God has given us important work to do in caring for the earth and its creatures. Show the children how they might make a thumbprint person by pressing a thumb or finger onto an ink pad and stamping it onto the creation poster. You might add arms and legs and face to the thumbprint to create a person, animal, or insect. Talk about thumbprints being unique, and how we are all special to God. Add caption to the poster, "God needs us all to care for the earth and its creatures." Remind everyone that God's Spirit is with us helping us to care.

2. God's creation collage or illustration (Psalm 8)

Materials: magazines, variety of art materials, scissors, glue, large sheet of construction paper for each child
Give each child a large sheet of construction paper. Invite them to make a collage celebrating God's creation by drawing, making, sculpting, cutting out, and writing things to show the great variety and wonder of creation. The collages can be called "God's Creation." Reinforce the concept that each of us is part of God's Creation. The children could add variety to the collage by incorporating texture (cut-out shapes, leaf rubbings, etc.)

or

Invite the children to depict by drawing, collage or painting how they can help care for God's creation.

3. God is with us in many ways

In advance: locate the book In God's Name *by Sandy Sasso, published by Jewish Lights (contact your library or religious book store) or songs such as "God Is Like" on* Seasons Growing Faith CD *[#5] and* Seasons Growing Faith Songbook; *or* Rainbow Songbook *[#15]; both available from Wood Lake Publishing, www. woodlakebooks.com.*

Today is Trinity Sunday, a day when the church celebrates three of the many ways God is experienced – Creator (Father), Christ (Son), Spirit, and a day when we can remember and celebrate that God is with us in many ways.

    In our Bible stories today we discover the many ways in which we experience God being with us.
* Read the book. Invite children to say which images they like the best and why.
* Sing "God Is Like"

Prayer

After the story, ask children and congregation to think of a time when they felt God very close – when they encountered God. Invite them to think about the sights and sounds, and then think about what God was like to them in that experience. What name would they give God? Children might like to choose a name from the storybook. Then invite them to call out their names for God popcorn style, that is, one after the other. Some names will be called out at the same time and that's okay. When the "popping" stops, say, "And God is …" *(hold up one finger so they will respond with the word, "One").* Amen.

Two Houses

(based on Matthew 7:21–29)

Invite the children to join you in making the actions and sounds that accompany the story.

One day Jesus and his friends sat together on a hillside. Jesus told them a story to help them understand how to live in God's way.
Once there was a man who wanted to build a house. He thought and thought about where he should build his house. He knew that rocks were hard and strong. He decided to build his house on rock. (*Place a large flat rock on a tray. Invite a child to place a paper house on the rock.*) Soon the rain fell (*make rain motions with hands*), the water rose around the rock (*pour water in tray*), the wind blew (*make blowing and wind sounds*) and the thunder became louder and louder (*clap hands loudly*). But the house stayed standing.

Jesus looked at his friends and said, "A person who lives God's way is like that wise person who built a house on a rock."

Then Jesus continued with his story.

Once there was another man who also wanted to build a house. He wanted to build his house fast. He didn't think carefully about where to build. This man built his house on the sand. (*Pour sand into a second tray and smooth out the sand. Invite a child to place a paper house on the sand.*) Soon the rain fell (*make rain motions with hands*), the water rose (*gently pour water on the sand*), the wind blew (*make blowing and wind sounds*) and the thunder became louder and louder (*clap hands loudly*). And, crash! The house fell down. (*Topple house.*)

Jesus looked at his friends again and said, "A person who does not listen to me and does not live in God's way is like this foolish person who built a house on sand."

"What an amazing story," said Jesus' friends. "Thank you, Jesus. You have given us a lot to think about."

Wondering about the story

What happens when you build a sandcastle by the seashore? What would happen if a real house was built on sand?

Discuss some reasons why a person might do good things, but not out of genuine love? (e.g. to be popular, to be famous, to look good, to cover up for lack of self-esteem, to gain favours from people, out of fear of punishment)

Who in your life is a lot like the person whose life was built on rock? When are you like this?

Season after Pentecost

Proper 4 [9]

Genesis 6:9–22; 7:24; 8:14–19

Psalm 46

Romans 1:16–17; 3:22b–28, (29–31)

Matthew 7:21–29

Storytelling props needed:

• two baking trays

• a large flat rock

• sand

• a jug of water

• two paper houses (pattern on page 156)

Paper House

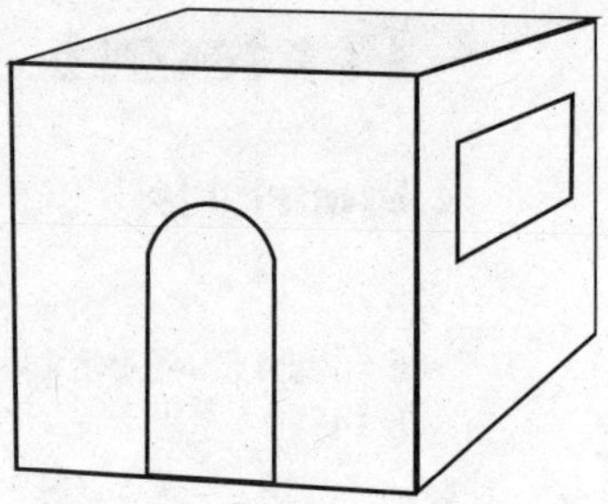

Materials
- card stock
- tape and scissors
- flat rock for each child

Instructions for storyteller
- Make 2 houses and place one on rock and one on sand

Instructions for children
- Photocopy on card stock or heavy paper.
- Cut out on solid lines.
- Fold on dotted lines.
- Tape sides together
- Bring a flat rock for every child
- place the house on the rock

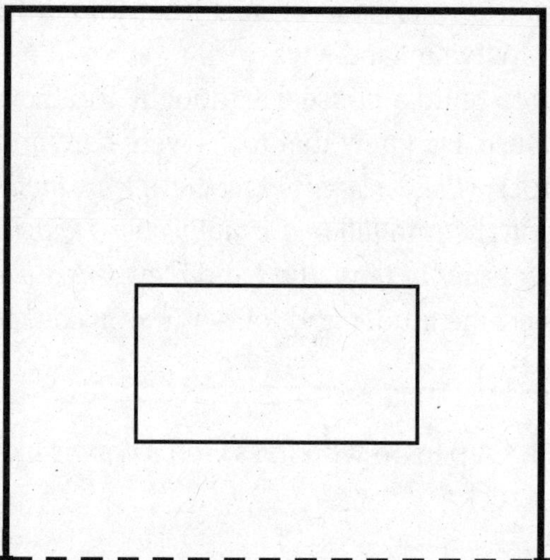

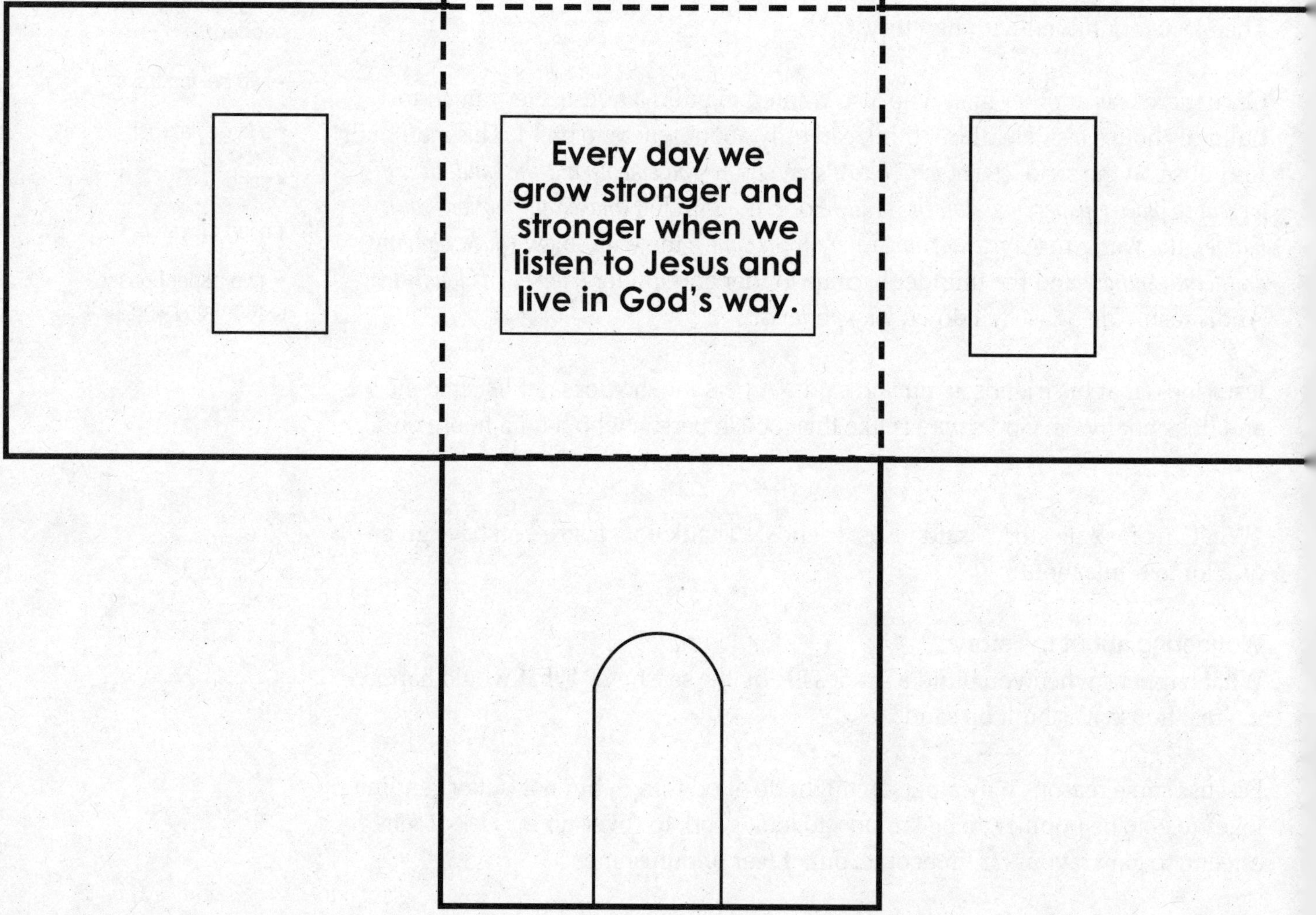

Every day we grow stronger and stronger when we listen to Jesus and live in God's way.

A House Built on Rock

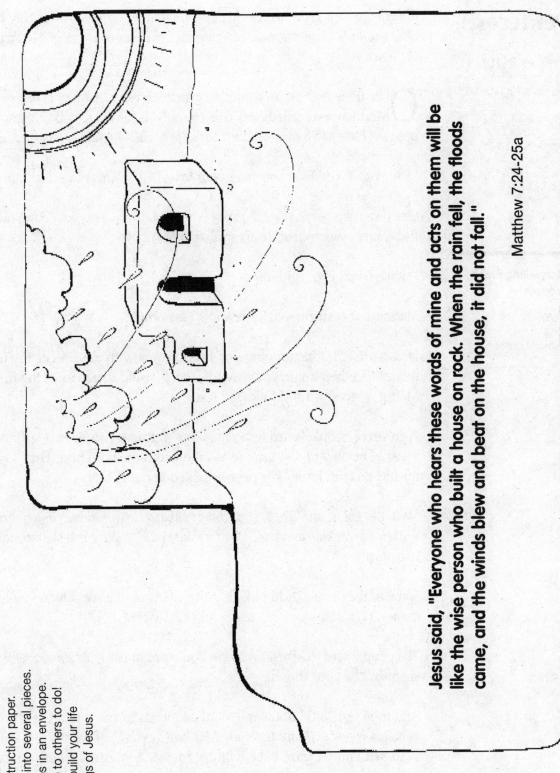

Jesus said, "Everyone who hears these words of mine and acts on them will be like the wise person who built a house on rock. When the rain fell, the floods came, and the winds blew and beat on the house, it did not fall."

Matthew 7:24-25a

Material
- construction paper
- felt markers or crayons
- glue and scissors

Instructions
- Colour the picture.
- Glue onto construction paper.
- Cut the picture into several pieces.
- Place the pieces in an envelope.
- Give the puzzle to others to do!
- Remember to build your life on the teachings of Jesus.

Season after Pentecost

Proper 5 [10]

Genesis 12:1–9

Psalm 33:1–12

Romans 4:13–25

Mathew 9:9–13, 18–26

Storytelling props needed:

• coins

• small basket

Jesus and Matthew

(based on Matthew 9:9–13)

(Distribute a few coins to each child. Mention to the children that during the story these coins will be collected from them. Ask for one child to be Jesus, one to be Matthew, and the rest to be the crowd.)

Once there was a man named Matthew. *(Present Matthew to the congregation.)* Matthew was called a tax collector. It was his job to collect money from the people. *(Have Matthew take a little basket from child to child as you speak in Matthew's voice.)*

"Pay your taxes! Everyone pay your taxes!" *(Children place their coins in the basket.)*

One day Jesus walked by the spot where Matthew was collecting money. *(Present Jesus to the congregation)* Jesus smiled at Matthew.

"Hello, Matthew," said Jesus.

Matthew was surprised. Jesus knew his name!

Jesus said, "Matthew, would you like to come with me, and be my friend? Let's have dinner together. Invite your friends, too. I would like to meet them." Immediately, Matthew stood up and followed Jesus.

A group of people heard Jesus speak to Matthew. *(Have the crowd children stand in a group.)* They heard Jesus invite Matthew to come with him. They saw Matthew get up and go with Jesus. The people looked at each other.

"What is going on?" they said. *(Invite children to look at each other, shrug, put their hands on their hips or chin and say, "What is going on?")* "Why is Jesus friends with someone like Matthew?"

Some of the people didn't like Matthew because he was always collecting their money. *(Place the crowd between Jesus and Matthew.)*

The people said to Jesus, "Why do you want to eat with someone like Matthew? He shouldn't be your friend!"

And then Jesus said to them, "Matthew needs to know that God loves him. I want to be his friend." *(Move Jesus and Matthew together.)* "I want to eat with him. I want to share with him. I want to be with his friends, too. And I want you to do the same."

The people heard what Jesus said. They knew these were important words. They would try to do as Jesus said. *(Place crowd beside Jesus and Matthew.)*

And Matthew? He was so happy to be Jesus' friend. Soon, he too, was telling everyone about God's love.

Come, Let's Have Dinner Together
(Matthew 9:9–13)

Jesus cared and loved everyone. Add more people who could be sharing a meal with Jesus. (Either draw the people or cut them out of magazines and glue them in place.)

Season after Pentecost

Proper 5 [10]

Mathew 9:9–13, 18–26

The Calling of Matthew

(based on Matthew 9:9-13, 18-26)

(Ask for a volunteer to be Matthew who will pantomime actions as the story unfolds – e.g. going to each person with hand outstretched "collecting taxes," acting sad and lonely. Another volunteer could pantomime Jesus' actions. Group members could be other tax collectors and religious leaders.)

Matthew was a tax collector. He collected money for the conquering Romans. Sometimes Matthew lied to the people and cheated them to get more money from them than he should. Then he kept this money for himself. That is how he was able to make his living. People didn't like Matthew at all because they didn't trust him.

Actually, Matthew didn't like doing what he did. But what could he do? Where could he go? This was the only thing he knew how to do. So day after day he sat at his tax booth collecting money from people as they entered the city – hated by everyone who came to him.

Then one day, Jesus came to town. Matthew had heard about him. People were talking about Jesus as teacher, healer, and prophet. Some people even called him God's special leader, the Messiah. Suddenly, things got quiet. A crowd was gathered around him. Matthew looked up. It was Jesus, looking right at him! Then he heard Jesus say to him, "Come, follow me. I will help you live and love in God's way."

Matthew knew that this was a way to change his life. Right away, he got up and followed Jesus, leaving his tax booth and his old life behind. "Jesus," Matthew said, "would you come and have dinner at my house?" Jesus agreed, and Matthew was so excited, he went and invited other people he knew, including some other tax collectors, to join them for dinner.

Some important religious leaders saw Jesus eating dinner with Matthew and other tax collectors and unpopular people. "Why is Jesus eating with these people and making friends with them?" the religious leaders wanted to know.

Jesus overheard what these religious leaders were saying. So he told them, "I have come to help people live and love in God's way. Matthew and his friends know they have done wrong, so I have come to help them. I'm like a doctor helping them become well again."

Wondering about the story

What are the surprises in this story?

What might happen if one of the religious leaders decided to follow Jesus?

What might Matthew say the next day to the Roman authorities? to his family? to Jesus?

Welcome!

Instructions

- Colour and decorate the welcome sign. Add other faces around the sign (either draw them or cut from magazines.)

Season after Pentecost

Proper 6 [11]

Genesis 18:1–15, (21:1–7)

Psalm 116:1–2, 12–19

Romans 5:1–8

Matthew 9:35—10:8, [9–23]

Storytelling props needed:

• several dolls or soft toys

Jesus Sends His Friends to Show God's Love

(based on Matthew 9:35 – 10:8)

(Place several dolls or soft toys around the room. Have children pretend they are a group of disciples.)

Jesus and his friends were doing so much travelling. They went to this town and helped people who were sick. They went to that town and told about God's love. They visited people over here. They talked to people over there. Jesus and his friends travelled everywhere.

Sometimes they met people who were very sick. *(Have children show how their face and body might look if they were sick.)* Sometimes they met people who were feeling sad. *(Have children show how their face and body might look if they were sad.)* Sometimes they met people who were feeling worried. *(Have children show how their face and body might look if they were worried.)* Jesus worked very hard loving and caring for everyone. But there was so much to do and so many people who needed help.

Jesus turned to his friends and said, "So many people need our help. Here is what I want you to do." And then Jesus began to call out the names of his friends. *(Point to one of the children in the group of disciples for each name you call out.)*

"John! I want you to go and teach the people about God's love."
"Peter and Andrew! Please go to the next town and help people who are sick. Show God's love."

"Sarah and Mary! Please go to the people who live by the river. Tell them God loves them! Share the good news!"

Jesus called out the names of all his friends. "(*Child's name*), go and show God's love."

And that's what everyone did. Some of Jesus' friends went to heal the sick. *(Have one child show how their face and body might look if they were sick and have the other children help them.)* Some of Jesus' friends went to help people who were sad or lonely. *(Have one child show how their face and body might look if they were sad and have the other children help them.)* Some of Jesus' friends went to be with people who were worried. *(Have one child show how their face and body might look if they were worried and have the other children help them.)*

Jesus had many, many friends who wanted to help show God's love to everyone. Jesus calls us to do that, too! *(Encourage the children to stand up, walk to a doll or soft toy in the room, cradle it, and say, "God loves you." Then carefully put the toy down and return to the story area.)*

Showing God's Love

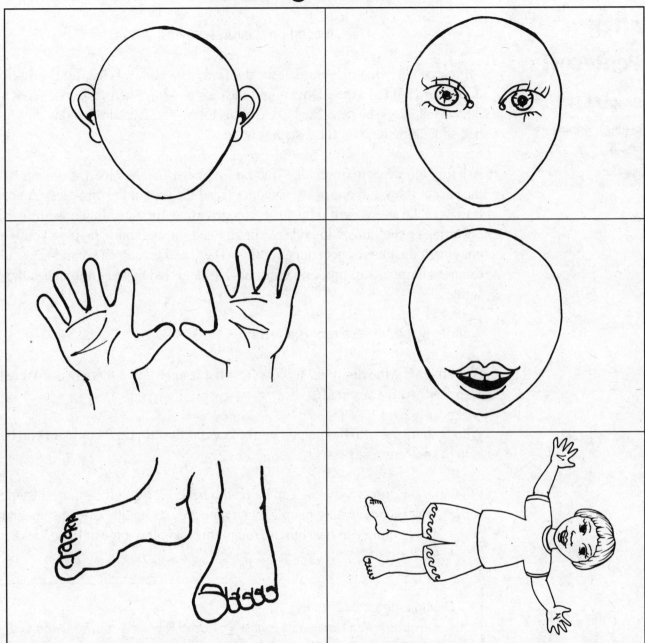

Dear family,
Your child is bringing home a pocket of little pictures. Each day, encourage your child to choose a paper from the pocket. Look at the body part pictured and think of a way to use that part of the body to help show God's love. For example, a picture of a pair of ears may remind us that we can listen to someone who needs to talk to us.

Materials
- 1 1/2 paper plates for each child
- yarn and felt markers
- hole punch or glue gun

Instructions
- Either stitch plates together by making holes around plate and threading yarn through holes or use glue gun to glue plates together, as shown. Write words "Showing God's love" at the top. Add yarn for hanging.
- Children colour and cut apart body parts and place in pocket with letter to family.

Jesus Calls Others to Share His Ministry

(based on Matthew 9:35–10:8, (9–23))

Ask people what they think Jesus did from day-to-day. What did the disciples do from day-to-day? How might the disciples have helped Jesus? What might it have felt like to be Jesus? to be one of his followers? Explain that one day, Jesus had something new for the disciples to do.

Ask for volunteers to dramatize "the rap" on page 165. Ask for a volunteer to read the part of Jesus and one or two others to read the part of the disciples. (An option is to have the everyone but the Jesus character take turns reading one line each. Encourage a rhythmic, rap-style reading.) Read through once, helping younger ones learn the lines or beat out a rhythm. Then read through a second time, adding dramatic emphasis, props, and costumes as suggested by the group to set the scene.

Wondering about "the rap" (page 165)

What might be the disciples' reaction to what Jesus wanted them to do? Were they surprised? scared? excited?

Who is someone who has helped you? How did they do this? How can you be of help to someone else?

What are some other ways we can help with healing? (e.g. giving hugs, listening, being a true friend, visiting people when they are sick, taking care of someone who is sick, giving money to the church) You might role-play some of these ideas.

Disciple detector activity
In advance: place a mirror in the bottom of a covered box (a shoe box would work well). Tell the children that today you have brought in a disciple detector, and ask if they have ever seen one. What do they think a disciple detector might look like? How might it work? *(build their excitement or suspense.)* Lift the lid of the box and have them come and peer into it. In a whisper ask how to describe what has been detected. When each child has had a chance to discover what the detector has revealed, invite volunteers to carry the box to some folk in the congregation and ask them to look in and see the results – what do they see?

In Jesus' time, some of the people were surprised about the people Jesus called to be his disciples, they thought that the people needed to look a certain way, and be a certain kind of person. They discovered that discipleship had nothing to do with how you looked, or whether you followed all the rules. What makes you a disciple is following Jesus and trying to live in God's way. Jesus sends all of us out to be his disciples.

Jesus Sends Out the Disciples

(based on Matthew 9:35 – 10:23)

Disciples

This is great. This is cool.
Jesus is the man. Jesus rules!
We hear him teach. We see him heal.
We know he's from God. We know he's real.
He's got the power. He's got the Spirit.
We're so happy to see and hear it.
The kingdom of heaven, he says, is near.
We can't wait for it to appear!

Jesus

Peace be with you, one and all.
I'm glad you've come and heard God's call.
Many steps we've taken. We've many more
    to take.
There's so much more work to do, for
    heaven's sake.

Disciples

We're right here with you, Jesus.
Whatever you need, just tell us.

Jesus

You've heard me teach. You've seen me heal.
You know the power of God is real.
The power I have, I give to you.
It's time for you to do the things I do.

Disciples

We can do the same things? We can teach
    and heal?
We can make others feel the way you make
    them feel?
We can help God's kingdom come? We can
    be like you?
Those are very awesome things you're
    asking us to do!

Jesus

Yes, it's true; believe it.
For you will have the Holy Spirit.
So have no fear;
you know that God is always near.
Go teach and heal from town to town.
Share the good news all around.
Give what you were given, freely and with
    love.
Take what kindness people give you, but
    take no notice of
the ones who may reject you or even slap
    you on the cheek.
Just know that you're loved by God, and let
    the Spirit speak.

Disciples

We promise to follow in your loving ways.
We promise to be faithful all our days.
We promise to be faithful all our days!

Other ideas for exploring the lectionary readings (Proper 6[11])

1. What do disciples do? Matthew 9:35–10:8, [9–23]

Disciples are followers of Jesus. One of today's Bible passages tells us what Jesus did. He travelled around teaching, proclaiming the good news of God's love, and healing the sick.

How do we teach others about God? *(church, Sunday School, living our lives in God's way, etc.)*

How do we proclaim the good news of God's love? *(showing others that God loves them no matter what by helping them feel loved and by being a forgiving person).*

How do we heal the sick? *(supporting hospitals in our offering, giving to food banks that provide good healthy food to the hungry).*

As disciples of Jesus, we try to do the things that Jesus did. We can do that as individuals and when we come together as a church for worship, education, and outreach.

2. "Ways of being God's people" collage

Materials: white paper, construction paper, decorative materials, hole punch, yarn, magazines
Either print or have children print the title on a sheet of paper and add pictures drawn and coloured or cut from magazines of people doing things that help and heal. Discuss how these are ways of being God's people. The picture collage could be mounted on construction paper, decorated, and hole-punched. Attach yarn so the picture can be mounted on a wall or window at home. Some children may be willing to have their pictures used as part of a bulletin board display.

3. Being a friend

Once a man had a pet bird. It had belonged to his wife, and she would let it fly around the house. It would sit on her shoulder when she went outside. When the woman died, the bird became the man's friend. He didn't want to lose it, so he tied a piece of string around its leg and held onto it all day long.

A boy called Mark lived next door. He watched the man with the bird on the string, and it bothered him. He got a pair of scissors and went over to the man's house. He knocked on the door. *(Make a knocking sound:)* The man opened the door with the bird sitting on his shoulder, the string tied to the bird's leg and then to the man's belt. Mark went into his neighbour's house and sat at the kitchen table like he'd done many times before. He looked at the man, and then at the bird.

"The bird wants to fly," Mark said.

"I know," said the man. "But if I let the bird fly, it will fly away and I won't have it any more."

"Birds need to fly," Mark said. "That's why God gave them wings."

"But I can't risk losing my only friend," said the man.

Mark took out his scissors and gave them to the man. "Let the bird fly free. I will be your friend."

The man took the scissors and cut the string from the bird's leg. The bird fluttered its wings and flew out the window. Mark put his hand on the man's shoulder. The bird flew in the window and landed on the man's shoulder.

The man smiled. "Now I have two friends."

You know, God calls us to look after each other, to meet the needs of those around us. That's part of being a friend. It's part of being a disciple.

Prayer

Dear God,
help us to be good friends and good disciples,
doing the things that Jesus did every day.
Amen.

God Loves Us So Much

(based on Matthew 10:24–39)

Season after Pentecost

Proper 7 [12]

Genesis 21:8–21

Psalm 86:1–10, 16–17

Romans 6:1b–11

Matthew 10:24–39

One day Jesus' friends were sharing some bread and fruit together. And while they were eating, they began thinking about all the stories that Jesus had told them. Stories about helping people. Stories about healing sick people. Stories about teaching people about God's love. John looked around at the friends.

"What are you thinking about?" asked John.

"Well," said Peter, "I'm thinking about all the people who need to hear about God's love."

"Me too!" said Andrew. "There are so many people!"

"We know how to do lots of things," said Peter. "We know how to sail our boats. We know how to catch fish. We even know how to fix our boats and nets when they are broken. But I'm just not sure about showing so many people about God's love. How can we ever let people know that God loves each of us so much?"

Jesus heard his friends' questions. He smiled at them.

"You're worried about this new job I have for you," said Jesus. "Well, there will be some good days when people will be so happy to hear your news. But there will also be days when people won't want to hear your news. They won't listen to you. When you are having a bad day and it seems hard to show God's love, you must remember that God is with you even on those days. God's love is with us everywhere."

As Jesus was talking, some sparrows flew down to share the crumbs from the bread that the friends were eating. (*Invite the children to find the sparrows in the room and "fly" them down into the storytelling circle.*)

Jesus pointed to the sparrows. "When you are having a day when showing God's love seems like a hard thing to do, just think about these sparrows."

"Sparrows!" said John. "What do sparrows have to do with showing God's love?"
"God loves even these little sparrows," said Jesus. "And if God loves little sparrows, imagine how much God loves you."

Everyone stopped to think about that. What wonderful news! Sharing God's love would not always be easy. But they knew that God loved them very much. God would be with them every day.

Storytelling props needed:

• copies of sparrow outline on page 170 to spread around the room for children to find

God loves us so much!

Instructions

- Cut out and decorate the set of figures.
- Cut out the title strip.
- Cut out a large construction paper heart.
- Glue the figures and the title on the heart.
- Beginning at each side of the heart, accordion fold each side to meet in the middle.
- Gently unfold the heart to reveal the message.

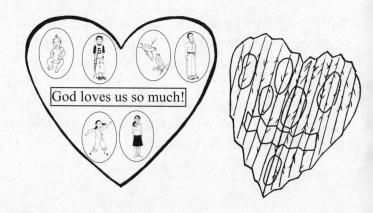

God is with us

(based on Matthew 10:24-39)

(Practice reading this story slowly with expression several times until you can make the actions and read it smoothly. Ask everyone to mimic your actions as you tell the story. Alternatively, give people different parts of the story to mimic and when they hear their part read, they do the actions. Have fun!)

This is the sparrow *(flap hands like wings)* that God made.

This is the nest *(cup hands)* that was made by the sparrow *(flap hands like wings)* that God made.

This is the egg *(make an oval with two hands)* that was laid in the nest *(cup hands)* that was made by the sparrow *(flap hands like wings)* that God made.

This is the baby *(open and close hands like a beak)* that came from the egg *(make an oval with two hands)* that was laid in the nest *(cup hands)* that was made by the sparrow *(flap hands like wings)* that God made.

This is young bird *(flap hands like wings uncertainly, then with confidence)* that grew from the baby *(open and close hands like a beak)* that came from the egg *(make an oval with two hands)* that was laid in the nest *(cup hands)* that was made by the sparrow *(flap hands like wings)* that God made.

This is the window *(make square shape with hands)* that fooled the young bird *(flap hands like wings uncertainly, then with confidence)* that grew from the baby *(open and close hands like a beak)* that came from the egg *(make an oval with two hands)* that was laid in the nest *(cup hands)* that was made by the sparrow *(flap hands like wings)* that God made.

This is the silence *(put both hands to side of head as if sleeping)* that followed the bump when the window *(make square shape with hands)* fooled the young bird *(flap hands like wings uncertainly, then with confidence)* that grew from the baby *(open and close hands like a beak)* that came from the egg *(make an oval with two hands)* that was laid in the nest *(cup hands)* that was made by the sparrow *(flap hands like wings)* that God made.

These are the people who felt sad *(point at one another sadly)* in the silence *(put both hands to side of head as if sleeping)* that followed the bump when the window *(make square shape with hands)* fooled the young bird *(flap hands like wings uncertainly, then with confidence)* that grew from the baby *(open and close hands like a beak)* that came from the egg *(make an oval with two hands)* that was laid in the nest *(cup hands)* that was made by the sparrow *(flap hands like wings)* that God made.

These are the people who felt joy *(make celebratory gestures)* when the sparrow flapped its wings and flew off again *(flap hands like wings)* so one day it could make a nest *(cup hands)* and lay an egg *(make an oval with two hands)* that would become a baby *(open and close hands like a beak)* that would become a young bird *(flap hands like wings uncertainly, then with confidence)* that would hopefully never bump into a window *(make square shape with hands)*.

This is the love *(hands across heart)* felt by God for the sparrow *(flap hands like wings)*, for all living creatures *(make all kinds of animal sounds)*, and for all the people of the earth! *(make a giant circle with your arms, then do a group hug)*.

Window Sparrow

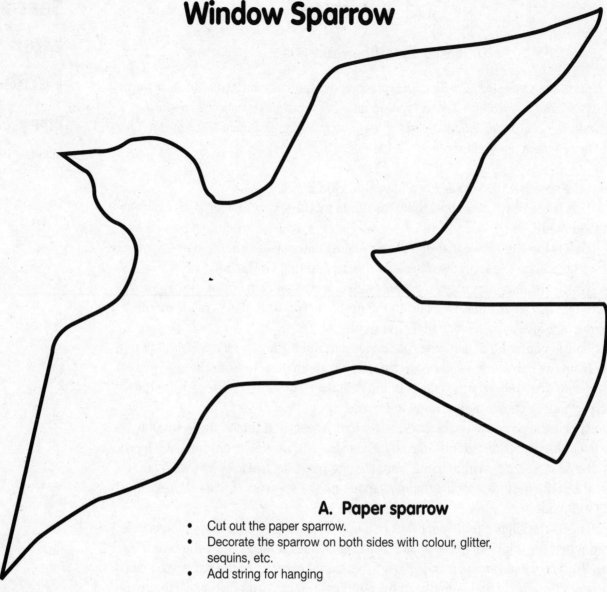

A. Paper sparrow
- Cut out the paper sparrow.
- Decorate the sparrow on both sides with colour, glitter, sequins, etc.
- Add string for hanging

B. Felt sparrow
- Cut out the paper sparrow and use as an outline for two felt sparrow pieces.
- Cut out the felt pieces and sew them together. Before the last stitches, stuff tissue paper inside.
- Decorate each sparrow on both sides with colour, glitter, sequins, etc.

C. Sparrow Mobile
- Cut out several paper sparrows and glue them to construction paper.
- Decorate the sparrows on both sides with colour, glitter, sequins, etc.
- Punch a hole in the upper part of each sparrow.
- Attach string to each sparrow and tie to a stick or piece of dowelling.

Material for A
- copies of sparrow
- colour glitter or sequins
- hole punch, glue and thread for hanging

Material for B
- felt pieces
- thread and needles
- tissue paper for stuffing
- colour glitter or sequins
- glue

Material for C
- construction paper
- colour glitter or sequins
- glue and hole punch
- string and dowelling or stick

Place your window sparrow on the inside of a window at home as a reminder of God's love and care. The window hanging will also discourage birds from flying into the glass.

Welcome!

(based on Matthew 10:40–42)

Hold the welcome sign in both hands with your arms extended. As each child walks under the sign say, "Welcome, [child's name]!" Invite the children to imagine that now they are joining many of Jesus' friends. Sit near "the gathering well." Say, "Let's listen to what Jesus is saying."

Jesus looked at his friends. They were such good friends! He knew they were working very hard to learn about living God's way. He knew they were learning about loving others. He also knew that being a disciple was not always easy. They all needed the friendship and care of others to help them do God's work.

"My dear friends," Jesus said, "remember, whoever welcomes you, welcomes me. And if you help someone else, you help me. We are in this together!"

"I can remember that," said Andrew. And then he sat up and gave John a hug. "Welcome," Andrew said to John. (*Pass a hug around the circle with the children turning to the person beside them, offering a hug, and saying, "Welcome!" Some children may prefer a pat on the arm instead of a hug.*)

"But," said Peter, "giving a hug and saying welcome is such a small thing!"

"It doesn't matter," said Jesus. "Small things can be big things, too. Giving a glass of water might seem like a small thing, but if a person is thirsty, very thirsty, then offering a glass of water is a big thing to do. You are showing God's love, and when you welcome another, God also feels welcomed."

The friends smiled at each other. One of Jesus' friends stood up, collected some water from the well, gave a cup to John and said, "Welcome." Then John turned to Andrew and gave him a cup of water and said, "Welcome." One by one the friends turned to each other, offered a cup of water and said, "Welcome." (*Use ladle to pour a cup of water from the well for each child and repeat the phrase "Welcome!"*)

Jesus held out his hands to his friends. "Thank you, dear friends."

Season after Pentecost

Proper 8 [13]

Genesis 22:1–14

Psalm 13

Romans 6:12–23

Matthew 10:40–42

Storytelling props needed:

• long cardboard sign saying "Welcome"

• The Gathering Well
Materials: bucket or other straight-sided container, brown construction paper, tape, marker, dowel or stick, string, small cup or container.

Cover the sides of the bucket with paper. Use markers to draw lines on the paper-covered bucket to resemble stone or brick work. Tie a cup or container to the stick or dowel and place across the top of the bucket so the cup hangs down inside the well.

• a small paper drinking cup for each child

• ladle or small spouted cut to dip water from the well

You Are Welcome!

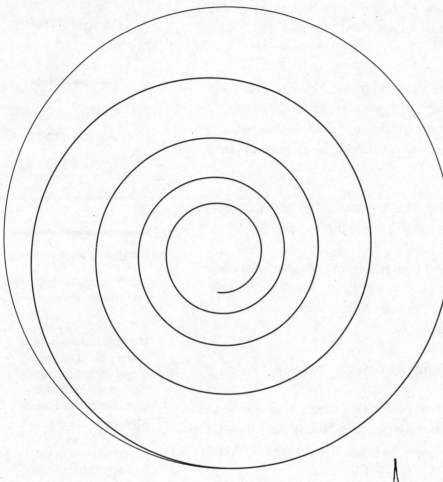

Materials
- cardstock or heavy construction paper
- tape and scissors
- yarn or string

Instructions
- From heavy construction paper, cut a circle about the size of a large plate. Then cut around and around the circle, spiralling into the middle, as shown.
- Or, enlarge and duplicate spiral pattern on this page onto bright paper.
- Decorate and cut out little pictures.
- Tie top end of the spiral with a piece of yarn or string.
- Tape the Jesus picture to the yarn at the top of the spiral.
- Lightly tape the figures, one at a time, to the bottom of the spiral.

When You Welcome Others, You Welcome God

(based on Matthew 10:40-42)

Season after Pentecost

Proper 8 [13]

Matthew 10:40–42

(Invite children to imagine that they are disciples travelling with Jesus. Encourage them to join in the actions during the telling of the story.)

Let's go, everyone! Jesus is on his way to a new town. *(Walk together around the room a couple of times.)*

We've been walking all morning, and we're tired *(sigh)* and hungry *(rub stomach)* and thirsty *(pant)*. Where will we find food and water out here in the hot countryside?

Look, just ahead. Jesus is talking to some shepherds. What are they saying to him? *(Hold up the sign and repeat together:* "Please come and stay. You're welcome here today.") How wonderful! The shepherds are leading us to a well where there is water. We all share a drink. *(ahhh!)* The shepherds share some bread with us. *(yum!)*

They lead us to a tree full of fruit and they offer us some. *(yum!)* It's cool and shady under the tree, so we lie down to rest. *(Lie down for a moment.)* While we rest, Jesus tells the shepherds how much God loves them. "By welcoming us," he says, "You welcome God. God will greatly bless you!"

Now it's time to go. *(get up)* We thank the shepherds *(say thank you)* and we're off again toward the next town. *(walk a while)* Here we are! I wonder what the people will be like here?

Crowds gather around Jesus as he heals many people and tells them about God's love. It's been a long day, and once again, we're tired *(sigh)* and hungry *(rub stomach)* and thirsty *(pant)*. Where will we find food and water and a place to stay here?

Look, there's a family talking with Jesus. What are they saying to him? *(Hold up the sign and repeat together:* "Please come and stay. You're welcome here today.")

How wonderful! So we follow them home where they give us fresh water *(ahhh!)* and food *(yum!)* and a place to sleep *(lie down for a moment)*.

The next morning, it's time to go again *(get up)*.

As we leave, Jesus tells the people, "By welcoming us, you welcome God. God will greatly bless you!"

We thank the family *(say "thank you")* and later, Jesus tells us this:
(read, or have an older child, read Matthew 10:40-42, possibly from The Message, *by Eugene H. Peterson).*

Storytelling props needed:

• make a sign with the words "Please come and stay. You're welcome here today."

• optional: copy of *The Message* by Eugene H. Peterson

My Giving Cup

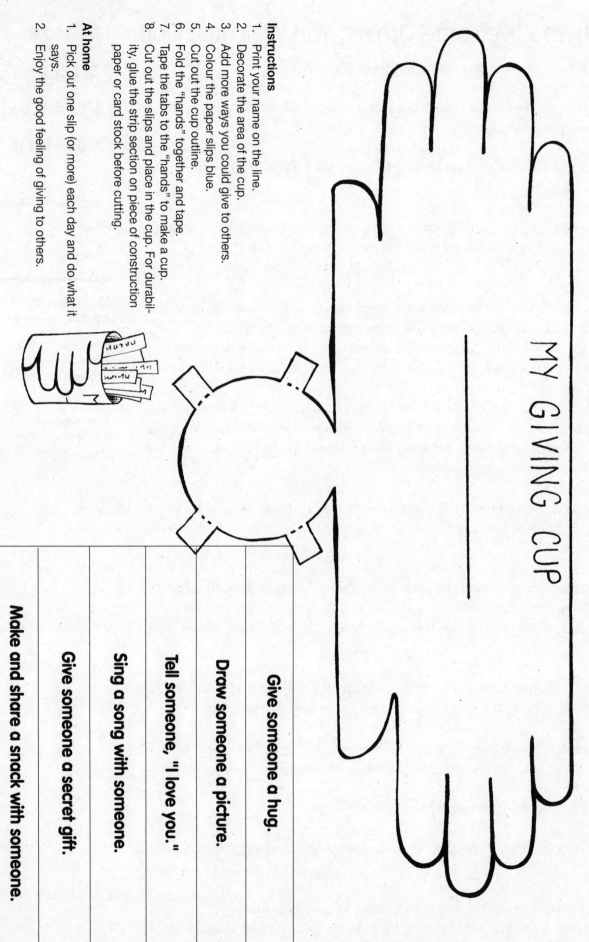

MY GIVING CUP

Give someone a hug.

Draw someone a picture.

Tell someone, "I love you."

Sing a song with someone.

Give someone a secret gift.

Make and share a snack with someone.

Instructions

1. Print your name on the line.
2. Decorate the area of the cup.
3. Add more ways you could give to others.
4. Colour the paper slips blue.
5. Cut out the cup outline.
6. Fold the "hands" together and tape.
7. Tape the tabs to the "hands" to make a cup.
8. Cut out the slips and place in the cup. For durability, glue the strip section on piece of construction paper or card stock before cutting.

At home

1. Pick out one slip (or more) each day and do what it says.
2. Enjoy the good feeling of giving to others.

Other ideas for exploring the lectionary readings (Proper 8[13])

1. What are some welcoming signs in our church? (Matthew 10:40–42)

Talk about (or walk around and look at) things that invite people into your church, and that make them feel welcome (doors, stairs, elevator, bulletins, greeters, smiling faces, passing the peace, signs to show where the restrooms are, a nursery, etc.). Are all of these welcoming things? How about an elevator or ramp, if there are stairs? Do people of all ages serve as greeters, so people know everyone is welcome?

Are there suggestions of how we do things (such as when to stand or kneel, having words to prayers printed in the bulletins)? Is there a sound system? Does someone provide signing? Are there lots of colours and dance and paintings, and gardens, for people who connect with those things?

Explore many things – even simple ones that may be taken for granted – that help people feel welcome in your church.

Jesus says that one of the most important things we can do is to welcome others. Let's keep thinking of ways we can do that.

2. Allowing people to share their feelings (Psalm 13)

We often share our happy feeling with God. How do we do that (sing songs, jump for joy, dance, celebrate)? What about our other feelings? One of our Bible readings today was written by people who were feeling very, very sad, and they told God about it. They were very upset – almost angry with God – because they felt the way they did.

Do you ever share other feelings with God? How? What does that feel like? The Bible reminds us that God accepts all of our feelings. Sometimes we're happy and want to sing for joy. Other times we're sad. Or we're hurt. Or we're angry about things going on around us.

We can share all of these feelings with God. And we can encourage others to share their feelings with God, too. Part of making people feel welcome in our church is letting them know that they can be themselves. We can be happy sometimes, and sad, and angry, and confused, and hopeful, and have all kinds of feelings. God accepts them all.

Prayer

Loving God,
we are glad that you accept us as we are
and welcome us always.
Help us to make our church a loving place
where everyone feels truly welcome.
Amen.

Season after Pentecost

Proper 9 [14]

Genesis 24:34–38, 42–49, 58–67

Psalm 45:10–17 or Song of Solomon 2:8–13

Romans 7:15–25a

Matthew 11:16–19, 25–30

Story props needed:

• people figures cut out from magazines (man, woman, children)

• fabric

Come, Be with Me

(based on Matthew 11:28–30)

(Use a piece of fabric to create a "stage." Have the people figures nearby (man, woman, children.)

One day a man came up to Jesus as he was walking. (*Invite a child to add the man figure.*) "Jesus," said the man, "sometimes I feel so sad. I wish I had a friend to help me when I am feeling sad."

Jesus touched the man on his shoulder. "Let me be your friend," said Jesus. And the man said, "Yes. Thank you, Jesus. Thank you for being my friend." (*Repeat the man's words together.*)

A woman who was feeling lonely came up to Jesus. (*Invite a child to add the woman figure.*) She said, "I am feeling so lonely. I wish I had a friend to sit and talk with me."

Jesus gently touched the woman's hand. "Let me be your friend," said Jesus. And the woman said, "Yes. Thank you, Jesus. Thank you for being my friend." (*Repeat the woman's words together.*)

Some children came to Jesus. (*Invite a child to add the children figures.*) "We would like to hear some stories," said the children. "We wish we had a friend who would tell us some stories."

Right away Jesus sat down with the children. "I have stories to tell you," said Jesus. "Let me be your friend." And all the children sat and listened to Jesus' stories.
"Thank you, Jesus! Thank you for being our friend!" said the children. (*Repeat the children's words together.*)

Now the man who was sad felt better. He knew that Jesus was his friend. He knew Jesus was always with him.

Now the woman who was lonely felt better. She knew that Jesus was her friend. She knew that she could think of Jesus and remember that he was always with her.
Now the children who wanted to hear stories felt better. They loved to learn about Jesus. They knew that Jesus was with them every day. They could tell stories together and remember Jesus.

Jesus was very happy that the people wanted to spend time with him. He hoped that lots more people would want to spend time with him too.

Come, let me be your friend

Materials

- crayons or markers
- scissors and glue
- construction paper
- craft sticks
- clear sticky tape

Instructions

- Cut out the set of pictures and decorate with crayons or markers.
- Tape a craft stick to the back of the group of children but not the Jesus figure.
- On a large sheet of construction paper, print "Come, let me be your friend" across the top.
- Glue the figure of Jesus near the bottom left edge of the paper.
- About a quarter of the way up from the bottom of that paper, place a strip of clear tape perpendicular to the bottom of the paper.
- Make a slit along that tape that runs across the paper but stops before it reaches the edges. (See illustration.)
- On the right side of the paper, insert the group of children into the slit and slowly move them towards Jesus. Have Jesus say, "Come, let me be your friend" as they move along.

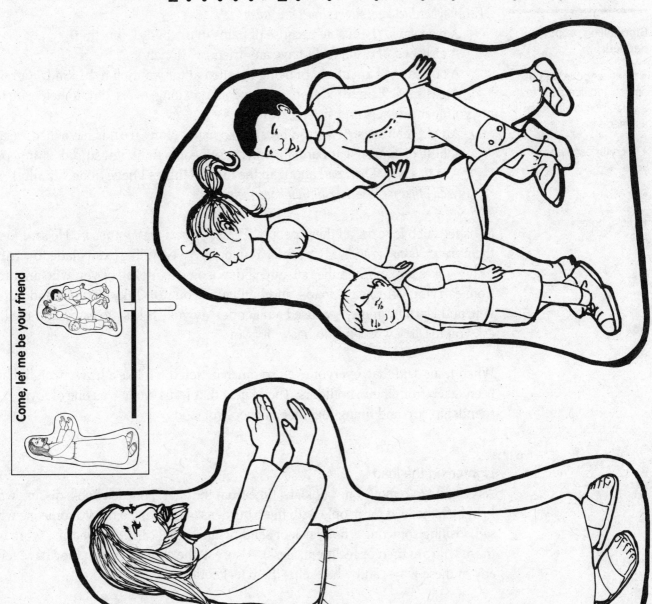

Season after Pentecost

Proper 9 [14]

Matthew 11:16–19, 25–30

Storytelling props needed:

• dowel or board to go across shoulders to create a yoke (pad it with foam as needed)

• bags for each end of yoke

• books

• sticky notes

Sharing the burdens
(based on Matthew 11:16-19, 25-30)

Invite the children to imagine being together on a hillside listening to Jesus. Read the story on the resource sheet. (Volunteers could read various parts.)

It's a beautiful morning, and we are sitting under a tree in the shade. A huge crowd is gathered around Jesus, and he is listening to the people tell him about the burdens they have in life.

One woman says, "My children and I don't have enough to eat." (*Print the word "hungry" on a sticky note, attach it to the back of a book, and have a child place it in one of the bags on the yoke. Do the same with the additional burdens, asking the children to identify what they are; suggestions are given:*)

A man says, "I am sore because of pains in my body." (hurting)
A girl says, "I don't feel I have any friends." (lonely)
A boy says, "I am afraid of being laughed at for wanting to be kind." (afraid)
A girl says, "I am tired from working all day long, every day, to help care for my younger brothers and sisters." (tired)
An old man says, "I am sad because so many of my friends have died." (sad)
A little girl says, "I am unhappy because people think I'm stupid." (unhappy)
A man says, "I feel bad about all the hurtful things I have done." (guilty)
(Add other ideas if the children have them.)

Jesus felt such love for all these people. (*"Jesus" places the yoke down.*) He said to them (*have "Jesus" read*): "My people! You look so weary, like oxen made to wear heavy yokes and work in the hot sun all day. Come to me, all of you who are tired from carrying your heavy loads, and I will give you rest. Take my yoke and put it on you, and learn from me, because I am gentle. My yoke is easy to carry, and the load I ask you to carry won't be too heavy for you."

When Jesus said that, everyone felt so much better. It felt like a heavy weight had been taken from their shoulders. They knew that Jesus' yoke was one of love, friendship, joy, and living together as people of God.

Lightening the load
Ask a child to remove one book at a time from the bags. For each book, discuss ways to lighten the load for people with these burdens (e.g. giving a hug to someone who is sad, visiting someone who is sick or sending a get well card, and sharing work with those who are tired or feeling useless). Also, ask the children when they have felt any of these ways, and what helps them feel better.

Other ideas for exploring the lectionary readings (Proper 9 [14])

1. Rebekah journeys with God (Genesis 24:34–38, 42–49, 58–67)

In advance: invite a teenage girl to present this short monologue in her own words. A biblical costume would be a nice touch, but it not essential.

Hi, my name's Rebekah, and I'd like to tell you my story. I used to live far away from here and one day I was getting water from the well. A man was there with a bunch of camels, and they all looked very tired and thirsty, so I helped him get water for himself and the camels. The man seemed quite impressed, and he came to our house for dinner.

It turned out that he was a long-lost relative, and he had wonderful stories to tell about Abraham and Sarah, and what had happened to them since they left our town years ago. He told us of the many ways God had been with them over the years. He told us that Abraham and Sarah had a son called Isaac, and that this man had come to find a wife for him. And he thought I would be just right!

Well, my parents and my brother and everybody else all started talking at once, trying to decide what would be best for me. I just sat in the corner, trying to take it all in. What was Isaac like? Was he nice? Was he good-looking? He lived so far away – would I ever see my family again?

That night I couldn't sleep a wink, wondering about all of these things. The next morning, everyone was still talking about what I should do. And then the strangest thing happened: they asked me what I thought! I wasn't used to that. In my time, people almost never asked girls for their opinion. But this time they did. And having had lots of time to think about it all, I said "yes!"

That's how I came to live here in Canaan and got married to Isaac. It's been quite an adventure, but I know that God is with me. When I get homesick, I can talk to God. When I worry about what lies ahead, God reminds me that I am not alone – that God goes with me every step of the way.

2. Working together (Matthew 11:28–30)

Materials: a sturdy chair and six to eight people
In advance: practice this experiment to make sure you are comfortable with it.
Place the chair in a clear spot and ask someone to sit on it; it would be better if the person is not too heavy.

Ask the children how much they think you could do with one finger. Do they think you could lift the chair with the person on it? Presumably they will say no. Ask the person on the chair: do you think I could lift you with one finger? Presumably they will say no, too. (*Try it and demonstrate how ridiculous this is.*)

What if I were to try it with eight fingers? Do you think that would work? (*Again, people will probably assume that you cannot.*) How about if eight of us tried with one finger each?

Invite your volunteers to gather around the chair. Have each person place one finger firmly under the chair – either the index or middle finger. Ensure that people are evenly spread around the chair so that the weight is supported equally. Ask the person on the chair if they think you can do it. Then, on the count of three, give the instruction to "lift." Because the load is spread, you should be able to lift the chair with the person on it.

Did the person on the chair trust that you could do it? Did the congregation believe it could be done? It is amazing, when we work together, how much we can do. Jesus helps us do that.

Prayer

Dear God,
Help us to trust you and to work together
to share your love with others. Amen.

Season after Pentecost

Proper 10 [15]

Genesis 25:19–34

Psalm 119:105–112

Romans 8:1–11

Matthew 13:1–9, 18–23

Storytelling props needed:

• one or two bird figures from page 170

• brown blanket

• several rocks

• strips of paper to represent weeds

• grass seed

Seeds That Grow

(based on Matthew 13:1–9, 18–23)

(Spread a large brown cloth on the floor. Place several rocks together in one area of the cloth and some paper "weeds" in another area. Have the children stand around the cloth.)

One day Jesus told this story to the many people who had come to see him… Once there was a farmer who had lots of seeds to plant. He walked out to his field with his large bag of seeds and got ready to scatter them on the soil. *(Give each child a handful of grass seed.)*

The farmer threw some seeds to the right. *(Children scatter some seeds on the cloth. Have some of the seeds land on the rocks.)*

The farmer threw some seeds to the left. *(Children scatter more seeds.)*
The farmer threw some seeds behind him. *(Children turn around and scatter some seeds behind them – but still on the cloth.)*

The farmer scattered the seeds in front of him. *(Scatter the rest of seeds.)*

Finally, there were no more seeds in the bag and the farmer returned home. *(Invite the children to sit down and look at all the seeds that were scattered. Notice how many there are.)*

Some seeds stayed on top of the ground. The birds flew by, saw the seeds and ate them. *(Have a child "fly" the paper bird onto the cloth beside some seeds.)*
Some seeds fell beside the rocks. *(Point to those seeds.)* They started to grow a little bit. Their roots went down and the leaves came up. But then the rocks were in the way and the plants couldn't grow any more.

Some seeds fell beside some weeds that were growing. *(Point to those seeds.)* The seeds were very crowded beside the weeds. They couldn't feel the sun or the rain. The seeds could not grow.

But some seeds fell down into the good soil. *(Place second cloth over some of the seeds.)* The birds didn't eat them. The rocks didn't get in the way. The sun shone on them. The rain rained on them. They grew and grew into more and more plants. These seeds had what they needed to grow good roots. This was going to be a HUGE harvest!

As Jesus finished this story, he looked around at all the people and said, "God cares about our growing and learning, just as God cares about the seeds that are planted in the earth."

Growing and Learning in God's Way

Instructions

- Look at each of the pictures and discuss how the people are growing in and learning about God's way.
- Colour the pictures.
- Use a pencil to draw along the path to the happy hearts.

start

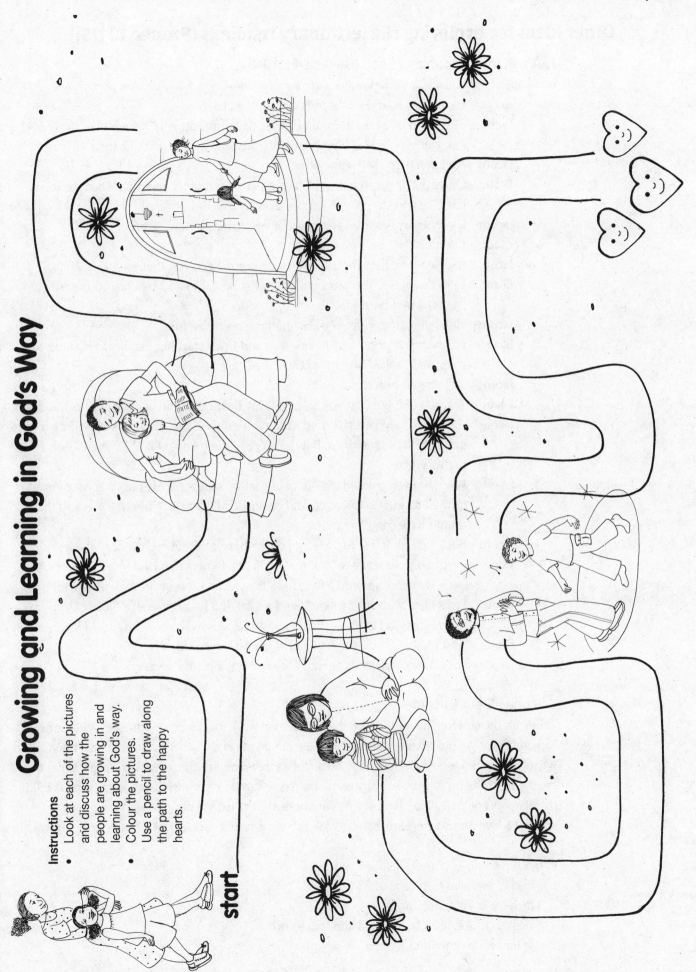

Other ideas for exploring the lectionary readings (Proper 10 [15])

1. A visit from Jacob and Esau (Genesis 25:19–34)

In advance: invite two men to prepare and share the following dialogue, in their own words.

Jacob: Hi, I'm Jacob, and this is my twin brother, Esau.

Esau: There you go again. I should be the one to introduce us, because I'm the oldest. *(to congregation)* He's always pushing his way to the front like that.

Jacob: No I don't! You're exaggerating!

Esau: Oh yeah? *(to congregation)* He's so pushy, our mother says that when we were born, he tried to push me out of the way and be born first.

Jacob: Okay, so I was a little anxious. But we're friends now, right?

Esau: Right.

Jacob: It took a long time for us to patch up our differences, though.

Esau: I should say so! You want to know what he did to me? He cheated me out of my rights as first-born son.

Jacob: He's telling the truth – I did something pretty awful.

Esau: I came home from hunting one day, and I was starving. Jacob was making some soup, and I asked him for a bowl.

Jacob: So I offered him some.

Esau: Yes, you did. But first you asked for my birthright – all of my rights as the eldest.

Jacob: For a while afterward, I tried to convince myself that, if he was so willing to give it up, he didn't deserve it. But the more I thought about it, the more I knew I was in the wrong.

Esau: Later, he even cheated me out of our father's blessing. He put on some of my clothes, disguised his voice, and convinced Dad to give him the blessing that should have come to me.

Jacob: But I paid for it. I felt so guilty, I didn't have a decent night's sleep for years.

Esau: Eventually we made up, but it wasn't easy. I knew that God loved both of us, but it was hard for me to feel God's love when I was so angry with my brother.

Jacob: I was filled with envy, jealousy, and anger. And I was miserable. Slowly I came to realize that God loved my brother and, if God loved him, then I should love him too.

Esau: And I knew I couldn't stay mad at Jacob forever, either.

Jacob: I'm glad we're friends again. *(They embrace, and leave together.)*

2. Using all our senses

Talk with the children about the idea that our senses work together: we can "see" with our ears sometimes, or go into a bakery and smell the fresh goods and almost taste them. In a noisy place we might not hear someone speaking to us, but as they point to things we can "hear" what they are saying. Sometimes people who are unable to see can hear very well, and know who is talking by the sound of their voice. People who cannot hear can "listen" through sign language.

God's love comes to us in many ways. We can see it, hear it, taste it, feel it, touch it, and grow in it.

Prayer

God of love and forgiveness,
thank you for caring for us.
Help us to see, hear, taste, smell and touch you
in the world around us. Amen.

Waiting and Waiting

(based on Romans 8:12–25)

(Ask for someone to be Priscilla and pantomime the actions while the storyteller narrates.)

Long ago there was a place where Paul's friends gathered as part of God's church. This was in the city of Thessalonica. Paul, who lived far away, would send them letters to encourage them and cheer them on. Sometimes they felt as if they had been waiting for a long time. They were waiting for the world filled with love and kindness just as Jesus said.

"When will the world be like Jesus said?" a boy asked. "Waiting is too hard!" *(Pause.)* One day a visitor arrived. Maybe she had some news about how long they would have to wait!

(Introduce Priscilla) "Hello, dear friends. My name is Priscilla. I bring you a letter from our good friend, Paul. Please come and sit with me." All the people gathered around. Priscilla saw a young woman who was going to have a baby and quickly made a place for her to sit. Then Priscilla began to read the letter from Paul. *(Unroll the scroll and begin to read.)*

Dear brothers and sisters,
I have good news for you! God hears your voices. God knows how hard it is to wait. God wants you to trust. The world that God wants for you is coming. We are all God's children. When the world is filled with God's love, it will be so wonderful! While you are waiting, be sure to love and help each other. Feel God's love in your hearts. Soon, soon it will be here.
Love from your friend,
Paul.

Priscilla leaned down to the woman who was going to have a baby. She held out her hand and gently helped the woman to stand. "It is like waiting for a baby to be born," said Priscilla. "We want so much for the baby to be here. We want to meet this new little boy or girl. Waiting feels so hard. But then the baby is born and we are so happy! We are so happy to see the new baby that we forget how hard it was to wait."

The people thought about what Priscilla said. They knew how happy they were when a new baby was born. There was always a big party to celebrate.

"Be patient," said Priscilla. "It will be wonderful just as Jesus promised. For now we can feel in our hearts the love that Jesus promised."

The people felt better. They knew they might have to wait a little longer. But they would help each other to wait. They would gather together to remember Jesus' words. They would plan a big party to celebrate the new baby that was coming.

Season after Pentecost
Proper 11 [16]

Genesis 28:10–19a

Psalm 139:1–12, 23–24

Romans 8:12–25

Matthew 13:24–30, 36–43

Storytelling props needed:

• colour and prepare a scroll as on page 184. Copy and glue or write the words to Paul's letter on the scroll.

Story Scroll

Instructions

- Cut out the printed strip and the set of pictures.
- Decorate with markers. (Option: decorate the pictures and then cut them out.)
- Open the scroll and glue the long strip along the top edge.
- Glue the small pictures underneath the strip.

To make a scroll

- Cut paper into approximately 50 cm/20 in x 28 cm/11 in strips.
- Glue one end of the strip to each long card-board tube.
- Roll the tubes toward each other and tie with a ribbon.

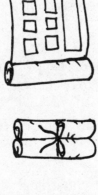

Let's fill the world with God's love

Together in God's Love

(based on Romans 8:26-39)

Season after Pentecost
Proper 12 [17]

Genesis 29:15-28

Psalm 105:1-11, 45b or Psalm 128

Romans 8:26-39

Matthew 13:31-33, 44-52

Teach the cue words, "Just remember…" and the response "God is with us." Practice several times before telling the story. Ask someone to be Priscilla and pantomime the actions.

One day, some people were gathered together. They were feeling worried and wanted to be with their friends. They needed to talk together.

"I want to feel close to Jesus," said a woman.

"I want to remember Jesus' stories," said a man.

Many other people said, "What are we going to do?"

Then a boy said, "Maybe our friend, Priscilla, can help us."

"He's right!" said the people. "Our friend, Priscilla, is still here in our town. Let's tell Priscilla how we are feeling."

And so the people went to find Priscilla. They told her how worried they were. They wondered if they had been living the way that Jesus had taught them.

"Dear friends," said Priscilla, "please sit here with me."

And then Priscilla helped the people feel better. She invited the people to join her in saying some comforting words.

"Just remember…" said Priscilla. **God is with us.**

"Jesus showed us how to live God's way. Jesus taught us about loving and helping each other. Just remember…" **God is with us**.

"Even when we are sad or worried we can remember Jesus' words of love. Just remember…" **God is with us.**

"Love one another. Help one another. Share together. That is living God's way. Just remember…" **God is with us.**

Priscilla smiled at her friends. "How are you feeling now?" she asked.

"Much better!" said everyone. "We remember Jesus' words. We remember how to live God's way. Thank you, Priscilla."

And the people said together, "Just remember… **God is with us!"**

Connected to God

Draw lines to connect the pictures. Why do they go together?

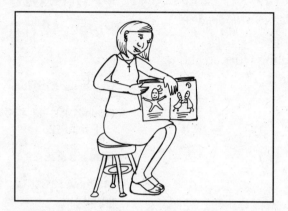

Other ideas for exploring the lectionary readings (Proper 12 [17])

1. Sourdough Bread (Matthew 13:31-33, 44-52)
Materials: a loaf of sourdough or French bread (optional)
In one of our Bible stories this morning, Jesus talks about how the Reign of God is like yeast. Just a little bit can go a long, long way.

Over 150 years ago a man in San Francisco, California, started making a special kind of French bread called sourdough. He used a little bit of yeast, some water, flour, and salt. He kept a bit of that dough, and used it to start another loaf, and another, and so on and so on, always keeping some of the mixture as a starter for the next loaf. Now that same company makes bread in several places, and every loaf of bread has flour, water, salt, and a little bit of sourdough "starter" that has continued on from the very first loaf of bread that they made over 150 years ago.

Each of us has a little bit of God's love inside of us – kind of like yeast. We share love with others, we pass it on, much like the sourdough bread. That love goes on and on, and affects lots and lots of people. *(If you brought some sourdough bread, offer a piece to the children, or make arrangements to share it during coffee hour after worship.)*

2. Water jug symbols (Romans 8:39)
Preparation and materials: a glass jug filled with water, food colouring, a basket, a few small colourful, waterproof objects that symbolize various aspects of our lives (Monopoly™ house; a "best friend" pendant; a marble to symbolize ball sports; balloon for fun times; coin to symbolize wealth.) Place items on a table or stand so everyone can see.

Invite children to use their imaginations and imagine that the jug of water is them and you. In our lives there are many different things that shape us and make us who we are. These things become part of us. Show the basket of symbols. Invite a volunteer to select one of them and place it in the jug of water. Explain that this object symbolizes something of part of who we are. What do they think it might symbolize? (Accept all responses.) Continue until all the symbols you have brought are in the jug.

Show the bottle of food colouring. Explain that this represents God's love. Drop a little colouring into the water. Now you can see that God's love is part of us.

Sometimes things happen which cause us to be separated from things in our lives. Invite a child to take out one of the symbols, and put it back into the basket. Encourage the others to think about what might happen to cause us to be separated from that particular thing: our friend may have a fight with us, our home may get burnt, our money may get spent… Continue until all the objects are back in the basket. But what do they notice? God's love is still there, still part of who we are. There is nothing that could ever separate God's love from us. No matter what might happen, God's love will always be with us. Open up the Bible to Romans 8: 39 and read it aloud.

Prayer
Help us to remember, God,
that nothing can keep us from your love,
and that we can help your love go on and on and on. Amen.

Season after Pentecost

Proper 13 [18]

Genesis 32:22–31

Psalm 17:1–7, 15

Romans 9:1–5

Matthew 14:13–21

Storytelling props needed:

• basket

• basket and fish from activity sheet on page 189 or 2 real buns and 5 pieces of real fish.

Enough to Share

(based on Matthew 14:13–21)

(Encourage the children to copy your actions as you tell the story.)

One day the people heard that Jesus was coming to their town for a visit. They began to gather together in a big wide open space outside. First there were just a few people. Then there were lots of people. Then there was a huge crowd of people waiting for Jesus.

Suddenly a woman in the crowd said, "Look, everyone! Here comes Jesus. Wave, everyone. Wave to Jesus! Hi, Jesus!" *(Children wave and call out to Jesus.)* "Let's go and sit beside Jesus." *(Children "walk" their fingers on the floor.)*

A boy called out, "Look at all the people!" *(Shield eyes with hands as if looking over a large crowd.)* "Jesus is talking," he said. "Let's listen to what he has to say." *(Cup hands behind ears.)* The people listened very carefully. They loved to hear Jesus' stories.

When the story was finished someone said, "I liked that story! Now I'm feeling hungry." *(Rub tummies.)* "I wonder what's for lunch? Do you have any food?" The people turned to one another to see if anyone had any food. *(Turn to one another and say, "Do you have any food?")*

Suddenly a girl called out, "Look! Jesus has a basket." *(Place basket in circle.)* "But it's a very small basket. I wonder if there is enough food for all of us?"

The people saw Jesus take some bread and some fish out of the basket. "Can anyone see how much there is? Let's count," said a man. *(Remove the loaves one at a time and count aloud with the children.)* "Now let's count how many fish were in the basket." *(Remove the fish one at a time and count aloud with the children.)*

Jesus took the basket with the five loaves and two fish and did something wonderful. *(Put loaves and fish back into the basket.)* Jesus thanked God for the food. Then he broke the loaves and fish over and over again. Soon there was enough for everyone.

Jesus handed the food to his friends. They began to walk around and invite people to take some food from a basket. "Hold out your hands, everyone," they said. "Here comes some food for us. Let's eat." *(Pretend to eat some fish and bread.)*

The people were amazed. "Wow!" they said. "Everyone had some bread and some fish to eat. Jesus took the fish and bread and made it enough for us all to share. There was even some food left over that could be shared on the way home. Thank you, Jesus!"

Food to Share

Materials
- a brown paper lunch bag for each child
- scissors and stapler
- felt markers

Instructions
- Use pattern below to create a basket
- print "Enough for everyone" onto the bottom of the basket as shown
- colour and cut out the fish and bread and place in the basket

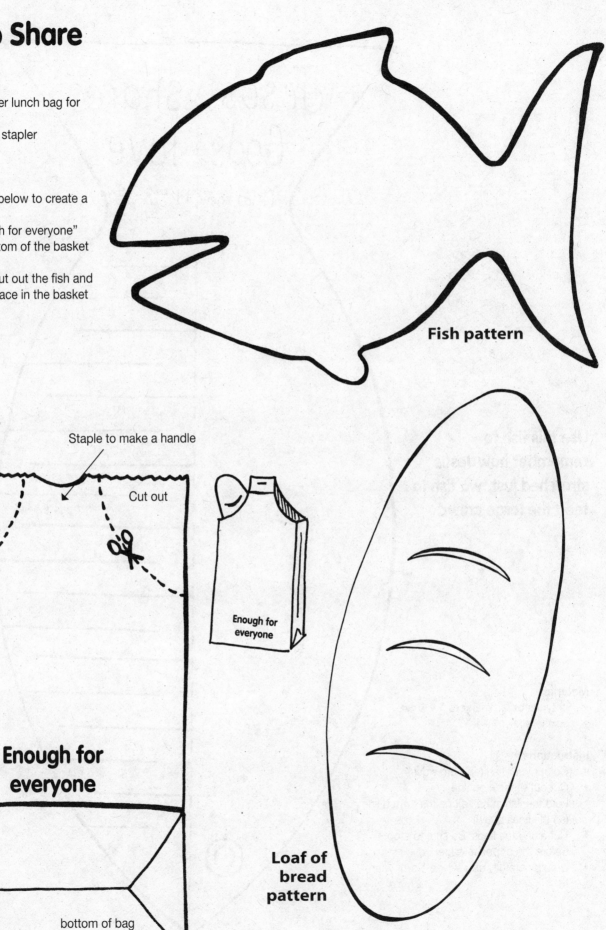

Fish pattern

Pattern for basket

Staple to make a handle

Cut out   Cut out

Enough for everyone

Enough for everyone

bottom of bag

Loaf of bread pattern

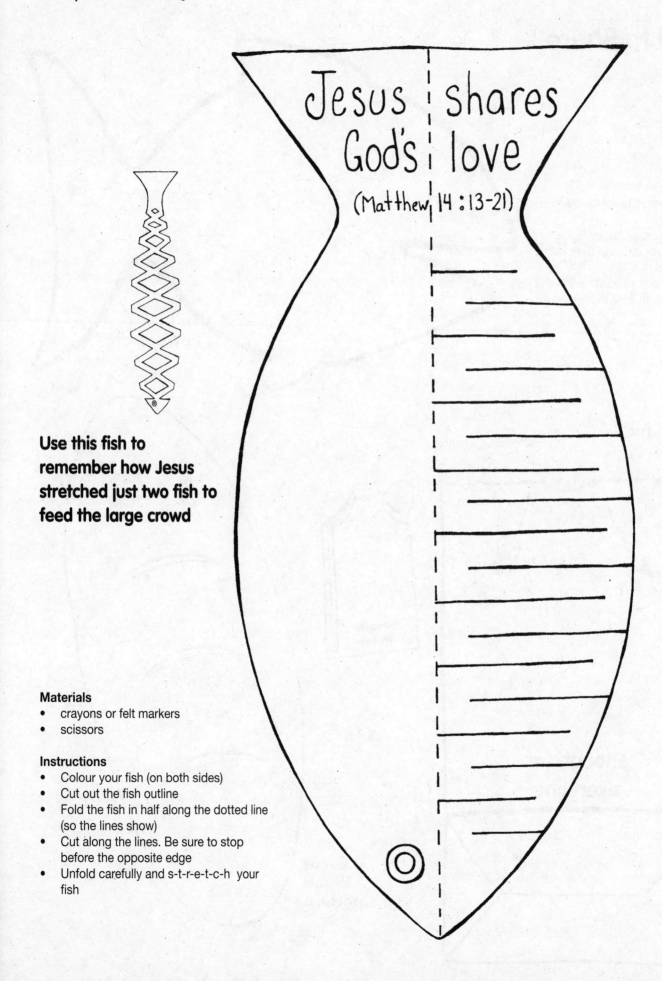

Jesus shares
God's love

(Matthew 14 : 13-21)

Use this fish to remember how Jesus stretched just two fish to feed the large crowd

Materials
- crayons or felt markers
- scissors

Instructions
- Colour your fish (on both sides)
- Cut out the fish outline
- Fold the fish in half along the dotted line (so the lines show)
- Cut along the lines. Be sure to stop before the opposite edge
- Unfold carefully and s-t-r-e-t-c-h your fish

Jesus Calms the Lake

(based on Matthew 14:22–33)

One day Jesus asked the disciples to get into a boat and go to the other side of the lake.

"I will join you soon," said Jesus to his friends.

And so the disciples got into the boat and set out on the lake. (*Spread the blue cloth. Place the boat with the disciples, including Peter, in the middle of the cloth. Invite the children to each hold onto an edge of the blanket.*)

The wind started blowing gently on the lake. The disciples saw small ripples in the water. (*Gently begin to move the cloth to create ripples.*)

The wind blew harder. The disciples saw small waves in the water. (*Continue to wave the blanket.*)

The wind blew harder! The disciples could see BIG waves in the water. (*Move the blanket to create waves big enough for the boat to bounce around.*)

Now the disciples were very scared. "This is a big storm!" they said.

Suddenly, they saw something amazing! They saw someone, on the water, coming toward them. "Who can this be?" they said. Then they heard Jesus call out to them. "Don't be afraid!" called Jesus. "It's me, Jesus." (*Lay down edges of blanket. Place Jesus figure on the blanket.*)

Peter called out, "Jesus! I want to come and join you!"

"Then, come," said Jesus and he held out his hand. So Peter did as Jesus asked him. (*Take Peter out of the boat and have him move toward Jesus.*) Peter went toward Jesus. Now, Peter hadn't really thought about what he was doing. He just walked toward his special friend, Jesus. But as he walked he looked away from Jesus. When he looked at the waves he became frightened and began to sink in the water. Peter called out, "Jesus, save me!"

Jesus reached out his hand and caught Peter. (*Put them side by side.*) "Don't you know that you can always trust me? Anything I ask you to do, God will help you to do it."

Then Jesus and Peter got into the boat with the disciples. (*Move figures together.*) And suddenly the wind slowed down to a whisper. (*Gently move the cloth.*) The waves settled down and went back to being a peaceful ripple. Everything was calm again.

Season after Pentecost

Proper 14 [19]

Genesis 37:1–4, 12–28

Psalm 105:1–6, 16–22, 45b

Romans 10:5–15

Matthew 14:22–33

Storytelling props needed:

• blue cloth

• boat and disciples from activity sheet on page 192

Disciples in the Boat

Paper boat

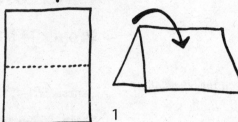 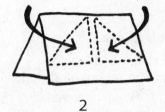 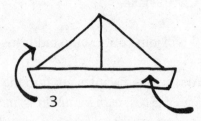

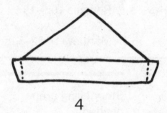 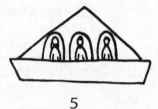

Materials

- construction paper
- tape, glue, and scissors
- crayons or felt markers

Paper boat instructions

1. Fold a rectangle of construction paper in half widthwise.
2. From the folded edge, fold in both corners, leaving a wide margin at the bottom.
3. Fold up the open, bottom edges on each side of the boat.
4. Tape the side edges closed.
5. Cut out and decorate the disciples and Jesus and place them in the boat. (These figures might be glued in place.)

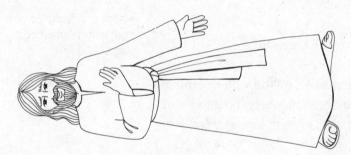

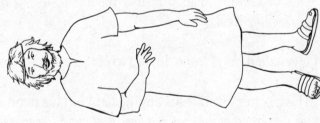

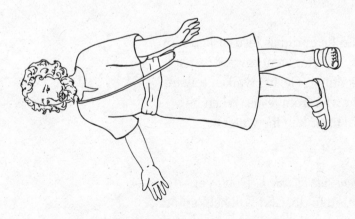

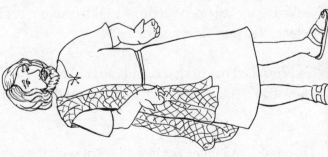

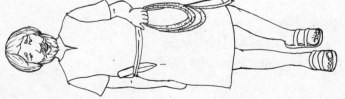

Praise God

(based on Psalm 133)

Season after Pentecost

Proper 15 [20]

Genesis 45:1–15

Psalm 133

Romans 11:1–2a, 29–32

Matthew 15:(10–20), 21–28

Storytelling props needed:

• rhythm instruments

(Sit in a circle. Have the rhythm instruments ready.)

All the people were so happy! This was the day to come together and worship God. This was the day to sing and dance. This was the day to praise God! They gathered their drums. They gathered their tambourines. They gathered the flutes and the horns. The people got ready to make music together. As they walked to the gathering place, the children danced in the road. Everyone was so excited!

Finally they were all together. The children sat together. They were waiting for their instruments. And here they were! A man and a woman walked among the children and handed them each a music-making instrument. Now they were ready to praise God. *(Give each child an instrument. Invite them to make practice sounds with their instruments. Then, give them a cue and practice placing the instruments on the floor in front of them.)*

The storyteller was ready to start. "Ready, children?" she asked.

"Ready!" said all the children together. They knew that whenever the storyteller said the words, "Praise God!" they should make music with their instruments.

"Welcome, dear friends," said the storyteller. "Let's praise God!" *(Children respond. Then, give them a cue when it is time to place the instruments on the floor.)*

"How wonderful it is to be with friends. Praise God!" *(Children respond.)*

"God blesses us. God's love shines on us. Praise God!" *(Children respond.)*

"Let us be glad and sing! Praise God!" *(Children respond.)*

"We are so happy! We love you, God! Praise God!" *(Children respond.)*

The people felt so happy. Together they had worshipped God. They praised God with their voices and their instruments.

What a wonderful day! Praise God! *(Children respond.)*

Dancing puppet

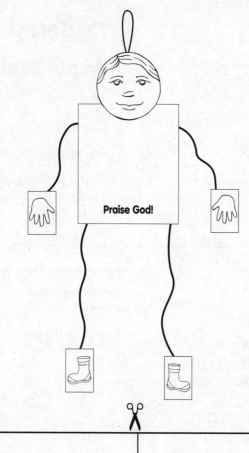

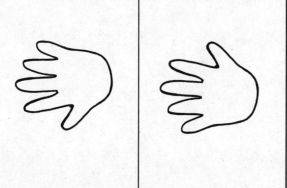

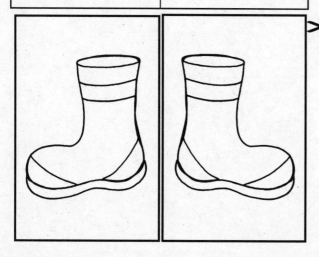

Praise God!

Materials
- crayons or felt markers
- fabric strips
- rubber bands
- tape

Instructions
- Cut out the body, hands, and feet.
- Decorate with crayons or markers. (Option: glue fabric scraps onto the body.)
- Cut four rubber bands and tape one end of each rubber band to a hand or foot.
- Tape the other end of the rubber bands to the body.
- For a handle, tape a complete rubber band to the back of the head.

All Together Now

(based on Romans 12:1–8)

Season after Pentecost

Proper 16 [21]

Exodus 1:8—2:10

Psalm 124

Romans 12:1–18

Matthew 16:13-20

Long ago there was a place where Paul's friends gathered as part of God's church. This was in the city of Thessalonica. Paul, who lived far away, would send them letters to encourage them and cheer them on.

One day the people were gathered together. They wanted to spend time with each other. They wanted to talk and share stories. Suddenly they heard singing.

"Who is singing?" the people asked.

Then they saw their friend, Priscilla, walking towards them. "Let's listen to Priscilla's song," they said.

Sing (tune: "Following the Leader" or use your own tune)
Paul sent us a letter, a letter, a letter,
Paul sent us a letter,
to help us live God's way.

When Priscilla had finished her song, she turned to everyone and said, "Dear friends. I have a letter from Paul. Come sit with me. I will read it to you."

The people quickly gathered around Priscilla and sat down. Priscilla began to read the letter.

My dear friends,
It is important for us to live God's way. God wants us to love each other. Share with each other. Help one another. And always care for each other. This is living God's way. We all have important work to do for God.
Love from,
Paul.

All the people looked at each other. They felt important. They would help each other to love God. That is God's way. The people were happy.

Storytelling props needed:

- make a copy of Paul's letter in the story

- glue this on the middle of a piece of paper

- roll paper up from both ends to form a scroll and tie with yarn

Use this as an activity after you tell the story to reinforce what you have talked about.

Our Gifts Help the Church to Grow

Materials: large paper figure created by tracing around a person lying on newsprint. Make one or two more figures and cut apart the body parts – feet, hands, head, arms, smiling lips, eyes, ears, etc.)

Unroll a large paper figure. Mention to the children that there are many parts to a person. A body can't be only arms, or only legs, or only eyes. Each part has special work to do. Invite the children to put together some of the parts. *(As you call out the children's names, invite them to attach the cut-out parts.)*

"(Child's name), you use your hands to help others. Please come and put some hands on our person."

"(Child's name), you are always willing to go and carry things for older people. Please come and put the feet on our person."

Continue to call out names and attach parts *(ears for good listening, smiles for being cheerful, eyes for looking for lost things)*. If necessary, add more than one of each part in order to give every child a turn. Then look at the completed figure. Mention that, just as parts of our bodies work together, all the parts of the church work together, too. We are all important parts of the church. We all help the church to grow.

God made ...
I'm the only one like me.

Materials
- felt markers, crayons, and pencils

Instructions
- connect all the dots to complete this drawing. Add some clothes and colour the figure.

Remember that God made you and loves you.

Start → 1 • ... • 13

• 4 ... 10 •

2 •
• 3

• 12
11 •

• 7

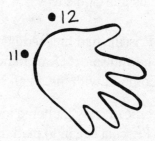

5 •
• 6

8 • • 9

Learning to be a Disciple

(based on Romans 12:9–21)

Season after Pentecost
Proper 17 [22]

Exodus 3:1–15

Psalm 105:1–6, 23–26, 45c

Romans 12:9–21

Matthew 16:21–28

Long ago there was a place where Paul's friends gathered as part of God's church. This was in the city of Thessalonica. Paul, who lived far away, would send them letters to encourage them and cheer them on.

Priscilla was very excited. Last week she had read a letter from Paul to all her friends. Now she had another part of the letter to show them. As she walked to the gathering place, she began to sing her song…

Sing *(tune: "Follow the Leader" or use your own tune)*

"Paul sent us a letter, a letter, a letter,

Paul sent us a letter,

to help us live God's way."

"Hurray!" the people said. "Priscilla has come again!" The people sat around Priscilla. They were ready to hear what else Paul had to say. *(Open the scroll and read the letter.)*

My dear friends,

Here is what is important if we are to be followers of Jesus…

Share. Jesus shows us how to share with each other.

Help. Jesus wants us to be kind and help each other.

Pray. Say thank you to God each day. Pray that God will help us live in loving ways.

Love. Always love God. Always love each other. And remember, God loves us very, very much! And God wants us to do our best.

Love from,

Paul.

Priscilla wanted to make sure her friends remembered Paul's letter. She decided to play a game with them. *(Invite the children to imagine they are with the people and Priscilla, and play the game.)*

Game Sit in a circle. Bring out the prepared box covered in crepe paper. Start the music and pass the box around the circle. When the music stops, the child holding the box begins to unravel the paper. Then, cut the paper, start the music and continue sending the box around the circle. Each time the music stops, the child holding the box continues to unravel the paper. When a word is uncovered, read it to the children and review what Paul had said in the letter. Continue until all four words have been uncovered. Share the treat.

After the game, Priscilla smiled at the people. The people smiled back. What a wonderful letter. They felt so happy to hear Paul's words. And the people began to talk about all the ways they could share, help, pray, and love.

Storytelling props needed:

• make a copy of Paul's letter in the story

• glue this on the middle of a piece of paper

• roll paper up from both ends to form a scroll and tie with yarn

Materials for game:

• a crepe-paper wrapped box with the words share, help, pray, and love printed on paper strips hidden at intervals in the wrapping

• music

Living Together in Love

Colour each picture and talk to your family about how the people in the pictures are "living together in love."

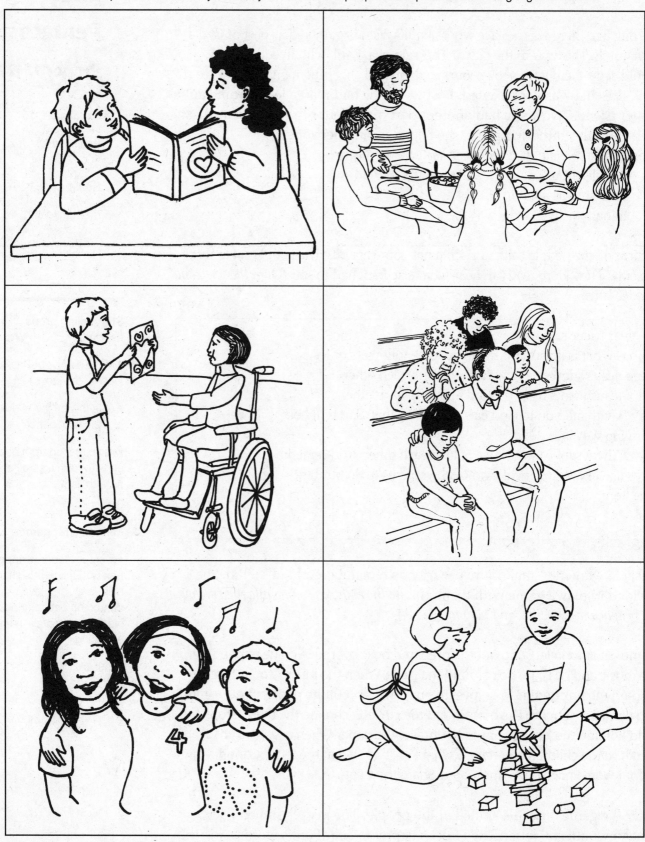

Following Jesus

(based on Matthew 16:21–28)

Season after Pentecost
Proper 17 [22]

Matthew 16:21–28

(Before telling the story, ask the children, "What does your face look like when you are happy? surprised? frightened?" Then, during the story, hold up the appropriate paper face and invite the children to respond with the appropriate facial expression.)

Jesus was a teacher, but he didn't teach about letters or numbers. He taught about God's love. Jesus was *happy* he could teach people about God. He taught people to help each other, to share, and to work together. Jesus had a group of friends who helped him. They were *happy*, too, because they could help Jesus.

One day, Jesus talked to his friends. "I must go to another city, a city called Jerusalem," he said.

All of his friends were *surprised*. "Why are you going there?" they asked. "It could be dangerous."

"Why are you so *surprised*?" Jesus asked them. "God wants me to go to Jerusalem, so I must go."

His friend Peter was *afraid*. Jerusalem was a big city. There were a lot of people there. Peter didn't know what would happen in Jerusalem. He did not want Jesus to go. "Don't go to Jerusalem, Jesus!" Peter cried. "I am *afraid*. I don't want you to go. Please stay here with your friends."

Jesus looked at his friends. He was *happy* to be with them. He thought about everything he had taught them. He thought about God and how much God loved him. That made him very *happy*. Jesus was not *afraid*. He knew God would help him. Jesus said, "Don't be *afraid*, Peter. I must go. God wants me to go." Then, Jesus gently put his hand on Peter's shoulder and said, "You are my friend, Peter, my disciple. Follow me."

Peter looked at Jesus. He knew Jesus cared for him. He would always follow him. Oh, how *happy* he was to share in God's love!

Storytelling props needed:

• craft sticks

• make a copy of the feeling faces on this page

• cut out and tape each to a craft stick

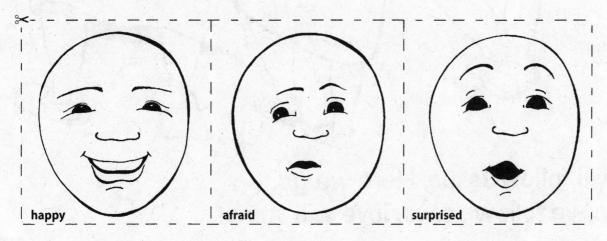

happy   afraid   surprised

Jesus, my friend

We will follow Jesus. Here we go.
When we follow Jesus, love will show!

A Heart Full of Love (game)

Preparation
- Cut out a large red construction paper heart.
- Cut it into 5 puzzle pieces.
- Glue a "Loving action" strip onto each piece.
- Cut out 3 other shapes from the same red construction paper.
- Glue an "Unloving action" strip onto each piece.
- Place all 8 puzzle pieces in a basket.

How to play the game
- Sit in a circle with the basket and puzzle pieces. Have a child remove one puzzle piece. Read it to the children and encourage them to decide if it is a loving rule or not.
- For a loving rule: everyone jumps out and shouts, "Yes, for love!"
- Place puzzle piece on the floor.
- For an unloving rule: everyone jumps up and stamps their feet and shouts, "No way!" Set the piece aside
- Continue until the heart shape is complete.

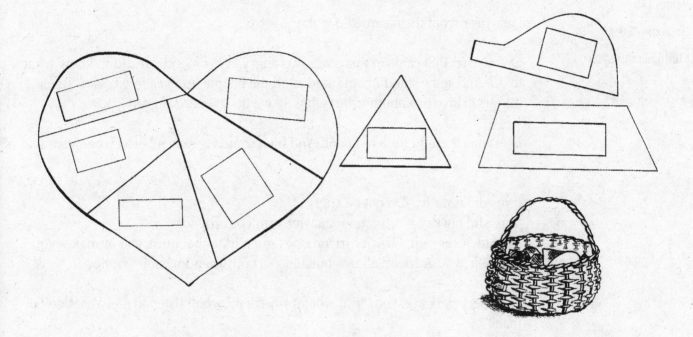

Loving actions	Unloving actions
When someone gives you an apple, say, "Thank you."	Walk across a carpet with dirty boots on.
Help each other.	Leave the tap running after washing your hands.
Pray for a friend who is sad.	When someone takes a toy from you, hit them.
Share a snack with a friend.	
Take only what is yours.	

Season after Pentecost

Proper 18 [23]

Exodus 12:1–14

Psalm 149

Romans 13:8–14

Matthew 18:15–20

Loving and Caring for Each Other

(based on Matthew 18:15–20)

A long time ago there was a place where Matthew's friends gathered as part of God's church.

The people came here to sing songs together and they pray together. Sometimes they shared food together and they always learned about Jesus together. These people were part of God's church.

Let's hear what they learned one day…

One person that came to this place was angry at his friend. He didn't know what to do. And so he stood up and said to all the people *(use an angry voice)*, "Jesus told us to love one another, but what do we do if we are angry?"

Everyone thought for a moment. And then someone remembered what Jesus had said.

Jesus did not say, "Do not be angry."
Jesus did not say, "You cannot quarrel with your friends."
Instead, Jesus said, "If your friend does something that hurts you or makes you sad, talk to your friend all by yourself. Tell your friend what is wrong."

The angry person asked, "But what if my friend won't listen to me? What do I do then?"

Then Jesus said, "Take someone else with you. Maybe your friend will listen to both of you together."

The angry person asked, "But, what if my friend *still* won't listen?"

Then Jesus said, "You will need even *more* help. You can always ask for help if you are having trouble with your friends."

The angry person thought, "Mmm…That's a good idea…Yes, I will ask for help. I don't want to stay angry with my friend."

Everyone smiled. Today they had learned something very important. They had learned about loving and caring for each other. Then everyone shared some food together.

How do you feel?

Cut out the strip and the slots in the figure's head. Thread the strip in from behind.

...when your friends share their toys with you?

...when somebody breaks something good that you just made?

...when somebody is angry with you?

...when somebody wants to be your friend?

...when somebody says "Thank you" to you?

...when somebody smiles at you?

...when somebody welcomes you into the room?

...when nobody plays with you?

...when a friend welcomes you into the room?

...when somebody pushes you over and you cut your knee?

Storytelling props needed:

• Scroll (see below)

Materials: shelf paper, dowelling, yarn, red construction paper.

Instructions: Prepare a scroll: cut shelf paper, approx. 20 x 40 cm (8 x 16 in.) Cut dowels slightly longer than the paper is wide. Glue or tape one dowel to each side of the paper. Print "Love others as much as you love yourself" across the paper. Add a red heart above the word "love." Roll the paper from each end toward the middle and tie with yarn.

A Loving Rule

(based on Romans 13:8–14)

A long, long time ago many people were confused. "Rules! Rules! Rules!" they said. "There are so many rules and laws, it's hard to remember them all! Why do we have so many rules?"

The people knew that it was important to have laws and rules but there were far too many to remember. "We need help," they said. "Who can help us?" And then one day, the people received a letter. "What does it say?" one of the people asked.

"Who can read it?" another asked.

Finally a man came forward. He opened the scroll, read what it said, and then looked up at everyone. "Love," he said.

"What do you mean?" the people asked.

The man looked at the scroll again and said, "Love. That's what it says." *(Have each child, one by one, come up and look at the scroll. When they see the heart they say the word "love" and sit down.)*

And then the man spoke again. "The letter means that all the rules are important but the most important is love. If we remember to love everyone as much as we love ourselves we will be following the rules."

"I can remember that," someone said.

"Me, too," said another.

And then they all said, "Let's shout it out together!"

And so they did. *(Have everyone shout, "LOVE!")*

Then they all went home smiling.

Materials
- card stock
- a paper plate for each child
- paper fasteners and glue

Instructions
- Make copies of activity sheet.
- Cut out a set of 3 pictures and an arrow for each child.
- Mount the arrows on stiff paper and cut out.
- Poke a hole in the centre of the paper plates and in the ends of the arrows.
- Glue the 3 pictures around the edge of the plate.
- Put a paper fastener into the hole in the arrow and then into the hole in the plate. Spread the ends of the fastener on the back of the plate.
- Remind the children that the completed spinner makes a "circle of love" – God, others, self.

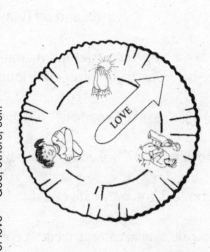

LOVE

LOVE

LOVE

Love Spinner

SELF	GOD	OTHERS
SELF	GOD	OTHERS
SELF	GOD	OTHERS

Season after Pentecost

Proper 19 [24]

Exodus 14:19–31

Psalm 114 or
    Exodus 15:1b–11,
    20–21

Romans 14:1–12

Matthew 18:21–35

Storytelling props needed:

• Scroll (see below)

Materials: shelf paper, dowelling, yarn, red construction paper.

Prepare a scroll for each child: cut shelf paper, approx. 20 x 40 cm (8 x 16 in.) Cut dowels slightly longer than the paper is wide. Glue or tape one dowel to each side of the paper. Print "**God Welcomes Everyone!** "f" across the paper. Add a red heart above the word "love." Roll the paper from each end toward the middle and tie with yarn.

• red heart-stickers or cut out of construction paper

• glue

Activity
• bring supplies for the children to make their own scrolls and print the words "God Welcomes Everyone!" inside. Add a red heart sticker.)

An Important Message

(based on Romans 14:1–12)

One day, a long, long time ago, a group of people in church were talking together. Soon their voices grew louder and louder.

"You must go," said one person. "You are doing too many things differently."

"What do you mean?" asked another person.

"Don't you see? You only eat vegetables! That's not right."

"Well, you are a meat eater. That is worse!"

"And another thing, you look at the calendar differently than we do. That's not right."

"I think *you* look at the calendar differently."

And so it went. The two groups of people argued and argued. They became more and more angry. They started arguing about other things as well. Each group thought they were doing what God wanted.

Suddenly a young child came into the room carrying a letter. (*Have a child bring over the scroll.*) The letter had just arrived and seemed to be very important. (*Have another child open the scroll.*)

"What does it say?" everyone asked together. (*Have the children repeat "What does it say?"*)

"What does it say?" everyone asked again. (*Have the children repeat it again.*) And then they knew. Deep in their hearts they knew what Jesus wanted them to know. In the letter it said, "God welcomes everyone!" (*Have children call out "God welcomes everyone!"*)

"Yes," they shouted together. "That is what we must remember!"

"Yes," they shouted again. "The love we share is more important than our differences."

"Yes," they shouted even louder. "God welcomes everyone!" (*Have children repeat it.*)

Differing Gifts

Choose which gifts you would like to share. Colour these pictures.

watering a plant

surprising someone

feeding a pet

hugging someone

painting a picture

entertaining a baby

More than That!

(based on Matthew 18:21–35)

Practice the phrase "More than That!" Each time you say "Was it this much?" that is the children's signal to repeat the phrase. When you add movement to a repetitive phrase such as "More than That!" children seem to learn more quickly. What could they do with their arms when they repeat the phrase? With their feet? With their whole bodies? Practice several times before telling the story.

A long time ago there was a place where Matthew's friends gathered as part of God's church.

They would sing songs together. They would pray together. And they would hear stories that Jesus told long, long ago. Let's hear one of those stories now…

Once there was a man who owed a king a lot of money.

Was it this much *(hold hands slightly apart)*? **More than That!**

Was it this much *(move hands further apart)*? **More than That!**

Was it this much *(stretch hands out as wide as you can)*? **More than That!**

Wow! That man owed the king a LOT OF MONEY!

The king asked the man to give back all of the money that he owed, but the man couldn't do it. He didn't have that much money. He didn't have *(stretch hands out as far as you can)* that much money, or *(move hands closer together)* that much money. He didn't even have *(move hands very close together)* that much money. The man begged the king to wait a while and let him try to get enough money.

The king knew that the man could never get that much money. *(Shake head.)* He could have become angry with the man, but he didn't. *(Shake head.)* The king said, "I know that you can't pay me the money that you owe me. I say that you no longer owe me anything, not this much *(stretch your hands out as far as you can)*, not this much *(move your hands closer together)*, not even this much *(move your hands very close together)*. Everyone makes mistakes. I will give you another chance. Let's start over. I forgive you."

God forgives us like that.

Does God forgive us this much *(hold hands slightly apart)*? **More than That!**

Does God forgive us this much *(hold hands further apart)*? **More than That!**

Does God forgive us this much *(stretch hands out as wide as you can)*? **More than That!**

Wow! God forgives us A LOT!

The people had learned something very important. They had learned about forgiving each other. They had learned to give each other another chance.

Celebrating God's Forgiveness

Colour the picture and add faces to the children. join hands in a circle like the children in the picture as you sing the song.

(tune: "Ring around the Rosie")

God forgives us so much.
God forgives us so much.
Loving. Caring.
We all jump for joy!

Season after Pentecost
Proper 20 [25]

Exodus 16:2–15

Psalm 105:1–6, 37–45

Philippians 1:21–30

Matthew 20:1–16

Storytelling props needed:

• make copies of the letter on this page

• cut out and fold on dotted lines, with text inside

• seal the letters with adhesive stickers

• make enough copies to give one to each child

Working Together

(based on Philippians 1:21–30)

Children love to hold a letter and imagine that they are reading it. Always start with someone who has the confidence to try it first. The others will easily follow.

Long ago there was a place where Paul's friends gathered as part of God's church. This was in the city of Philippi. Paul, who lived far away, would send them letters to encourage them and cheer them on.

The people would gather together often because they wanted to sing praises to God and learn more about the way Jesus lived. Let's hear what happened when they arrived at their house church one day…

First person: It's here! It's here! Another letter from Paul.

Second person: It's been a long time since we have seen our good friend Paul. He taught us so many ways to live in the way that Jesus did. I wonder what he has to say this time?

First person: Is everyone here? (*Look around at everyone and have them say "yes."*) Good. We don't want anyone to miss what Paul has to say. Let's open the letter now. (*Open the letter and read it.*)

Second person: Let me read it this time. (*Read the letter again.*) Soon everyone wanted a turn. Everyone wanted to read what Paul had written to them. (*Pass the letter around and encourage each child to "read" it aloud.*)

First person: Paul is right. We must work together side by side. Then we will be able to help each other to learn and grow.

Second person: Let's help each other to remember Jesus' teachings and follow in God's way. That will make God's church strong.

Everyone liked the sound of that so much that they decided to join hands and shout it out as loud as they could. (*Have everyone join hands, jump around in a circle, and shout, "Let's work together!"*)

(*Give the children a copy of Paul's letter to take home to show their family.*)

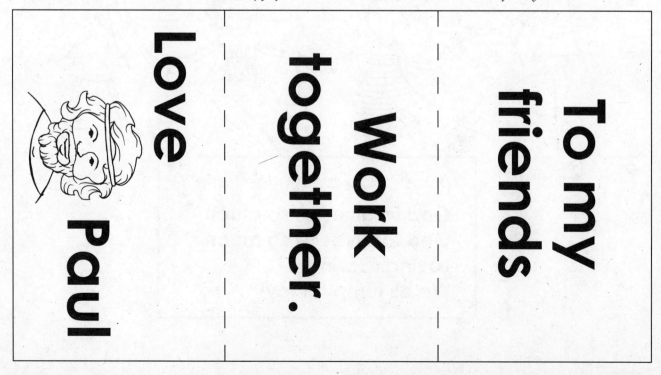

Love
Paul

Work together.

To my friends

Working Together – Side by Side

This room needs tidying. Let's help each other. Use a crayon to draw along the path. As you meet each person along that line, draw a happy smile on the face. Now all these children will joyfully help you clean up the room.

We Work Together
(tune: "Frère Jacques")

We work together. We work together.
Side by side. Side by side.
Jesus showed us how to live.
Jesus showed us how to love.
In every way, in every way.

Season after Pentecost
Proper 20 [25]

Matthew 20:1–16

A Generous Farmer

(based on Matthew 20:1–16)

Once there was a farmer who owned a very large field. "I need some help," he said. "This is too much work for me." So off he went to find some workers in the town. He knew exactly where to go. If people needed work, there was a special place near the market where they would stand and wait.

Soon the farmer arrived at the market- place. He saw several people waiting. "Come here," he said. "If you work for me today, I will give you a silver coin so that you can buy food for your family."

The people were glad to be chosen and went to work right away. *(Tape a group of farm workers on the flip chart.)*

About lunch time, the farmer noticed that there were more people who needed work. "How would these people feed their families if they cannot get work?" he thought. And so the farmer hired them, too, to come and help in his field. *(Using reusable adhesive, add one group of workers to the poster.)*

Later, in the afternoon, the farmer noticed there were still more people waiting to find work, so he invited them, too, to work in his field. *(Add another group of farm workers on the flip chart.)*

Finally, when there was only one hour left to work, the farmer noticed that there were *still* people waiting in the marketplace. "Did you not find any work today? Come. There is still time for you to work for me." And so they, too, went and worked in his field. *(Add another group of farm workers on the flip chart.)*

At the end of the day when the work was finished, the farmer called all the workers together. "Here," he said. "I have one silver coin for each of you. *(Hand out a coin to each child.)* Thank you for helping me in my field today."

"Wait! That's not fair!" cried the first group of helpers that had worked all day. "We worked more than all the other people here. We should get more money!"

The farmer shook his head sadly. "Listen friends. I haven't cheated you. You knew you were going to get a silver coin. I want to pay these other workers as much as I have paid you. They need to buy food too. Now, everyone will have enough."

All the workers looked at the coin in their hand. It was true. They all had enough to feed their families now. They looked at each other and then looked at their coin again. Then, they turned around and walked home. This farmer had been very generous. It was hard to understand!

Storytelling props needed:

- coins

- flip chart

- copies of farm workers on page 213. Colour them if possible.

- make extra copies of the farmworkers for children to colour so they can tell the story

Farm Workers

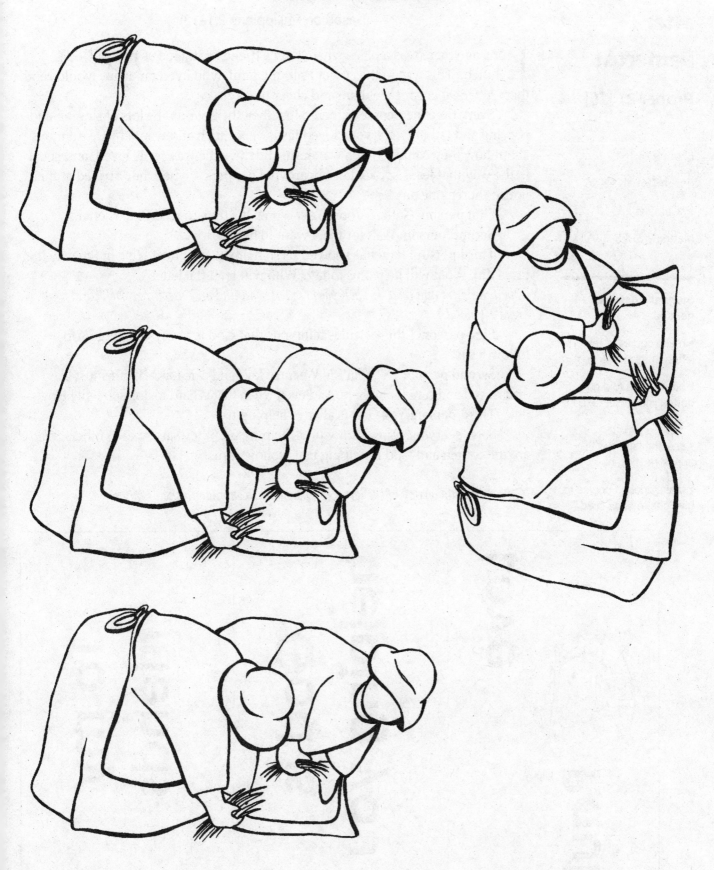

Season after Pentecost
Proper 21 [26]

Exodus 17:1–7

Psalm 78:1–4, 12–16

Philippians 2:1–13

Matthew 21:23–32

Storytelling props needed:

• make copies of the letter on this page

• cut out and fold on dotted lines, with text inside

• seal the letters with adhesive stickers

• make enough copies to give one to each child

God Helps Us
(based on Philippians 2:1–13)

Long ago there was a place where Paul's friends gathered as part of God's church. This was in the city of Philippi. Paul, who lived far away, would send them letters to encourage them and cheer them on.

Every time the people gathered together, there would be lots of singing and praying and talking. Everyone loved Jesus very much and wanted to learn more about how they could live the way Jesus did, love the way Jesus loved, and speak in the way that Jesus spoke. Let's hear what happened when they arrived at their house church one day…

First person: Gather around, everyone. It's time to read Paul's letter.

Second person: Wait for me. I want to hear it, too.

Third person: Paul has showed us so many ways how to live in the way that Jesus did. What will he tell us today? Who will read the letter?

(Open the letter and read it. Then pass the letter around and encourage each child to "read" it aloud.)

First person: I think Paul is telling us that God is always helping us to follow Jesus.

Second person: Yes! That's it! We must love and care for each other just like Jesus loved and cared for others. And even when that is hard to do, God will help us.

Third person: Yes! God is always helping us.

Soon everyone joined in. "God is helping us," they said to each other. "We are the church and God is helping us to follow Jesus."

(Give each child a copy of the letter to take home to share with their family)

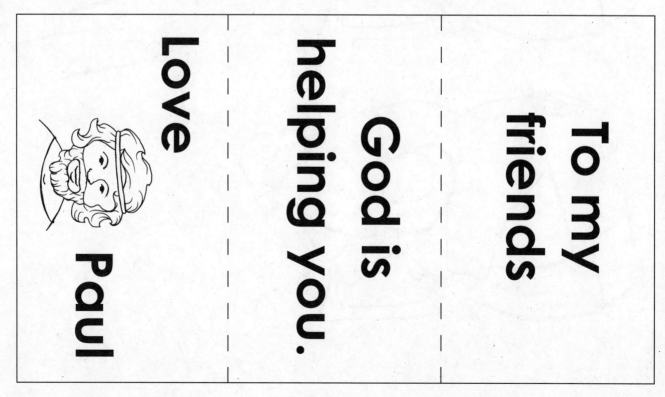

Love

Paul

God is helping you.

To my friends

Acting like Jesus

Draw in faces to show how people would feel if you…

…drew a picture for them.

…shared an apple with them

…sat down and looked at a storybook with them.

…shared your best toys with them.

…blew some bubbles together.

…helped them tidy their rooms.

…walked away and wouldn't play with them.

…surprised them with a special hug.

…said, "Have a nice day."

Season after Pentecost

Proper 21 [26]

Matthew 21:23–32

Storytelling props needed:

• bowl of grapes

The Son who Changed His Mind

(based on Matthew 21:23–32)

One day a farmer was out walking in his vineyard. Everywhere he looked he could see huge clusters of grapes on the vines. "It looks like these grapes are ripe," he said. He gently picked a few grapes and popped them into his mouth. *(Pass around the bowl of grapes and show the children how to "pop" one into their mouth.)*

"Mmm, these grapes are delicious! They must be picked right now. I don't want them to spoil on the vine." The farmer knew how important it was to pick the grapes at just the right time. Most of the grapes would be made into juice and wine.

"My sons will help me, I'm sure," he said. And so off he went to find them. Soon he found his oldest son.

"Come and taste these grapes," he said. "They are so delicious and they are very ripe. I need your help, son. The grapes must be picked before they rot and fall to the ground."

The son picked a big juicy grape and popped it into his mouth. *(Have the children "pop" another grape into their mouth.)*

"Mmm, these grapes are delicious! But I'm sorry, Father, I don't want to do that right now." And off he went to play. But the more the son thought about it, the more he knew how much his father needed him. He quickly put down what he was doing and went into the vineyard to work.

The farmer then went to find his second son. Soon he saw him sitting by a tree.

"Come and taste these grapes," he said to his son. "You will see how tasty they are. It is important that the grapes be picked now. Will you come and help?"

The second son leaned over and picked a grape. He popped it into his mouth. *(Have the children "pop" another grape into their mouth.)*

"Mmm, you are right. The grapes need to be picked now. I'll come in a few minutes."

All day the farmer and the first son worked hard picking grapes. And the second son – the son who said he would come and help – never came!

Yes!

What would you like to say "yes" to and really mean it?
Take crayons and decorate your "yes!" pages.

eating grapes

picking grapes

drumming

dancing

washing a car together

baking together

watching an animal

watching insects

Instructions
Practice the hand signing shown below for the words "No" and "Yes" and then use them when reading the rhyme below. Have fun with these actions.

Yes and No Rhyme
(based on Matthew 21:23–32)

One son said, "Oh, yes,
Father, I'll go."
He first said "yes"
but changed to mean "no."

One said, "I won't go."
Then couldn't rest.
He first said "no"
but changed to mean "yes."

The "yes" became a "no."
The "no" became a "yes."
It was all backward
and really a mess!

Do you ever say "no"
but then change to a "yes"?
In this story which one
did the best?

Jesus teaches us
to act and say
the things that show
we live in God's way.

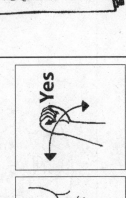

Yes

No

Season after Pentecost

Proper 22 [27]

Exodus 20:1–4, 7–9, 12–20

Psalm 19

Philippians 3:4b–14

Matthew 21:33–46

Storytelling props needed:

• make copies of the letter on this page

• cut out and fold on dotted lines, with text inside

• seal the letters with adhesive stickers

• make enough copies to give one to each child

We Love Jesus!
(based on Philippians 3:4b–14)

Long ago there was a place where Paul's friends gathered as part of God's church. This was in the city of Philippi. Paul, who lived far away, would send them letters to encourage them and cheer them on.

One night everyone decided to gather on the rooftop. It had been very hot all day. It felt good to feel the little breeze around them as they listened to stories and prayed to God. Each time they gathered, they learned more about living the way Jesus did, loving the way Jesus did, and speaking the way Jesus did. Let's hear what happened when they met at their house church one day…

First person: When I look up at all these stars, I think about God.

Second person: Yes, I do too. And I remember how much we have learned by following Jesus. Jesus helped me to know God.

Third person: Oh, yes. And Paul helped us to know Jesus. Let's read another part of Paul's letter tonight. Who wants to read it this time? (*Open the letter and read it.*)

First person: Paul is right. Jesus is our very special friend. In fact, Jesus is our best friend! I have so much love for Jesus that I feel it deep inside me and all around me.

Second person: I feel that way, too. I think we should all have a chance to read the letter again. (*Read the letter and then pass the letter around and encourage each child to "read" it aloud.*)

Third person: Let's celebrate the love we have for Jesus.

With big smiles on their faces, they joined hands and prayed to God. "Thank you, God, for your very special gift of Jesus."

(*Give copies of Paul's letter to children to take home and share with their family.*)

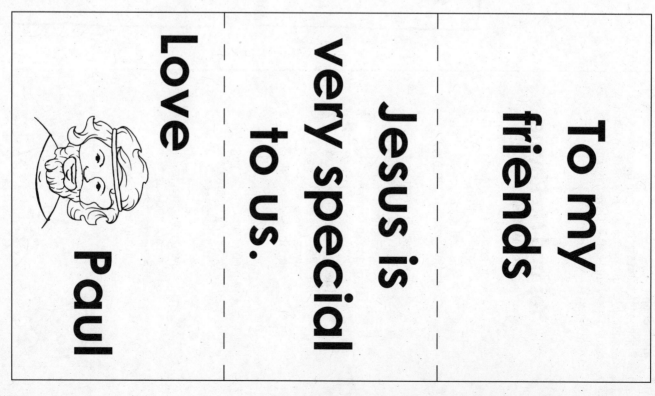

Love
Paul

very special to us.

Jesus is

To my friends

Jesus Brings Us Together

Instructions

- Colour the pictures and imagine what each person loves and knows about Jesus. How does Jesus bring people together? Draw yourself in this picture and print what you love about Jesus.

- Draw a line with hearts from you to Jesus.

**Season
after
Pentecost
Proper 23 [28]**

Exodus 32:1–14

Psalm 106:1–6, 19–23

Philippians 4:1–9

Matthew 22:1–14

**Storytelling props
needed:**

• make a copy of Paul's
letter in the story

• glue this on the middle
of a piece of paper

• roll paper up from both
ends to form a scroll and
tie with yarn

Celebrating in God Always
(based on Philippians 4:1–9)

Long ago there was a place where Paul's friends gathered as part of God's church. This was in the city of Philippi. Paul, who lived far away, would send them letters to encourage them and cheer them on.

All the women came. All the men came. All the big children and the little ones came. They all came and stood together to pray and sing and celebrate God's love. Each time they gathered, they learned more about living the way Jesus did, loving the way Jesus did, and speaking the way Jesus did. Let's hear what happened when they met at their house church one day…

First person: I have had such a busy day today. I've been worrying about so many things. I'm glad we're finally together again.

Second person: Did you notice how many people are looking worried today? I wonder what is bothering them.

Third person: Why don't we read more of Paul's letter? Paul always supports us in helpful ways. Perhaps he knows what we can do. (*Open the letter and read it. Then pass the letter around and encourage each child to "read" it aloud.*)

First person: That's it! When we're worried, we can talk to God.

Second person: And when we are sad or angry, or happy or excited or afraid, we can talk to God.

Third person: It's like God is always ready to give us a great big hug when we most need it.

And then everyone stopped to imagine God's hug. They knew God loved them. They could feel it deep inside them and all around them. It was a wonderful peaceful moment to celebrate in God always.

(*Give copies of Paul's letter to children to take home and share with their family.*)

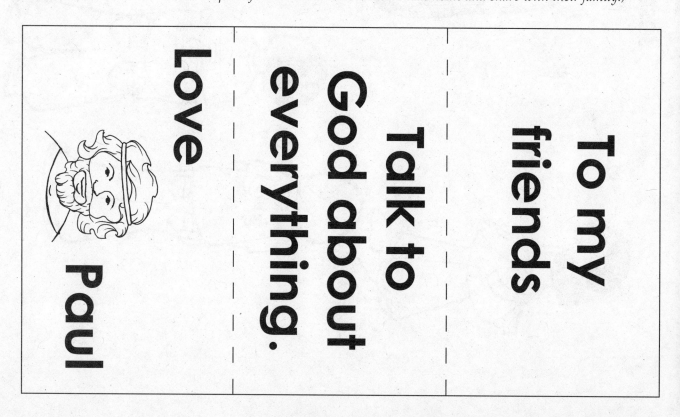

I can talk to God every day.
I can talk to God about everything.

Monday

Tuesday

Wednesday

Thursday

Friday

Saturday

Sunday

Praying Every Day

Materials
- cardstock or construction paper
- magnetic tape *(optional)*
- cloths pin/clothes peg for each child

Instructions
- Cut out and decorate the calendar.
- Strengthen it by gluing it onto heavier paper.
- On the back, press a piece of magnetic tape to the top and the bottom of the calendar. (Optional)
- Cut out and decorate the group of children. Glue the picture onto a clothes pin/clothes peg.
- Each day move the clothes pin and remember to talk to God.

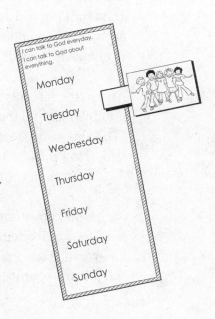

Season after Pentecost

Proper 23 [28]

Matthew 22:1–14

Storytelling props
needed:

• copies of figures on
page 223 (enough for
all the children.) Colour
them and hide them
around the room but
not in places too diffi-
cult for children to find.

• wedding invitations

• sheet of poster board
and tape

The Invitation

(based on Matthew 22:1–14)

One day a king's son was getting married. The king was very happy. He planned a big party to celebrate.

He asked the cooks to make a wedding cake and lots of delicious food.
He asked his servants to decorate the big hall.
He asked the musicians to come and play music.
He asked the gardeners to plant more beautiful flowers.
It was going to be a very special party!

Then, when everything was ready, he sent his servants to invite all his friends and relatives to come to the wedding banquet. (Hand out wedding invitations.) And then they waited. They waited and waited. No one came!
Again, the king sent his servants to invite his relatives and friends.
And again, the servants went out and called, "Come now! Come to the wedding banquet." (Invite the children to join with you in the invitation, saying, "Come now to the party.")

"Oh no! I cannot come!" said one. "I must go to my farm to take care of the crops and animals."

"Oh no! I cannot come!" said another. "I have too much business."
Each person they asked had the same answer. (Encourage each child, one by one, to say "Oh no! I cannot come!") No one could come. Everyone had an excuse for not coming to the party.

The king was sad. "Who will come and celebrate with us?" he asked. The great hall was all ready for a party. The food was cooking.
Then the king had an idea. He called to the servants again. "Go out and invite anyone you can find. Invite the homeless people, the beggars, the sick people. Everyone is invited!"

And so the servants went along the streets and alleys, the lanes and country roads. It didn't matter if the people were poor or sick or poorly dressed. All were invited! "The king's son is getting married. Come to the wedding banquet," the servants said. (Have children search for hidden figures and tape them one at a time to a poster board. As you tape each figure have the children say "Welcome to the party.")

So, people came from the streets and filled the hall with happy sounds. They ate the good food and celebrated the wedding of the king's son. The king had enough room for everyone and enough food for everyone. He was glad that people could come and join the happy celebration.

The Invitation Story Figures

Dear God,
you invite us to eat food from the earth,
and share food with our friends.
We give thanks for your gift
of love without end.
Amen.

Season after Pentecost

Proper 24 [29]

Exodus 33:12–23

Psalm 99

1 Thessalonians 1:1–10

Matthew 22:15–22

Storytelling props needed:

• make copies of the letter on this page

• cut out and fold on dotted lines, with text inside

• seal the letters with adhesive stickers

• make enough copies to give one to each child

Hearing Encouraging Words

(based on 1 Thessalonians 1:1–10)

Long ago there was a place where Paul's friends gathered as part of God's church. This was in the city of Thessalonica. Paul, who lived far away, would send them letters to encourage them and cheer them on.

The people remembered when Paul had visited them. Now Paul was far away, but he still wanted the people to know that he cared about them. Paul knew how much the people wanted to live the way Jesus did, love the way Jesus loved, and speak in the way that Jesus spoke. So, what do you think Paul did to let the people know how much he cared for them? *(Listen to their responses.)*

Paul wrote letters to the people in Thessalonica. Paul knew how hard the people worked to spread the news of God's love. The people followed Jesus' ways. They loved Jesus. They told others about Jesus. The people lived God's love. And Paul was very proud of them. He wanted them to know it and so he sent another letter to them. Let's find out what this letter said…
(Open the letter and read it. Pass the letter around and encourage each child to "read" the letter aloud.)

The people looked at each other. "Yes," they said. "We are amazing! We are doing God's work. And we are doing our best!"

The people laughed and danced and celebrated. *(Have children "dance.")* "Yes," they said. "God chose us to tell others. And that's what we are doing!"

(Give copies of Paul's letter to children to take home and share with their family.)

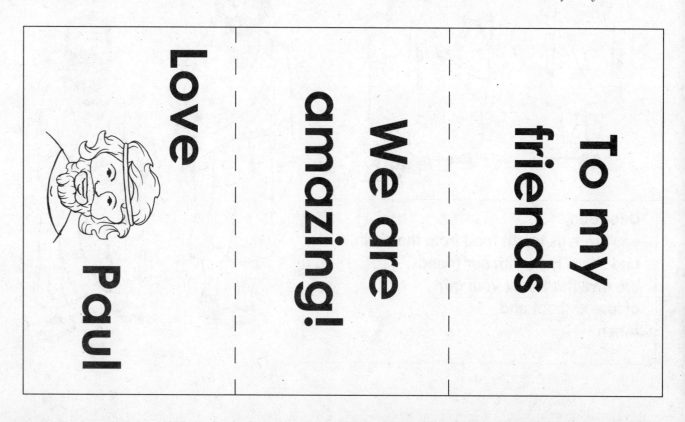

I AM AMAZING

AND I AM DOING MY BEST

Materials
- various art supplies so children have a choice at decorating their poster

Instructions
- Decorate and colour this poster of encouragement to hang in your room

Season after Pentecost

Proper 24 [29]

Matthew 22:15–22

———

Storytelling props needed:

• a coin for each child

The Face on the Coin

(based on Matthew 22:15–22)

Many people liked to follow Jesus. Some people would follow Jesus into the countryside. Some people followed him when he walked by the seashore. Some people followed him when he went into the small towns and villages.

Everywhere Jesus went, there were people who wanted to follow him. People wanted to be with Jesus and hear his teachings and see what he would do. They wanted to be Jesus' friend. One day some important leaders noticed how popular Jesus was.

"I don't like it," said one leader.

" I don't either," said another. "Too many people are following Jesus."

And then another worried leader said, "People might start listening to Jesus instead of us. What are we going to do?"

They thought and they thought and they thought. They must do something! Finally, one of the leaders jumped up and said, "I know. Let's trick Jesus into saying something that will make the people angry! Then the people won't follow him anymore."

"Yes. What a good idea!" they all said at once. And off they went in search of Jesus.

"Jesus, we have a question for you. We know you are very wise. Tell us Jesus, is it right to pay a lot of money to the king?"

Now these leaders knew that in their country there was a rule that everyone had to pay money to the king. The king was not a good king but everyone knew that they had to obey him. But the people also wanted to love and obey God. The leaders didn't know how the people could obey the bad king and also obey God. This was a tricky question!

Jesus thought about the problem. Then he said, "Show me a coin."

"How strange," the leaders thought. "Why does Jesus want to see a coin?" They handed a coin to Jesus. (*Give a coin to each child.*)

Then Jesus asked, "Whose picture is on the coin?"

The leaders said, "The king's picture is on the coin."

Jesus smiled, "Well, then, give this money to the king. It belongs to him. Give God what belongs to God."

The leaders were surprised! Jesus had found a way to answer them without being tricked. The king should receive the money but at the same time everyone knew that everything belongs to God – everything in the whole world. Jesus knew that. And so did the leaders!

Everything belongs to God.

belongs to God.

_____

Instructions: Add your name to this picture to finish the sentence. Add your eyes, nose, and mouth. Colour your clothing.

Other ideas for exploring the lectionary readings (Proper 24 [29])

1. What Do You See? game (Matthew 22:15–22)

Ask the children to look around and notice that everything and everyone belongs to God. Then, play a game similar to "I Spy." Begin with the leader saying "I see something that belongs to God and it is *(blue)*." The children then guess what it might be. When it is found, everyone then says *"(The blue flower)* belongs to God." Encourage the children to take a turn saying what they see that belongs to God.

2. Self-portrait (Matthew 22:15–22)

Materials: copies of the activity sheet on page 227 onto transparency film. Overhead projector, felt markers

The scripture asks us to give to God that which is God's. To help the children think about giving themselves to God, make self-portraits. Give each child the resource sheet, read the title to them, and help them print their name in the appropriate place. Invite them to use markers or crayons to colour in the figure to look like themselves. Then, if possible, use an overhead projector and project each completed picture onto the wall. Identify who it is and then have everyone call out, *"(Child's name)* belongs to God."

3. Fruit baskets for housebound people (1 Thessalonians 1:1–10)

In Paul's letter to the church in Thessalonica, he thanks the Christians there for the way they have imitated the work of Jesus, and become an example to all the believers in that area. One of the ways that we can imitate the work of Jesus is to use all that we have and are for God.

Since giving to God involves giving to others, young children might share their care by preparing fruit baskets for some of the housebound people in your congregation. If you have access to the church kitchen, take the children there. First, ask all the children to wash their hands and then wash the fruit. Remove excess water. Line the bottom of the baskets with paper towels. Involve the children in choosing fruit and arranging in the basket. Tie a ribbon to the basket. Arrange to deliver the fruit baskets or to have someone from your congregation do so. Perhaps there are children and parents who could accompany you when you make deliveries.

Prayer

Thank you, God,
for helping us to learn about you.
Amen.

Gentle Love

(based on 1 Thessalonians 2:1–8)

Long ago there was a place where Paul's friends gathered as part of God's church. This was in the city of Thessalonica. Paul, who lived far away, would send them a letter to encourage or cheer them on.

Each time the people came together they would sing and pray and laugh and tell stories. They would help each other learn more about how to live the way Jesus did, love the way Jesus loved, and speak in the way that Jesus spoke. Paul knew that the people loved each other in gentle ways and he was very proud of them.

Let's find out what Paul's letter said one day…
(Open the letter and read it. Pass the letter around and encourage each child to "read" the letter aloud.)

When everyone had read the letter, some people wanted to read it again. *(Invite those children who want to read it again to read it now.)*
"That is a good reminder," said one of the people. "Jesus taught us many ways to be caring and gentle with each other. Now it is our turn to do the same."

"We must gently care for all of God's world," said another.

With that, everyone joined hands. They thanked God for all the love that surrounded them. They knew that they would try their best to pass that love on in gentle ways.

(Give copies of Paul's letter to children to take home and share with their family.)

Season after Pentecost

Proper 25 [30]

Deuteronomy 34:1–12

Psalm 90:1–6, 13–17

1 Thessalonians 2:1–8

Matthew 22:34–46

Storytelling props needed:

• make copies of the letter on this page

• cut out and fold on dotted lines, with text inside

• seal the letters with adhesive stickers

• make enough copies to give one to each child

To my friends

We are gentle with one another.

Love Paul

Plant Stakes

_____
gives me gentle care.

I am in good soil.
I am watered.
I have sunshine.

_____
gives me gentle care.

I am in good soil.
I am watered.
I have sunshine.

_____
gives me gentle care.

I am in good soil.
I am watered.
I have sunshine.

_____
gives me gentle care.

I am in good soil.
I am watered.
I have sunshine.

_____
gives me gentle care.

I am in good soil.
I am watered.
I have sunshine.

Materials
- Plant pots, potting soil, and seeds for each child
- craft sticks and tape

Instructions
- Print a child's name on each label.
- Tape each label to a craft stick.
- After the seedlings are planted, place a stake into each container.

What Is Most Important?

(based on Matthew 22:34–46)

Season after Pentecost
Proper 25 [30]

Matthew 22:34–46

Storytelling props needed:

• a copy of the sh'ma on page 232

Everyone was talking about Jesus. "Have you heard what Jesus says? You should go and hear him preach," someone said.

"You can understand every word he says. He speaks so simply," said another. "I heard he is going to the temple. Let's follow him," said another.

Soon a whole crowd had gathered in the Temple waiting to hear Jesus speak. They sat quietly and waited. They looked around. Everyone was waiting.
Finally one of the religious leaders stood up and looked at Jesus. "Jesus," he said, "I have a question for you. There are many books full of God's laws. But what is the most important law?"

Now this was a very tricky question. The law of God had been written down by many religious teachers. There were books full of tiny laws as well as big laws. There were so many laws to remember. You can't do this. You must do that. You can't do this. You must do that. On and on it went. But there was one law that Jesus and all Jewish people recited every day. *(Have the children repeat the verse. Have the children help create some actions as you say the verse, "Love God with all your heart…")*

How would Jesus answer the question? The crowd waited and wondered. Which law would he choose? All the laws were important. How could Jesus choose just one? *(Have the children repeat the verse with the actions you have created together, "Love God with all your heart…")*

Jesus thought about the law that he learned when he was a little boy. He knew it by heart and had said it every day. This was the law that Moses had asked the Jewish people to remember always. What do you think Jesus said to the religious leader? *(Have the children repeat the verse with actions, "Love God with all your heart…")*

"Yes," Jesus said, "the most important thing is to love." And then Jesus said, "Wait. There is another important part to loving."

Everyone wanted to hear what else Jesus had to say. They moved closer so they wouldn't miss his words.

Jesus looked at everyone and then said, "Love your neighbour and love yourself." The religious leaders were amazed. Jesus had answered the question well. He was a good and wise teacher.

Materials
- construction paper
- magnetic tape
- glue and scissors

Refrigerator Magnet Instructions
- cut out and glue the scroll onto construction paper
- add magnetic tape to the back

The Sh 'ma

Love God
with all your heart
with all your soul
with all your strength

Deuteronomy 6:5

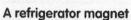

A refrigerator magnet

Love Message

We want to share our love with you. God loves you. Share your love with others.

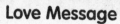

Instructions Print your message of love in the space above. Cut out it out and decorate it. Give it to someone who needs to hear what you printed.

God's Love in Us

(based on 1 Thessalonians 2:9–13)

Season after Pentecost

Proper 26[31]

Joshua 3:7–17

Psalm 107:1–7, 33–37

1 Thessalonians 2:9–13

Matthew 23:1–12

Long ago there was a place where Paul's friends gathered as part of God's church. This was in the city of Thessalonica. Paul, who lived far away, would send them letters to encourage them and cheer them on.

There was a lot of singing. There was a lot of praying. There was a lot of storytelling. For all the people wanted to help each other learn more about God's love. They wanted to live the way Jesus did, love the way Jesus loved, and speak in the way that Jesus spoke. This time, when they all gathered, there was a lot of excitement in the air. Another message had arrived from Paul. They missed their good friend, Paul. He cared about them so much and he always helped them to see what good work they were doing. Paul was so proud of them. Let's find out what Paul's letter said one day…

(Open the letter and read it. Pass the letter around and encourage each child to "read" the letter aloud.)

"Wait," said some of the people listening to Paul's words, "we want to read the letter, too." *(Read" the letter again.)*

After listening to Paul's message over and over again, the people hugged each other. They knew that God loved them. They knew that they were part of God's family. And now they knew that other people could see God's love in them, too. "Let's dance," they said. "When we love others, people see God's love in us. That's worth celebrating!" And so that is what they did. *(Everyone dance.)*

(Give copies of Paul's letter to children to take home and share with their family.)

Storytelling props needed:

• make a copy of Paul's letter in the story

• glue this on the middle of a piece of paper

• roll paper up from both ends to form a scroll and tie with yarn

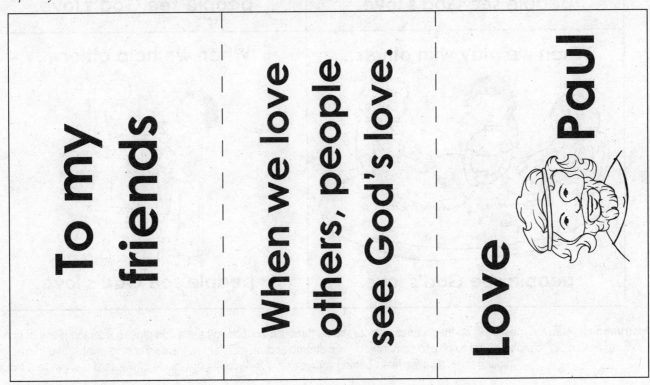

To my friends

When we love others, people see God's love.

Love Paul

Message Cards

When we care for others...

people see God's love.

When we sing with others...

people see God's love.

When we share with others...

people see God's love.

When we love others...

people see God's love.

When we play with others...

people see God's love.

When we help others...

people see God's love.

Instructions: Read the messages on the pictures. Colour the pictures. Cut out the pictures and glue to a folded piece of construction paper to make a card to give to someone in your church and/or your family. Inside the card print "Love from _____(your name)." Draw a heart beside your name. (Or decorate the inside of the card the way you like.)

Other ideas for exploring the lectionary readings (Proper 26[31])

1. Jesus' footsteps game (Matthew 23:1–12)

(Create a path with paper footprints, setting the footprints a few feet apart. If possible, make the path go under tables, over chairs, and around objects. Place game strips in Bibles along the path.)

Invite the children to pretend they are following Jesus' footprints. When they reach a Bible along the path, invite them to sit down, open the Bible and pull out a game strip. Read to them what it says and then

Game strips for "Following Jesus' Footprints"

✂ Jesus said "You must show your love not just talk about it."

Jesus said "The most important thing is to love."

Jesus said "Love your neighbour and love yourself."

Jesus said "Everything belongs to God."

Jesus said "God welcomes everyone."

together think of an example of a loving action that follows what Jesus said. Continue along the path until the next Bible. Repeat until all the strips have been taken out of the Bibles. (The children might also take turns creating a new trail that leads to the Bibles each time.

2. Collage (1 Thessalonians 2:9–13)

Give each child a prepared paper heart with the phrase, "Through our caring actions, we show God's love," printed on them. Read the phrase and talk about what it means. Provide copies of the people figures on page 244, and/or a variety of pictures of people from magazines and invite children to choose some to glue onto their heart shapes. As they choose each person encourage them to imagine what caring activity that person might be doing. (*Note:* older children might find and cut out their own people pictures from magazines.)

3. Service project (1 Thessalonians 2:9–13)

Find out whether your church or a social service agency (homeless shelters, safe houses for victims of domestic violence) in your community could use "personal care packets" to distribute to people it serves. Consult with them about what would be needed.

Materials: personal care products, resealble bags, art supplies and paper for creating a note or card

One way that Christians love and serve God is through our work in the world. Talk about some of the service projects that are happening or have happened in your church. Tell the children about the service project they will help with today.

Help children prepare the "personal care packets" to be distributed through service agencies in your community. Set out the resealable bags and personal care items and show the children how to put one of each item (e.g. a tube of toothpaste, a toothbrush, a bottle of lotion, shampoo) into the bag. Have the children create a note or a piece of art to include in the bag. Seal the bags, and put them into a box to be distributed.

Prayer

Dear God,
you gave us Jesus to teach us the way.
Help us teach others what we learned today.
Amen.

Season after Pentecost

Proper 26[31]

Matthew 23:1–12

Storytelling props needed:

• books

Matching Words to Actions

(based on Matthew 23:1–12)

Long, long ago there were some very important leaders who wanted to know everything about God. "We must read all we can," they said. *(Have some children bring over several books and place them in the centre.)* And so they read. They learned many things about God and living in God's way.

"We must read more. We want to know everything," they said. *(Have some children bring over more books and place them in the centre.)* The books told them a lot about God. *(Have children bring over more books.)* Soon they had everything they could find. *(Have children find the rest of the books in the room and place them in the centre.)* They read and read and read. They learned how much God loved everyone and how much God cared for everyone. They learned all about loving.

"Now we know how God wants us to live. Let's make sure we are all thinking the same way," they said. And so they started to talk to each other. They talked and talked and talked. "No one has learned as much about God as us," they said.

They began to think they knew everything there was to know about God.

Now, Jesus saw what was happening. These leaders were reading and reading about God. They were talking and talking about God. And they were teaching and teaching about God. But there was one big problem! They were not doing what they were saying! The leaders were so busy telling the people what to do – they forgot to love the people. They made heavy loads to carry and then made other people do the work. They liked wearing fancy clothes, sitting in the best seats, and being called important names. But they weren't kind and loving. They only cared about themselves.

Jesus sadly looked around him. He loved the leaders. He wanted those leaders to understand what God wanted. And so he said to them, "You mustn't just learn about living in God's way, you must live that way too."

Instructions

- Make copies of the picture and pre-fold them along the dotted lines so that the picture of Jesus is hidden at the back. Give each child a pre-folded picture and read the question to them. Discuss what they see in the pictures and encourage them not to peek underneath while they colour them. When finished colouring, have them open the picture up and turn it over to reveal the answer – Jesus. Invite them to add a picture of themselves beside Jesus.

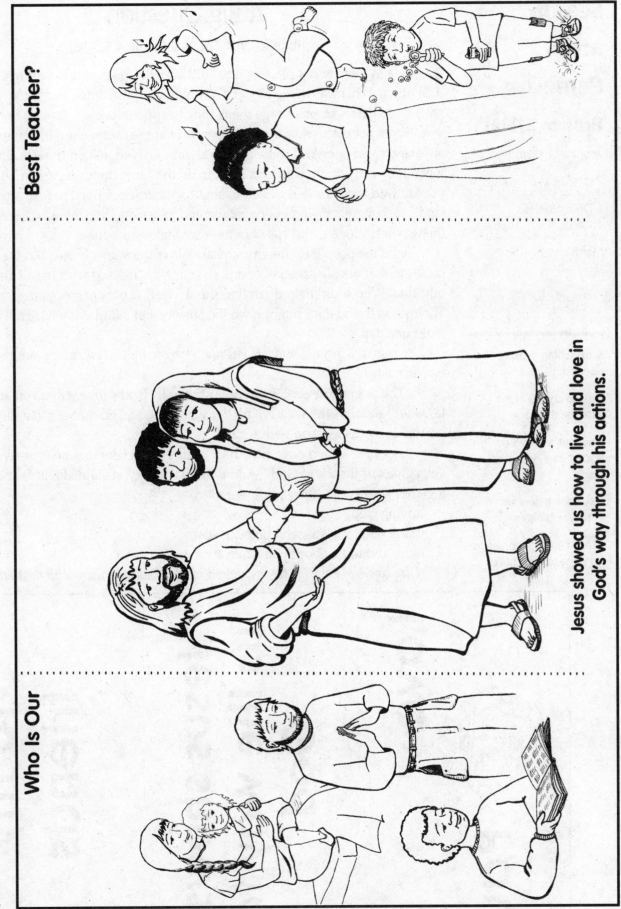

Best Teacher?

Jesus showed us how to live and love in God's way through his actions.

Who Is Our

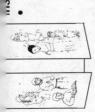

Season after Pentecost

Proper 27[32]

Joshua 24:1–3a, 14–25

Psalm 78:1–7

1 Thessalonians 4:13–18

Matthew 25:1–13

Storytelling props needed:

• make copies of the letter on this page

• cut out and fold on dotted lines, with text inside

• seal the letters with adhesive stickers

• make enough copies to give one to each child

A Big Question

(based on 1 Thessalonians 4:13–18)

Long ago there was a place where Paul's friends gathered as part of God's church. This was in the city of Thessalonica. Paul, who lived far away, would send them letters to encourage them and cheer them on.

Some people always arrived very early at the house church. Some people always arrived late. And some people always arrived just on time. But no matter when they arrived, they always liked to do the same things together. They liked to pray to God together. They liked to sing together. They liked to hear stories about God's love together. And everyone wanted to learn to live the way Jesus did, love the way Jesus loved, and speak in the way that Jesus spoke.

Now the people in this church had lots of questions to ask. But there was one question that people asked over and over again, "Is Jesus with us?" This was a big question! Who could help them find the answer? *(Listen to the children's responses.)* Their good friend Paul might have the answer. Let's find out what Paul said in his letter one day…

(Open the letter and read it. I Pass the letter around and encourage each child to "read" the letter aloud.)

"This is good news," the people shouted. "God's love will go on and on and Jesus will show us the way. No matter where we are, no matter what happens to us, we will be with God and with Jesus."

"Hooray!" called out a little boy. "Our big question has been answered. Let's give our thanks to God." And with that, everyone joined hands and prayed together. *(Say the following prayer together.)*

Loving God,
thank you for Jesus who helps us learn
more and more about your love. Amen.

(Give copies of Paul's letter to children to take home and share with their family.)

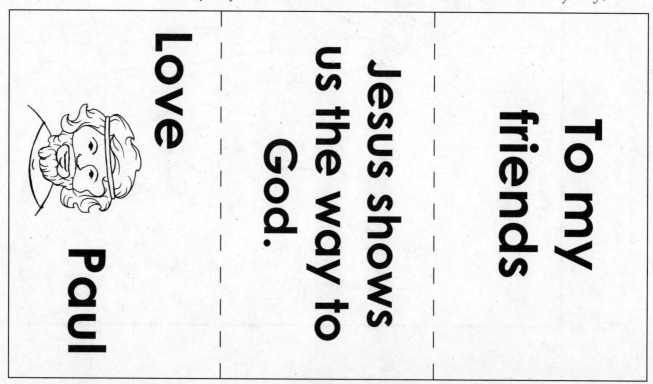

Love

Paul

Jesus shows us the way to God.

To my friends

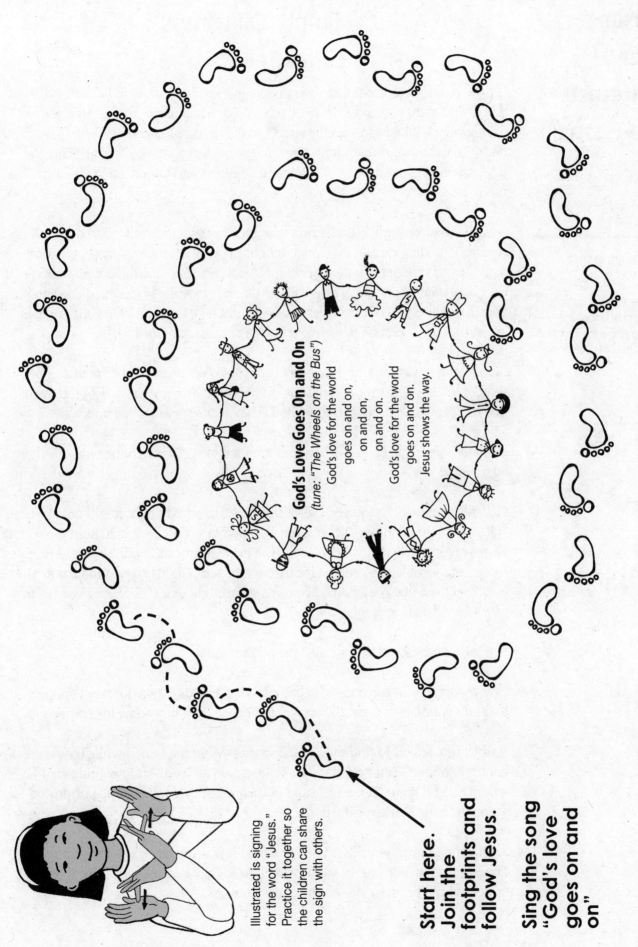

Jesus Shows the Way

God's Love Goes On and On
(tune: "The Wheels on the Bus")
God's love for the world
goes on and on,
on and on,
on and on.
God's love for the world
goes on and on.
Jesus shows the way.

Illustrated is signing for the word "Jesus." Practice it together so the children can share the sign with others.

Start here. Join the footprints and follow Jesus.

Sing the song "God's love goes on and on"

Storytelling props needed:

• make ahead a sample clay or play dough oil lamp to show the children (see page 241)

Empty Oil Lamps

(based on Matthew 25:1–13)

It was a very important day. Two people in the village were to be married and that night was to be the big party. As soon as the sun went down, the bridegroom walked through the streets to the house of his bride. Then they both walked through the same streets to the bridegroom's house and there the celebration began. There was eating and drinking and dancing and singing. What fun!

Now there were some bridesmaids who had a very important job to do for that celebration. They carried oil lamps to light the way for the wedding party. (*Invite the children to pretend that they are the bridesmaids.*) First, they filled their lamps with oil. (*Have children pretend to fill lamp with oil.*) Some of the bridesmaids decided to take extra oil. Some of the bridesmaids did not take extra oil. (*Divide the children into two groups – ask one group to pretend to put extra oil in their pocket.*)

Before long it was dark and the stars came out. "We must light our lamps now," someone said. "The groom will soon arrive." (*Children pretend to light their lamp.*) The bridesmaids sat down and waited. They waited and waited and waited.

"Where is he?" one bridesmaid asked after a while. "I thought he would be here by now."

"I'm worried," said another. "I didn't bring extra oil. My light might go out soon." "Oh, dear," said another. "If our lamps go out we won't be able to light the way." They waited and waited and waited. The bridegroom still hadn't come. And then something terrible happened! One by one, the lamp lights started to go out. The oil had been used up. Wait! Some bridesmaids brought extra oil. (*Have those children pretend to fill up their lamp again.*)

"Please give us some of your oil," the others said.

"We're sorry," said the ones who had planned ahead. "There just isn't enough oil to fill up your lamps as well. You will have to go and buy some for yourselves."

So they hurried off to find more oil. But guess what happened while they were gone? (*Encourage their answers.*) The bridegroom arrived! And the bridesmaids who were still there, lit the way, and everyone happily followed the bride and groom into the house for the party.

Later, when the other bridesmaids returned it was too late. Everyone was gone. They were all inside and the door was closed. They had missed seeing the bridegroom. They had missed the party. They had missed out on all the fun.

Ten Young Women

(Invite the children to show their fingers as you say this poem. Repeat several times.)

10 young women, with lamps burning fine,
One ran out of oil and then there were 9.

9 young women said, "The bridegroom is late!"
One ran out of oil, then there were 8.

8 young women said, "Now it's past eleven!"
One ran out of oil, then there were 7.

7 young women, with brightly burning wicks,
One ran out of oil, then there were 6.

6 young women asked, "When will he arrive?"
One ran out of oil, then there were 5.

5 young women, standing in the room.
"Finally he's coming! Here comes the groom!"

5 young women, with lamps burning bright,
went to the wedding and shared their light.

Just like them, we can show God's way
by our words and actions every day!

Self-hardening Clay

Materials
- 500 ml (2 cups) sand
- 250 ml (1 cup) cornstarch
- 10 ml (2tsp.) powdered alum (available at craft store)
- 375 ml (1 1/2 cups) hot water

Instructions
- Mix sand, cornstarch and alum. Add hot water and stir vigorously.
- Cook over medium heat until thick, stirring constantly.
- Store in airtight container when cool. Unhardened clay can be stored in the fridge.
- Mold, then dry in the sun for several days. Dries very hard and waterproof.

Making an Oil Lamp

The oil lamp was used in the home every day. Olive oil usually provided the main source of oil. The wick was made of various materials, including flax.

Materials
- self-hardening clay(see recipe below)
- thick cloth strips or commercial cotton wick

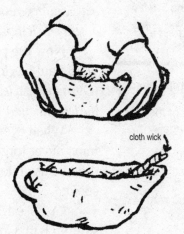

cloth wick

Instructions
- Form clay into a ball and pull sides out from centre to shape lamp. Pinch one end to make a handle and the other end to make a spout.
- Allow to dry.
- Add cloth strip for the wick

(Note: these lamps are for play. If you are actually lighting them, the lamps must be made with clay and kiln dried. Pour oil into receptacle and allow the oil to soak through wick. *The teacher must light it.*

Variation
- instead of olive oil and a wick, set a candle inside the lamp shape.

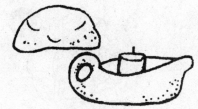

Season after Pentecost

Proper 28 [33]

Judges 4:1–7

Psalm 123

1 Thessalonians 5:1–11

Matthew 25:14–30

Storytelling props needed:

• make copies of the letter on this page

• cut out and fold on dotted lines, with text inside

• seal the letters with adhesive stickers

• make enough copies to give one to each child

• a flashlight

• make a copy of the letters on pages 210, 218, 220, 224, 229, and 238. Prepare as above, and tie together in a bundle.

We Are the Church

(based on 1 Thessalonians 5:1–11)

Long ago there was a place where Paul's friends gathered as part of God's church. This was in the city of Thessalonica. Paul, who lived far away, would send them letters to encourage them and cheer them on.

For a long time, the people had been receiving letters from their good friend Paul. Today someone had gathered those letters and was going to read them to everyone again. Let's hear what those letters said. I wonder if we will remember them… *(Invite a child to choose one letter from the bundle and open it. Read it aloud and have children respond "Yes, yes" and then repeat the one-liner in the letter. Repeat with the other three letters.)*

Now the people felt really happy. They had remembered Paul's letters. But wait! Paul has left another letter today. Let's see what this letter says…
(Open the new letter and read it. Pass the letter around and encourage each child to "read" the letter aloud.)

When everyone had read the new letter, one woman spoke up and said, "We must never forget that we are the church together. We try to live the way Jesus did, we try to love the way Jesus loved, and we try to speak in the way that Jesus spoke."

"Yes," said another. "We are spreading God's love in the world. We are shining with God's love!"

"Let's light all the lamps and dance in the light. Let's feel God's love all around us and deep inside us," the people sang together. And that's exactly what they did. *(Invite one child to hold a flashlight and shine it on the children as they all dance in the light.)*

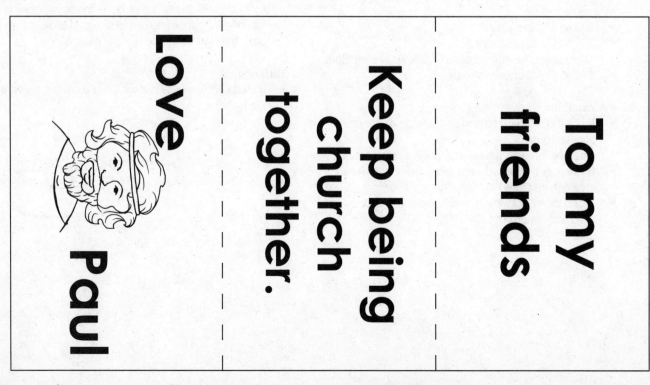

Love Paul

Keep being church together.

To my friends

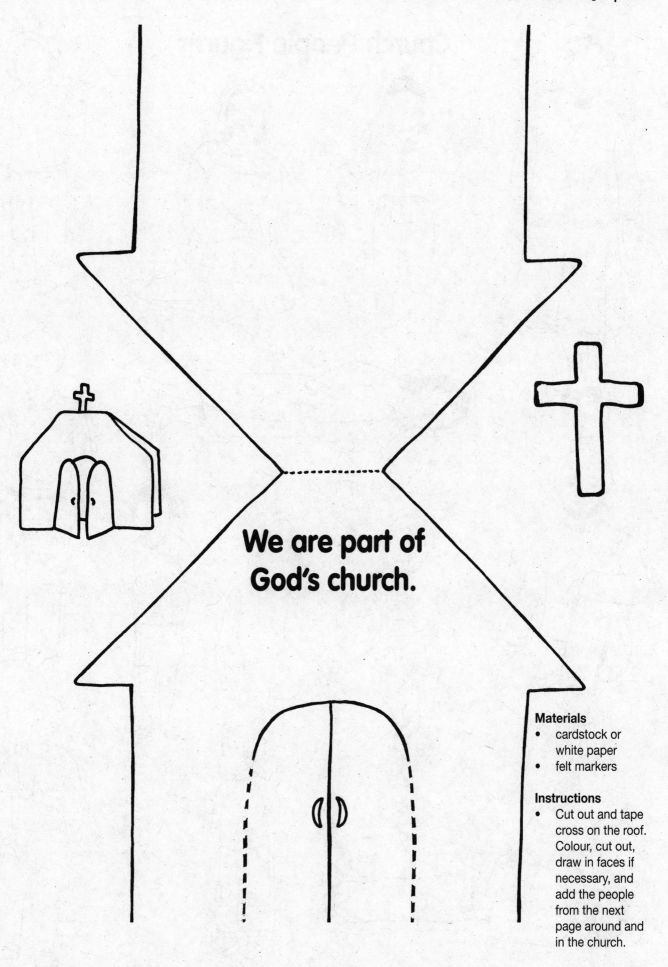

We are part of God's church.

Materials
- cardstock or white paper
- felt markers

Instructions
- Cut out and tape cross on the roof. Colour, cut out, draw in faces if necessary, and add the people from the next page around and in the church.

Church People Figures

The Parable of the Three Servants

(based on Matthew 25:14–30)

Season after Pentecost

Proper 28 [33]

Judges 4:1–7

Psalm 123

1 Thessalonians 5:1–11

Matthew 25:14–30

(Invite volunteers to be the landowner, the three servants, the shopper in the market, and the neighbour. Ask them to mime the actions suggested in this story.)

Once there was a landowner who was going on a long, long trip. *(The landowner pretends to pack.)* Before he left, he called together three of his servants. *(The three servants stand beside the landowner.)* He gave each one some money. *(The landowner hands out the coins to the servants.)*

To the first servant, he gave five pieces of money.

To the next servant, he gave two pieces of money.

To the third servant, he gave one piece of money.

"Take good care of this money," he told them. Then, he went away. *(Landowner waves, walks around the room, and sits down.)*

The first servant looked at all the money she had. She knew exactly what she would do with it. She took the five pieces of money and spent all of it to buy some vegetable seeds. Then she planted them in a garden. When the vegetables were ready to harvest, she picked them all, took them to the market and sold every vegetable. *(The servant pretends to buy seeds, putting the five coins on the table; then pretends to plant the seeds, pick the vegetables, and take them to market. The shopper pretends to buy the vegetables and gives the servant ten coins.)* Now she had ten coins, five more than when she started!

The second servant looked at the money he had. He knew exactly what he would do with it. He bought a cow. Every morning he would milk the cow and sell the milk to his neighbours. *(The servant pretends to buy a cow, putting the two coins on the table; he milks the cow and takes the milk to a neighbour. The neighbour pretends to buy the milk and gives the servant four coins.)* Now he had four coins, two more than when he started!

The third servant looked at the money she had. She had only one piece of money and was afraid she would lose it. So, she hid the coin. *(The servant hides the coin somewhere in the room.)*

Much later the landowner returned home. *(Landowner comes back.)* He was very interested to know what his servants had done with his money. So he called them in, one by one.

The first servant skipped into the room and happily told the landowner how she used the money. Then, she reached into her pouch and handed ten coins to him. *(The servant mimes the action, holds out the coins, and then everyone counts aloud.)* "My," said the landowner, "you did very well. I gave you five coins and now you have ten! You have made my gift grow."

The second servant walked into the room and happily told the landowner how he used the money. Then, he reached into his pouch and handed four coins to him. *(The servant mimes the action, holds out the coins, and then everyone counts aloud.)* "My," said the landowner, "you did very well. I gave you two coins and now you have four! You have made my gift grow."

The third servant slowly entered the room and nervously told the landowner what she did with the money. "I was afraid I would lose the money," she told him, "so I hid it." Then, she reached into her pocket and handed one coin to him. *(The servant mimes the action, holds out the coin, and then everyone counts aloud.)*

"I am very upset!" said the landowner. "I gave you one coin and you hid it! It doesn't do any good there."

Storytelling props needed:

• 22 coins

Other ideas for exploring the lectionary readings (Proper 28 [33])

1. Heifer Project International www.heifer.org (Matthew 25:14–30)

A modern example of putting love into action and seeing it grow is found in the *Heifer Project International*. *Heifer Project* gives a young animal to a poor farmer. That person takes care of the animal. When it grows up, it might produce milk or wool. When the animal gives birth, the farmer passes on the first offspring to another person in need. Each person who receives an animal passes one on to someone else. That's how the investment grows. A dairy cow given to a family in need is a great gift because it can produce enough milk for the family to drink, plus extra to sell. With money from the milk, the family can buy medicine, clothes, and home improvements.

The animals and training that *Heifer Project* provides to the families improve their quality of life in many ways. Income is generated through the sale of animal products such as milk, eggs, and wool. By-products such as manure can be used to power cooking stoves or used as fertilizer to improve crop production. Multipurpose animals like camels, buffalo, and cows are reliable sources of lifesaving milk and milk products beneficial in combating malnutrition. These animals also provide energy by hauling heavy loads and can be rented to neighbours for extra income. Small animals, such as chickens require little space and consume crop by-products or insects unsuitable for humans.

The idea of giving families a source of food rather than short-term relief caught on and has continued for more than 50 years. As a result, families in 115 countries have enjoyed better health, more income, and the joy of helping others. For more information about *Heifer Project* visit www.heifer.org.

Take a very large glass jar and put a few coins in it. Talk about how the money from the jar could be used to buy an animal to help others. Make a poster with animals on it to go with the jar that tells what the coins will do. Then, take the jar and set it out in the entry way of the church. Invite others to share in the investment. Encourage everyone to watch their investment of a few coins grow from week to week.

2. Open-ended response centre (1 Thessalonians 5:1–11)

Materials needed: variety of art and craft supplies (construction paper, felt and fabric scraps, variety of paper scraps, used magazines, felt markers, crayons, paints, scissors, glue, etc.)

In Paul's letter to the church in Thessalonica he calls the Christians "children of the light" and tells them to encourage one another and build each other up. What can we do to spread the light of God's love this week? Invite the children to use the art and craft materials to create a symbol of their response to this question. As a closing, sing together "This Little Light of Mine."

Song

This little light of mine, I'm gonna let it shine (x3) (*pretend to hold a candle in hands and then wave the candle around)*
Let it shine, let it shine, let it shine. (*cup hands and then open up arms three times)*

Hide it under a bushel. No! I'm gonna let it shine (x3) (*cover one hand with the other hand and then open up your arms 3 times)*
Let it shine, let it shine, let it shine. (*cup hands and then open up arms three times)*

Prayer

Dear God,
thank you for the gifts you give each of us.
Help us to know how to share them with others.
Amen.

The King Who Felt the People's Love

(based on Matthew 25:31–46)

Season after Pentecost

Proper 29 [34] (Reign of Christ Sunday)

Ezekiel 34:11–16, 20–24

Psalm 100

Ephesians 1:15–23

Matthew 25:31–46

A long time ago there was a place where Matthew's friends gathered as part of God's church.

They would sing songs together. They would pray together. And they would hear stories that Jesus told long, long ago. Let's hear one of those stories now…

Once there was a king, who loved all the people. The one thing that the king wanted more than anything else was for the people to love each other.

Every day the king watched the people, and whenever he saw any of them showing love, he smiled, and felt the love too.

The king watched the people all day long.

Sometimes the king saw somebody giving food to a person who was hungry. That is love! The king rubbed his tummy as if he had just eaten a delicious meal – umm. *(Invite the children to do it too.)* The king smiled, and felt the love too.

Sometimes the king saw somebody giving a drink to a person who was thirsty. That is love! He licked his lips as if he had just had a refreshing drink – aahhh. *(Invite the children to do it too.)* The king smiled, and felt the love too.

Sometimes the king saw somebody making a new friend. That is love! He watched a while longer. *(Pause to enjoy the picture together.)* It is good to make new friends. The king smiled, and felt the love too.

And sometimes the king saw somebody giving warm clothes to a person who was cold. That is love! As he watched, he felt warm. *(Hug yourself contentedly and invite the children to do it too.)* The king smiled, and felt the love too.

The king loved the people so much. When the people showed their love for one another, the king felt as though they were loving him, too. He was very, very happy. *(Pause.)*

At the end of the story, the people in Matthew's church turned to each other and smiled. They knew that when they helped others, they were helping God. They were helping to build a world of God's love.

Season after Pentecost

Proper 29 [34]

(Reign of Christ Sunday)

Matthew 25:31–46

Storytelling props needed:

• binoculars made from cardboard rolls as show for storyteller and all children.

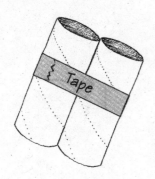

When You Love Others Like This

(based on Matthew 25:31–46)

Once upon a time there was a king who reigned over a large country. He loved his people very much and was always interested in what they were doing. One day he received a special pair of binoculars. "This will be fun," he said. "Now I can see how my people are living." And he ran to a window in the top of his tower and looked out over the land. He put the binoculars to his eyes. *(Have the children look through their binoculars and then do the same as the king.)* He looked to the right. He looked to the left. He looked up. He turned around and looked behind him. Everywhere he looked it was beautiful. And then he looked for his people.

He looked very hard and soon he noticed someone offering some food to another person. "Ah," he said. When you love others like this, you love me too! You have made me very happy."

And then he looked through the binoculars again. "Oh, dear," he said. "It looks like someone is very thirsty. But wait, I can see someone helping him. Someone is bringing him some water." *(Everyone looks through their binoculars.)* "Ah," he said. When you love others like this, you love me too. You have made me very happy."

Again, he looked through his binoculars. This time he noticed a woman holding a little baby. He watched her walk up to a house and knock on the door. She looked lost and afraid. Soon the door opened. She was welcomed in. *(Look through the binoculars. Encourage the children to repeat the king's response.)* "Ah," he said. When you love others like this, you love me too. You have made me very happy."

The king was beginning to enjoy this. He looked through his binoculars again. "What's this?" he said. "Oh, no. That person must be very cold. He isn't wearing much clothing." And then he smiled. "I shouldn't have worried. Here comes someone carrying a coat for him." *(Repeat as before.)* "Ah," he said. When you love others like this, you love me too. You have made me very happy."

"I wonder what I will see this time?" the king thought as he put the binoculars up to his eyes again. He looked through a window into a house across the town. He saw someone lying in bed, very sick and worried. As he watched her, he noticed that her face began to light up. Then the sick woman turned to see a child come into the room with a bouquet of flowers. *(Repeat as before.)* "Ah," he said. When you love others like this, you love me too. You have made me very happy."

The king knew it was time to go but he wanted to look through his binoculars one more time. He knew of a place where there were many sad and lonely people. He wanted to see how his people were cared for there. He strained his eyes until he found the prison. "Yes!" he said, "I see someone listening. I see someone caring. My people are loved." *(Repeat as before.)* "Ah," he said. When you love others like this, you love me too. You have made me very happy."

The king turned around and climbed down the stairs. He put the binoculars away. There was no need to use them anymore. He had seen his people caring for one another. He was happy. When they showed their love for one another, he felt as though they were loving him too.

Instructions: Read the phrases to the children and talk about the six pictures. Mention that these children around Jesus could be themselves and their friends. Invite them to colour the figures and put in names in the boxes of who the children might be.

Matthew 25:40

When you love others like this ...

you love me too.

We are helping to build a world of God's love.

Showing Love Heart Basket

When we love each other

we love God too.
(based on Matthew 25:40)

When we love each other

we love God too.
(based on Matthew 25:40)

When we love each other

we love God too.
(based on Matthew 25:40)

When we love each other

we love God too.
(based on Matthew 25:40)

Materials
- large construction paper heart for each child
- stapler and hole punch
- ribbon or pipe cleaners for handle
- crayons or felt markers
- scissors

Instructions
- Give each child a large paper heart to decorate. Roll the hearts into a cone shape and staple. Punch holes and attach a ribbon for a handle. Decorate the sets of pictures and place them in the baskets.

Appendix

LECTIONARY YEAR A & THE GOSPEL OF MATTHEW

The first Sunday of Advent heralds a new year in the life of the church and each of the three years of the *Revised Common Lectionary* cycle brings a new gospel. In Year A the readings are primarily from the gospel according to Matthew.

Matthew's gospel was compiled during the last third of the 1st century. At the time in which it was written, the lines between Christians and Jews were not firmly established. Believers in Jesus did not form a different religion but were seen as part of the Jewish community. Much of the unique material in Matthew reflects that fact.

Two foundations of Matthew's gospel are the great teachings of Jesus, including the Sermon on the Mount and the parables of the Kingdom or Reign of heaven. Within the gospel there is a sense of conflict between those who believe in and follow Jesus – who reached out to the marginalized – and those who speak about being holy but do not act on behalf of the poor.

The gospel is also very concerned with seeing Jesus as the fulfilment of Hebrew prophecies. In the stories of Jesus' birth and childhood, Matthew makes frequent references to the prophets, as he sees parallels being lived out in the events of Jesus' life. Matthew also makes frequent mention of Jesus as a descendant of David, more so than any other gospel.

Matthew may well have been written for Jews by a Jewish reformer. However, in the almost 2000 years since it was written, its portrait of Jesus challenging his own Jewish community has often been reinterpreted to justify anti-Semitism. Using Matthew as their proof text, some Christian religious leaders have taught that Jews, because they killed Christ and rejected his gospel, were incapable of a spiritual life and even not fully human. The persecution of Jews in the Middle Ages and the Holocaust of the last century were concrete results of this kind of misunderstanding. As we look again at Matthew, we can avoid these kinds of interpretations by remembering that the author of this gospel was challenging religious leadership and interpretation within his own tradition, not denigrating the very people and community into which he and Jesus had been born. Indeed, we can learn much from this gospel if we, in the spirit of the original writing, seek to apply it to ourselves, our own religious communities, and our own religious leadership.

– from *The Whole People of God* curriculum resource, 1999, Copyright © Wood Lake Publishing Inc.

Give Glory to God

Sing this song as written or in a "leader-response" form. Everyone should join in singing the "Glory to God" lines. Use a variety of rhythm instruments to give this song even more energy and allow children to participate fully.

Chorus: Glory to God! (clap) Glory to God! (clap)

Opt. Descant vs. 2, 4, 5 Glo - ry to God!

Sing songs of praise___ and give glo-ry to God! (clap)
Speak out for jus-tice and give glo-ry to God! (clap)
Love one a-no-ther and give glo-ry to God! (clap)
Do acts of kind-ness and give glo-ry to God! (clap)
Care for the earth___ and give glo-ry to God! (clap)

Opt. bass vs. 3, 5 Glo - ry to God!

We Are the Church

Words and Music: Richard K. Avery & Donald Marsh

Index

Helpful Books and Resources from Wood Lake Publishing

www.woodlakebooks.com

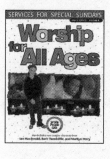

Seasons Growing Faith CD and Songbook: Music for the Very Young, Donna Scorer and Cathie Talbot, ed., 26 songs, 32 page songbook, 5.5 x 8.5", coil binding, soft cover, $28.95 set.

Rainbow CD and Songbook: Favourite Music for All Ages, Alan C. Whitmore, ed. Music for community, church, camp, or family and friends gathered around the piano. 96 pages, 8.5 x 11", coil binding, soft cover, CD $19.95.

Lectionary Story Bible (Year A), by Ralph Milton with full-colour illustrations by Margaret Kyle. Adept at handling even difficult material, Ralph Milton writes stories that are positive and life-afirming, use inclusive language, and portray a God of love to children and adults alike. 256 pages, 6.75 x 9.75", hardcover, $30.00.

Worship for All Ages: Services for Special Sundays, compiled by Marilyn Perry for The Whole People of God Library series. Shares Bible passages, visually and actively, while keeping children involved and adults inspired. 112 pages, 8.5 x 11", softcover, CAN$24.95/USA $19.95.

Creative Worship: Services from Advent to Pentecost, by Ian Price & Carolyn Kitto. Poems, readings, songs, and other ideas to build creative worship services covering major seasons of the Christian Year. 128 pages, 8.5 x 11", softcover, $24.95.